Tugmutton Common: The Life And Times of William Pateman

John Pateman

The Pateran Press
11 Windsor Close
Sleaford
Lincolnshire
NG34 7NL

November 2008

ISBN 978-0-9560812-1-6

Acknowledgements

Tony Baker
Cherie Batty
Joan Bright
Brenda Brincat
Frances Brown
Paul Coates
Bob Collins
Jim Davey
Dr E. Colin Dawson
Barry Dighton
Colin Fenton
Sylvia Harvey
Janet Keet Black
Kay Newman
Annette Pateman
Bill Pateman
Graham Short

Dedication

This family history is dedicated to the memory of William Pateman and the Tugmutton Gypsy community of Farnborough, Kent.

Contents

1. Introduction...1

2. Bastard Green...21
   - Betsy Pateman (1880-1881)
   - Emmie Pateman (1882-1956)

3. Tugmutton Common...41
   - Phillis Pateman (1883-1902)
   - Hannah Pateman (1884)
   - Robert Pateman (1885-1960)
   - Mary Ann Pateman (1886-?)
   - Charlotte Pateman (1887-?)
   - Phoebe Pateman (1889-?)
   - Jane Pateman (1890-?)
   - Celia Pateman (1892-1894)
   - John Pateman (1893-1900)
   - Polly Pateman (1894-1900)

4. Willow Walk..61
   - Betsy Pateman (1896-1897)
   - Elvy Pateman (1897-1950)
   - George Pateman (1899-1921)
   - Daisy Pateman (1901-1976)
   - Rose Pateman (1903-1993)
   - William Pateman (1904-1966)

5. Farnborough Village..81
   - Mary Pateman (1876-1901)
   - Henry Pateman (1880-1961)

6. Stow Cottages..102
   - Noah Pateman (1883-1949)
   - Walter Pateman (1886-1917)
   - Alice Pateman (1889-?)
   - Phoebe Pateman (1892-?)

7. Cobden Road...122
   - William Pateman (1894-1900)
   - Amy Pateman (1896-?)

8. The Boswells...142
9. Fellow Travellers..163
10. Chronology..184
11. Family Tree...187
12. Sources..188

1. Introduction

This is the story of the Tugmutton Gypsies of Farnborough, Kent. They included: William Pateman (my great grandfather) and his brothers John and James; Mercy, Jane and George Reynolds (married to William, James and Mary Pateman, respectively); and Urania Lee and Levi Boswell, the self-styled 'King and Queen' of the Kent Romany Gypsies. For many years they lived at Tugmutton, or Leg of Mutton Common, a large field on the edge of Farnborough shaped like a leg of lamb. During the summer they traveled around Kent picking hops, fruit and vegetables, and in the winter they would return to their cottages at Tugmutton and earn their living as pedlars and hawkers.

William Pateman was born in 1857 at Rochester, Kent. His father was Robert Pateman (1821-90) and his mother was Mary Ann Enis (1819). William's siblings were Mary Ann (1840-1844), Alice (1842-1892), John (1844-1883), James (1846-1926), Mary Ann (1851-1929), Elizabeth (1855-1916), Henry (1856-?), Anne (1858-?), Walter (1859-1943), Louisa (1861-?), Thomas (1861) and Noah (1866-?). For more information see *Hoo, Hops and Hods: the life and times of Robert Pateman and his family.*.

In 1871 William was living with his family in an old stable on a brick field at Becks Lane, Beckenham, Kent. In 1881 William was living in a van on the side of Orpington Lane, Farnborough with his wife, Mercy Reynolds, and their first two children, Mary (1876-1901) and Henry (1880-1961). Williams' brothers, John and James, were also living at Farnborough and John died there in 1883. Robert Pateman died at Farnborough in 1890 and was buried at St Giles church. There are 13 members of the Pateman family buried at St Giles. In 1891 William was living in Stow's Cottages, Church Lane, Farnborough Village. In 1901 William was living at 4 Cobden Road, Farnborough. He later moved to Chislehurst Road, Orpington where he died in 1921.

There are three main reasons why Gypsies settled at Farnborough: it was well known for its Horse Fairs; it was noted for its osier beds; and it was a good location for a winter base. Gypsies from all over Kent would bring their horses to buy and sell. They would run their horses up and down the High Street so that the would-be buyer could see their performance. Apparently this was a very popular spectacle for the villagers to watch. Each year till well before the war, a Gypsy Horse Fair was held in the village, the horses being trotted along the High Street for prospective buyers to see.

Galer: 'I wonder why we find so many Gypsies in this district? One may answer this question in various ways. For instance, at Farnborough there were noted 'osier' beds, and osiers were used for making cane chairs and baskets. No doubt the banks of a river made a suitable camping ground because water was a necessity for man and beast, and Gypsies were some of the greatest horse dealers. Their medical knowledge of animals was as renowned as any Harley Street specialist for his knowledge of the human body. By the way, the Pilgrim's Road from Winchester to Canterbury follows the course of a river as far as it can, for this same purpose of water for man and beast. Now a better answer would be that this district is near London for winter time activities, and a good starting off point for the spring and summer activities, that is for 'picking purposes.'

Farnborough was one of many Gypsy communities which established themselves on the fringes of Kent at the end of the nineteenth century. Locations such as Farnborough provided a good base from which they could travel down into Kent to work on the land picking fruit, vegetables and hops. They would then return to Farnborough and winter over on the edge of London where there were more opportunities to sell their goods such as pegs, skewers and baskets. In his book *Low Life Deeps* (published in 1881, the same year that William Pateman first arrived in Farnborough) James Greenwood describes this annual migration:

Some Secrets of Gypsy Life

'It may not be generally known that at a certain time of the year an important movement takes place amongst certain people dwelling in our midst. Numerically they are not great, but, as is well known, on account of their peculiar habits and customs, and their means of obtaining a livelihood, they exercise considerable influence on a large section of the community.

The people in question are the Gypsies, and just now, according to their invariable custom, they are engaged in preparing for their summer campaign, which lasts from April until the end of the following October. It is quite a mistake to imagine that they regard the "broad canopy of heaven" as such a mighty good thing that they cannot have too much of it. The "rollicking Romany", the hero of jail bird vocalisation, the "child of the forest glade, roaming abroad like a bird or a bee", of more polite and romantic eulogy, is not so "green" as – just for the look of the thing and to uphold his theatrical reputation – to pass the frosty months by which Christmas is bounded camped out in the wintry wilderness. A pitch on a common, or in a snug lane, and by a country wayside, may be all very well when the yellow gorse is ripening under the sun to the complexion of a Maltese orange, and when the hedges are so amply cloaked in verdure, as to afford prime screening for a hen roost robber, or a misappropriator of family linen; but when first frosts powder the short nipped grass, and leaves fall thick, and the rook nests are left naked aloft in the black boughs, the bold Gyspy feels that his faith in mossy banks and bosky brakes is shaken, and that, after all, though haystacks may in their season be all that can be desired in the way of shelter, there is another season when chimney stacks and their cosy associations are to be preferred.

Not that the Gypsy will consent to do violence to the fine free spirit with which nature has invested him by becoming a house dweller. No; as close as you please to the skirts of civilisation – indeed, if the said skirts are so immediately adjacent as to admit of his dipping his honest hands in the pockets thereof, he has no objection – but four walls and a roof are not to his fancy. It is the same with the women as the men. I recently overheard two middle aged flowers of the forest discussing the matter in their encampment in the vicinity of Lock's Fields, Walworth. Both were sun bronzed, and both wore coral ear rings, and their straw bonnets hind side in front. Both were at ease, and comfortably disposed for leisurely chat. The one was seated in a barrow, for which her ample form was an easy fit, and the other was partaking of her mid day meal, and was evidently actuated by a determination to adhere, as far as circumstances would permit, to those rural domestic rites and ceremonies to which her heart inclined. She was squatted on a wisp of hay bands by the side of a recumbent donkey, whose four legs hedged her in, and she had utilised the flanks of the docile creature to serve as a table. There were bread and butter spread on it, and about a quarter of a peck of turnip radishes. There was a bald shiny patch on the donkey's hip set round with hair, and this served as a convenient salt cellar, and every time his mistress dipped a radish into this repository and proceeded to scrunch it up, there was an expression in the animal's half closed eyes that betrayed his consciousness that now she was enjoying herself, and the satisfaction the reflection afforded him.

"And how's old Cooper a doin' since he give up the wan and took to the housel?" inquired the female in the wheelbarrow. "He's growing wus and wus," replied her friend with a grim serve him right too expression in her beady eyes. "He was right enough on wheels; why didn't he stay on em?" "Ah, to be sure. I know what I should expect would shortly happen to me if once I trusted myself atween lath and plaster."

"But it ain't the laths, and it ain't the bricks, my dear," rejoined her friend "its summat in the mortar that works its way into your cistern, and that's what'll bunnick up old Cooper, you mark my words." I don't believe that she meant "cistern", though certainly she said it. If I might hazard a guess, I think she intended to convey her impression that there was something in the composition of mortar that was injurious to the human system, and that old Mr Cooper was in danger of becoming a victim to rashly entrusting himself within its influence. If to be "bunnicked" means worse than this, the mortar is responsible.

As soon as the cold weather sets in the members of the various Gypsy tribes whose head quarters are London and its suburbs, may be seen with their brown babies and their houses on wheels, the gay green and yellow paint with which their panels are bedecked, dulled and blistered by the sun of a long summer, leisurely making their way to the winter settlements. These are not few. There are two or three at Camberwell, and one at a place called Pollard's Gardens, near the Waterloo Road. Peckham boasts of several; they may be found at Homerton, in the back slums of Lambeth, and among the potteries between Notting Hill and Shepherd's Bush. Lock's Fields, Walworth, is a favourite spot with the fraternity, and has been since that remote time, when Lock himself, standing at the door of his farmhouse, was able to take an uninterrupted view of his cows in the open meadows.

Now, one might traverse the said "fields" from end to end and find nothing more suggestive of cows than the heels and paunches of the animals in question exposed for sale in the grimy little shops that plentifully dot the neighbourhood; while, as for grass, not a solitary blade would meet the eye except in the form of those saucer size bits of turf retailed at a penny each, and which imprisoned larks speedily convert into the frowsiest of hay with their hot feet as they madly dance to their own pitiful piping. The Gypsies are expected at these places, and the 'bits o' waste' are reserved and kept vacant for their winter hiring. If the said bit o' waste includes a bit o' hedge, and anything of a ditch, no matter how inodorous or overgrown with green duck weed, they are regarded as advantages. Nothing else except a stable for the one or two old horses and a donkey is needed. The house on wheels serves as kitchen, parlour, and all, including bedroom for the elders of the family. As for the younger fry, half a dozen or so may be easily packed hammock-wise in the hay bag that is slung beneath the house to the fore and aft axle trees; and should there be one or two still unprovided for, there is always a spare bed in the stable.

It is not so easy to understand how the numerous party is provided for by day. Should the question be asked how a livelihood is obtained, the short answer is "clothes pegs". If they are produced at all, however, it must be by some necromantic process of manufacture, for no Gypsy is ever seen engaged with such implements and materials as are ordinarily used. Perhaps, however, "clothes pegs" is merely a slang phrase of "Romany", and signifies living by one's wits, or by other folks' lack of them. This would appear the more probable since, when in town, papa Gypsy may invariably be found at the horse market at Islington on Fridays, while mamma Gypsy is busy every day going her rounds and modestly concealing the light of divination and prophecy which possesses her under a simple hand basket, containing cottons and laces and hairpins.

Readers of the daily newspaper may always know, on turning to the police reports, when the merry Gypsy band have returned to town for the winter. Things do not appear to work smoothly with the fortune tellers of the tribes at first starting. Perhaps exhuberance of spirits at finding the "pastures new", as represented by silly housemaids and kitchen wenches, as green and promising as ever, causes them to be rash and recklessly grasping in their dealings; or, maybe, sufficient time has not yet elapsed for the weak minded damsels to have forgotten the stories of barefaced swindle and extortion exposed and made public last season. At all events, it somehow happens that early winter is bad for the fortune telling trade.

It was at Lock's Fields that I recently scraped acquaintance with an interesting family of Gypsies, 33 in number, including grandfather and grandmother and great grandmother.: and the old lady – 89 last birthday, and with a face as hard looking and as wrinkled, though many shades darker, than a walnut – was as eager to "be off and get a sniff at the wholesome green leaves and the daisies" as the youngest of her tawny kindred. There was a tremendous bustle among them. There were houses on wheels and a cart; and, turning the corner to reach the "bit o' waste" where the vehicles found standing room, the wind came at me so powerfully impregnated with paint and turpentine as nearly to take my breath away. All the adults of the party were literally up to their eyes in brilliant colours – grinding and mixing and laying on first coats and second coats, and picking out wheel spokes and panels; while the great grandmother was the proud custodian of the three brass knockers, which she had splendidly polished, and which, as I was informed, she wrapped in a flannel petticoat, and took to bed with her of a night, to preserve them from marauding fingers.

As the whole family were, however, not engaged in the work of decoration previous to making a start, business as well as pleasure had to be thought of, and the nature of the approaching campaign was disclosed on every side. Here an industrious youth was high busy, stripped to his waist, but with the inevitable black short pipe between his lips, fashioning cockshy sticks out of hardy loppings of green elm; while his brother, and doubtless partner in the innocent pastime, was sorting and mending, with the aid of a glue pot, a big bagful of damaged cockshy toys, and which, as was in confidence confided to me, had been bought in the "ditch" (Hounsditch) that morning for two shillings. At a little distance off was another youth, whose simple implements of business were a little dab of clay, a bit of stick, and a threepenny piece; and having stuck the stick in a hollow made in the clay, and balanced the coin atop of it, he went a little way off and practised knocking the three pence off by throwing another bit of stick at it, his object being to hit the coin so that it should not fall into the hollow. As he did so he kept up in under tone a sort of incantation.

"Don't be afeard, gen'elmen's sons, hev a shy: try your luck and never say die. Every time you knocks off the little silver bit it is yourn, and on'y a penny a shy. In the hole's for me; outside the hole, which iver way, east, west, north or south, is for you – a penny a shy, and three to one in your favour".

He was a shock headed, heavy featured, lubberly youth of about 15, and, of course, smoked a short pipe; but it was plainly perceptible that his eyes were red with weeping, and that both his great ears, as though in sympathy, were red too. Every time he aimed at the little silver coin perched on top of the stick, it fell outside the hole; instead of exhibiting satisfaction, however, he scratched his head in despair, and growled, "Bust and beggar the jiggerin' thing, why the 'ell don't it fall into the hole?" and then he would put up the bit of stick again inclined a little more forward or backward, according to his fancy. It was evident that he was practising a "little game", in which, opportunity serving, the public were to be invited to join, the plan being that any one was to have as many "shys" at the three penny piece as he had a mind to, at the rate of a penny a shy, the winnings to be the said coin, provided it was so knocked off that it avoided the basin in which its support was stuck, and the manipulator's object was to adjust the stick at such an artful angle that shy how he would, the customer was bound to facilitate the descent of the three penny into the hollow, and so lose his penny. It seemed to be a new branch of the cheating profession to the lad who was practicing it, and that his progress towards perfection was not rapid; but what on earth did he find to cry about? I discovered presently.

"Don't be afeared, gen'elmen's sons; hev another shy!" sighed the despairing youth, brushing a trickling tear from the side of his nose with the back of his dirty hand! "Try yer luck, and never say die;" and this time he threw, and the coin fell into the hole. His eyes brightened as he stuck up the stick just as before, and threw again, and with the same result. Again, and still again, and every time the three penny piece was faithful. There was a middle aged giant with great hairy arms engaged in sand papering a newly painted van wheel a short distance off, and to him the lad presently cried "*Now* come and hev a try!"

And the hairy giant came, and, kneeling down, took wary aim. At the very first try he tipped off the three penny piece and sent it flying, whereupon he seized on the youth's large ears, and wrung them as though they had been two wet sponges, and his aim was to squeeze every atom of moisture out of them, after which, and never heeding the maddened bellowing of the tortured one, he returned to his wheel, and next instant was sandpapering away as though he were the father of the most contented family in the world.

"Bust and beggar and double bust the blessed threepenny!" roared the youth rebelliously; but at that instant he fortunately glanced in the direction of the sand paperer, who had caught up a spoke brush, and was poising it for a throw; so he judiciously altered his tune, and, once more adjuring imaginary gentlemen's sons not to be afeared, he gulped down his grief, again applied himself to learning his business. But one of the oddest bits of information I picked up at the Lock's Field encampment was, that, simmering in knavery as Gypsies are, from the time when they are old enough to lisp lies to the gay company on a race course, until they arrive at the dead ripe age of the infatuated old lady who took the brass knockers to bed with her, they still believe, or seriously affect to believe, in the fortune telling powers of their own women. Over a beer can I put the question fairly to the Herculean sand paperer, and he replied that though she was his own grandmother, he should be very sorry to aggravate the old lady – who, at that moment, was breathing tenderly on the brazen nose of the dog's head that was part of one of the knockers, and rubbing it bright again with the corner of her shawl – to the extent of bringing on his head her malediction.

"Do you think she really could tell you your fortune if she tried?" "I'm sure of it," he replied, in a whisper. "Then why don't you let her do so?" I suggested. "Well, I'll tell you why," he replied, after reflecting on the matter for several seconds, with his face in the beer can, "I'll tell you why. Every man, mister, has ups and downs in life afore him, as well as behind him; and though it might be werry pleasant to be put up to the hups aforehand, a man mightn't feel ekal to be put up to all the downs what's in store for him. Life's very much like bacon," continued the hairy armed philosopher, intently regarding the ale in the can as though the revelation appeared in the liquor, "there's fat to it and there's lean to it, and him as tries to make a division makes a mess of it. It's best to put the two together and take it streaky. That's what I think about life, and that's why I don't see any pull in having my fortune told." And this opinion was accepted as the correct one by the six or seven young men and old who were present, and they, one and all, expressed their implicit belief in the women of the tribe as fortune tellers, "if they chose to give their mind to it."

"Then they don't always do so," I remarked. "'Taint likely," replied a young fellow, "it can't be expected that they'll go chucking away their talents for a tanner or so a time. It would be a reg'lar insult to the stars to go to 'em and consult 'em at such a cag-mag price. They'd very likely chuck you over if you tried it on with 'em, and tell you all wrong, and serve you right too. But them as pays handsome and deals square, is dealt square by, and gets what they bargains for, as true as this here in my hand is a paint brush."

I should like to have had another hour of the society of my interesting friends, but at that moment there came trooping a dozen or so of another tribe who had just broken up their encampment at Peckham, and so, wishing them a prosperous summer, I bade them good bye, casting an encouraging glance, as I came away, on the youth who was still ruefully on his knees before the bit of stick and the hollowed clay, enjoining gentleman's sons to try their hands, and never say die".

Tugmutton

James Pateman was born in a tent at Cliffe, on the Hoo Peninsula, in 1846. He travelled around Kent, Surrey and Middlesex with his family. In 1861 they were living in a van at the Notting Hill Potteries. In 1881 James Pateman was living in his vardo at Bastard Green, Farnborough, with his wife, Jane Reynolds, and their daughter, Betsy. In 1891 James was living at 5 Tugmutton (later 5 Willow Walk), on the side of Tugmutton Common. He lived at Tugmutton for 45 of his 79 years. His neighbours were Urania and Levi Boswell. All but one of James's eighteen children were born at Farnborough and many of them were baptised, married or buried at St Giles. James was buried there in 1926.

We do not know when Gypsies first started to live on the Farnborough Commons, including Tugmutton, but it could have been one of the traditional stopping places that Travellers had been using for centuries. What we do know is that the enclosure movement in the nineteenth century made it more difficult for Gypsies to live on the Commons. Once the Metropolitan Commons Act was passed in 1866 it was only a matter of time before most of the common land within the Metropolitan area – which included London and its environs such as Farnborough – were subject to enclosure. This made it easier to move non-parishioners and itinerants such as Gypsies off the Commons.

The Farnborough Commons Protection Committee was formed on 17 June 1887, six years after James and William Pateman arrived in Farnborough. The committee contained local business men and farmers such as J.H. and W. Fox (members of the Fox family which owned a brewery at Green Street Green), and J.W. Stow, fruit grower. Interestingly, one of the committee members – H.N. Penfold, beer retailer - had a Gypsy surname.

It is clear from the minutes of their very first meeting that the Committee's main target was the Gypsies 'and the debris left by a succession of Gypsy encampments.' The Committee was concerned about 'the indecency occurring in the Gypsy camp'. Mr Penfold 'spoke in favour of forming a ditch and bank around the frontage of the common with gates etc. so that no vans could be drawn upon it.'

Notices were put up on the common saying that 'if any persons were found camping on the same after 12 noon on the following Monday they would be forcibly removed by the overseers and the police.' Letters were written to the Chief Commissioner of Police and to a solicitor - Mr Birkett - seeking advice on 'the shortest and best mode of procedure to eject these trespassers'.

Mr Birkett was engaged by the Committee to prepare a 'memorial' which was signed by the Farnborough gentry and businessmen in favour of enclosing the commons. This memorial was sent to the Land Commissioners with the appropriate fee and, in return, a draft scheme of enclosure was produced for advertisement in the local area. Some objections were received but the scheme was introduced into the Commons via a Bill on 26 March 1888 and by 12 June that Bill had passed through all its stages and was ready for the Royal Assent. The first meeting of the Farnborough Commons Conservators was held at the Board School on 9 July 1888. At their meeting on 9 April 1889 the Clerk reported that 'he had banked up the common at the places where vans were drawn on and had also begun to take off the flints and make the Common tidy.'

The Conservators continued to meet until 1904. During its sixteen years of existence the Farnborough Commons Conservators exercised their full and petty powers over the Commons which they were entrusted with by Act of Parliament. These self selected guardians of the Commons made life difficult not only for the Gypsies, but also for anyone else who had previously made use of the Commons. The placing or storage of hop poles, flints and manure on the Commons was prohibited, and gravel could not be extracted without the Board's permission. A Ranger was appointed and given a note book to record infringements of the bye laws and any actions he had taken. Everything was reported to the regular meetings of the Conservators – they met 39 times between 1889 and 1904. Notices were put up on the Commons telling people what they could (or mostly could not) do and legal action was threatened (and taken) against offenders. The planting and pruning of trees was regulated and people were not able to ride carts or vehicles of any kind across the Commons.

The core of the Conservators – Messrs Stow, Fox and Wilson were at the first meeting in 1888 and the last meeting in 1904 – re-elected themselves back onto the Board. This small group of rich and powerful men had total control over the Commons and the only people with any rights were those who owned land around the Commons before the Enclosure Scheme was agreed. Banks were dug to prevent vans from pulling onto the Commons and gates were put around the gravel pit. The Commons Act 1876 and local bye laws gave wide ranging powers to Boards of Conservators, who could prevent local Councils from taking gravel to build highways.

Not content with owning the cottages where William Pateman lived (and some of his children were born), Mr. Stow also wanted to control the Commons where James Pateman lived (until he and the rest of the Gypsy community were forced into cottages on the edge of the Common at Willow Walk). But there was one law for the Conservators and another for the rest of the community – people could not dump rubbish on the Common, but Mr. Stow did; people could not build roadways on the Common, but Mr. Fox did; people could not put fences on the Common, but Mr/ Wilson did. Mr. Fox was also able to put a gate in his fence on the Common and lay a waste pipe from his brewery to the gravel pit – privileges which were not afforded to the rest of the community.

The Conservators spent much of their time enforcing petty restrictions which they did not apply to themselves. At least one Conservator could not live with these double standards and resigned saying that the Board were a "mean spirited body". Eventually the Board collapsed as a result of its own contradictions. It became like King Canute, trying to hold back the forces of progress in the shape of the Gas Co., the Water Co., the Telegraph Co., the railways and the road builders, all of whom needed access to the Commons for one reason or another. After taking a resident to court in 1904 for removing gravel from the Commons, the Board won the case but bankrupted themselves in the process and, as a result, their powers were transferred to the Parish Council.

The Farnborough Commons Conservators first met in 1888 (seven years after James Pateman arrived on Tugmutton) and their last meeting was in March 1904 (just five months before the birth of James Pateman's last child, William, in August 1904). So how did the Enclosure of the Commons affect James Pateman and the other Gypsies of Tugmutton Common? We know that James Pateman was living on 'Bastard Green' in 1881 but by 1891 he had moved into one of the cottages in Willow Walk. This move from living on Tugmutton Common to living in a cottage on the edge of the Common may well have been prompted by the enclosure of the Farnborough Commons. Many Gypsies would have resented this forced move but what were their rights with regards to stopping on Common land? It is a misconception to believe that the Commons were available for the use of all. Unless otherwise specified in some sort of charter (which is rare) commons were only available for the use of the commoners of the Manorial Landowner, and then quite often constrained by open / closed periods that reflected the particular use.

Commons could only be closed by Act of Parliament, such as the Metropolitan Commons Act. These Acts had to prove that the commoner's rights had fallen into disuse, or that some particular right had been exhausted (for example, "turbary", when all the peat had been removed), or that the commoners as a total body were willing to forego their "rights of common". This last did sometimes result from coercion, either by bribery or by pressure on the commoners who might have something to lose. This could be that a particular commoner was a tenant farmer of the same Manorial Landowner.

Only when the Manorial Landowner could prove that by whatever reason the common rights had been "extinguished" could he enclose legally under an Act of Parliament. Some were closed illegally, but were usually resisted by the commoners, and the courts could force the Manorial Landowner to take down the fences etc., and illegal enclosure was quite rare.

Whoever used the Commons, for whatever purpose, if they were not the legal commoners, they were trespassers. So Gypsies did not have any right to stop on a common. Even a legal commoner on a particular common did not have that right, nor any other rights except those conferred on him according to the practice of that common. Common rights included the right to graze stock (not often sheep), to take turf for firing, to dig marl or gravel, to take "morefall" which is fallen firewood, to take bracken for bedding, and one or two obscure items. These could be in a permutation of one or more.

Nor was there any right to stop on the verge of a highway, except where authorities, seeking to control such stopping, brought out bye laws that put a time limit on stops. That conferred some kind of permission, although the authorities did not have the right to give permission, as the roads, until comparatively modern times, belonged to the adjoining landowners, and stopping on them was a trespass. If the landowners were different on each side, they each owned as far as the centre of the highway.

In August 1887 one of the Farnborough landowners, Lord Derby, raised an objection to the enclosure scheme 'with regard to the road side waste'. This objection was considered in terms of: 'if it is not waste of the manor it is part of the road. Conversely, if it is not part of the road then it is waste of the manor and unless therefore Lord Derby is Lord of the Manor he cannot claim the ownership of it. In any case Lord Derby will not be entitled to enclose up to within 30 feet of the centre of the road. At the nearest telegraph pole westward of the Secretary's cottage, Lord Derby's hedge is 60 feet from the centre of the road.

The only right of use on a road, available to everyone, was that of "way", to pass along in other words. Some ancient drove roads may have had a right of grazing also. In November 1887 H. Wilson informed the Farnborough Commons Protection Committee 'In my conveyance to Lord Derby I gave him all my estate and interest (if any) in the road side strips but subject to the rights (if any) of the Public and the Highway Surveyors.

So William Pateman had no more right to be living in a "van on the side of Orpington Lane" in 1881, than James did to be living on "Bastard Green". Within a few years both had moved into cottages – William into Stow's Cottages (Church Lane) and later Cobden Road, in Farnborough Village; and James into 5 Tugmutton (later 5 Willow Walk) where he lived next door to Levi and Urania Boswell. I do not know what the value was of the cottages in Willow Walk, Tugmutton, when the Patemans and Boswells lived there. But I do know what their value is today. 1 Willow Walk (originally two cottages) was put on the market in October 2005 for £209,950. I wonder what James and Levi would have made of that!

Fellow Travellers

William and James Pateman joined an established community of Gypsies at Farnborough and Tugmutton. This included the Arnold, Coates, Lewis and Reynolds families, all of whom married into the Pateman family and with each other. But the most famous residents of Tugmutton were the Boswells, in particular Urania and Levi Boswell, the 'King and Queen' of the Kent Romanies, who lived at 7 Willow Walk at the back of Farnborough Workhouse (later to become Farnborough Hospital). James Pateman lived at 5 Willow Walk for many years and would have been good friends and neighbours of the Boswells.

A well-known family of Gypsies, reputed to be true bred Romanies, was the Boswells, who lived in a little bungalow at Willow Walk, Tugmutton Green, which is at the back of Farnborough hospital. For over 200 years the family carried on the business of providing 'fairtackle' to county families in connection with private sports gatherings. Levi Boswell was known at every horse fair and fete in the county and was reported to be without equal as a horse dealer. He had a herd of donkeys and for over 70 years the family had a stand for donkeys on Blackheath, just opposite the main gates of Greenwich Park. Kanza Boswell was 8 years old when he first helped his father Levi, with the donkeys, and every morning the donkeys were driven to Blackheath and in the evening back to Farnborough.

Levi Boswell died in 1924 at the age of 77 and the local newspaper reported that there was an attendance of over a thousand at his funeral, which took place at St Giles church, Farnborough. But his funeral was surpassed by that of his widow who died nine years later, when she was 81 years of age. She was Mrs Urania Boswell and was generally known as Gypsy Lee and although she resided at Farnborough, normally spent six months of each year traveling with fairs and circuses as a palmist and fortune teller. It was said that she forecast her own end, and it was estimated that there were 15,000 present at her funeral, for Gipsy Lee was the 'queen' of all the Kent Gypsies.

A report of Levi Boswell's funeral appeared in the *London City Mission Magazine*: 'At St Giles Churchyard Farnborough. Levi Boswell the 'Gypsy King' was laid to rest amid the lamentations of his tribe. The old chief was 78. He ended his days at Bromley in an encampment with the Borrovian name of Tugmutton, where he enjoyed the ministrations of the City Missionary. According to custom the dead King wore bright yellow socks and a red muffler and was buried with much pomp and ceremony. The casket half hidden with flowers, was in a hearse drawn by six horses with postilion richly covered in purple and gold.

To the graveside flocked Gypsies from near and far. Men who had never seen their chief in life; women who loved him; children who in later years will build a legend around his name and the outsiders, a thousand strong, assembled to witness the obsequies of a Romany King. Chals (Gypsy fellows), chiefly horse dealers and showmen, broke down with emotion. The crippled widow nee Urania Lee, known as the Queen of Kent, was an apathetic figure, leaning on crutches and supported by her six children, two of whom are diminutive cripples. The departed chief was one of many in the clan the Boswell's and Lees (the two clans have intermarried for 300 years) who died in the faith, resting wholly and consciously on the finished word of Christ.'

Levi Boswell's funeral is also mentioned in *Gypsies of Britain*, as an example of a 'funeral sacrifice'. One of these was after the funeral of Levi Boswell on 8 May 1924 at Bromley, Kent. Levi, who had two crippled sons, had lived in the neighbourhood for close upon thirty years and was well known and well liked by many people. By profession he was a horse dealer – he had a truly remarkable knowledge of horses even for a Gypsy and a great reputation for honesty and he was also a showman, and these two callings naturally brought him into touch with the gorgios. His funeral procession was interesting. *The Daily Mail*, 9 May 1924:

'He went to his rest wearing – as marks of his chieftainship of the clan Boswell - bright yellow socks and a muffler of brilliant red. Buried with him, according to custom, were also many little gifts most treasured by him. These were placed in the coffin secretly, and the members of his family are pledged never to disclose what they are. The coffin, half hidden among flowers, was in a hearse drawn by six black horses richly caparisoned in purple and gold. On one of the front horses rode a postilion wearing a tight fitting black tunic and purple knee breeches and a black jockey cap. The widow rode in a motor car with her two sons, who, like herself, are crippled and use crutches. She wore a black dress with a bodice of Victorian fashion and a heavily plumed hat. On foot followed a long procession of relatives.'

The colours red and yellow are the Gypsy colours, but the use of yellow at British Gypsy funerals is unusual. After Levi's funeral there does not seem to have been a holocaust – no burning of living wagon or slaughtering of horses – but many of his personal possessions and all his clothes were destroyed by fire.

Urania Boswell lived in Farnborough in a little bungalow in Willow Walk for six months of every year. The rest of the time she was traveling with the fairs and circuses as a palmist and fortune teller. Gypsy Lee was born in Brighton in 1852 as Urania Lee and married Levi Boswell who died in 1924. Gypsy Lee, who was baptized into the Anglican Church, left six children: Herbert and Kenza who were cripples, Levi, Mary Ann, Norah, who was an invalid, and Ada; also a brother Job Lee. She was the daughter of Gypsy Lee of Brighton, who was a palmist and fortune teller. It is said that Gypsy Lee foretold her own passing and saw a death bird sign just a short while before she died. She had been laying ill in bed for a short while when she saw a rain thrush sitting in a tree and she said 'My time is near. This is the first time we have seen a rain thrush for three years. My time is near and then we will have rain for a couple of days. Tomorrow I will say adieu to you all'. Next morning at 7.30 she said 'Goodbye to you all I am finished' and passed on. The funeral, which was arranged by Mr Owen of the village, was one of the largest funerals Farnborough has ever known.

Another milestone had been reached in the history of Farnborough Village. The date was 28 April 1933 and the event was the funeral of Gypsy Lee the Queen of all Kent Gypsies. As the funeral procession started at the cottage of Mrs Urania Boswell on Starts Hill the children of Farnborough School were allowed to join at 2.30pm the 15,000 people who had traveled from all over the country to see this grand funeral. The children were back in school again by 3pm.

On 28 April 1933, at Farnborough, Kent, Urania Boswell was buried. Urania was the daughter of Gypsy Sarah, the Brighton 'Queen', and Abraham Lee, who was, according to some of the papers, the original Gypsy Lee. Be that as it may, Urania Boswell – she was generally known as Reni – undoubtedly came of the aristocracy of English Gypsydom and married into an equally renowned family. And her funeral did attract much attention. The crowds that gathered were variously estimated at 15,000, 20,000 and 50,000, but it is beyond question that some hundreds of Gypsies attended and that the mourners did number fifty two. As with her husbands funeral, so with hers, the coffin was drawn by six horses draped in black and with a postilion, dressed in black and wearing a black jockey cap, mounted on one of the front pair.

The crippled sons, Herbert and Kenza, her daughter Nora (who got up from a hospital bed to come) and her brother Job Lee followed in one car, and another son and daughter, Levi and Georgina, with some other relatives in a second car. But the outstanding feature of this funeral is that after it was over the living wagon and the possessions of the deceased were not destroyed. Having regard to the lineage of Reni and the family into which she had married, this departure from tradition was described as 'truly astonishing, and shows all too clearly the waning strength of Romani customs in this country.' Instead of burning it was decided that the waggon should be left exactly as it was when she died until it rotted away. It was supposed that this decision may have been taken to show some faint remnant of the traditional Romani attitude towards the dead, but as it was an exceptionally well furnished wagon, and it was probably not left untouched for long.

Urania Boswell was a wealthy woman. She was reputed to have left £15,000 or so – though there has been some argument about the actual amount – and she is reported to have had a hundred £5 notes kept in her wagon. She also owned considerable house property. The money in her wagon was divided between her five children.

Death means a great deal to Gypsies and their expressions of grief are sometimes more unrestrained than that of Gorgios whose accounts of Gypsy funerals rarely seem to agree, and very little reliance can be placed upon newspaper reports. Sometimes, as at the funeral of Urania Boswell at Farnborough, Kent, on 28 April 1933, which was very widely reported, every account differs, so much so that it is difficult to believe that they refer to the same event. One newspaper described the mourners at this funeral as a 'gay and happy throng', and went on to say that this was the Gypsy custom (another described them as 'silent and respectful', another as 'weeping aloud'), but it is hard to believe that the mourners at any Gypsy funeral have been 'a gay and happy throng'.

Goldings, Napoleons and Romneys

Farnborough was well known for its fruit growing. The 1878 *Post Office Directory* notes that 'The chief crops are wheat, barley, and oats, and there are a great number of fruit gardens. 200 acres of land are planted with strawberries." The *Directory* also lists a number of commercial residents: William Clark, fruit grower; William Durling, fruit grower; Alfred Fox, fruit grower; Charles Giles, grocer and fruit grower; William Griffin, farmer and fruit grower; Samuel Johnson, fruit grower; James and Robert Sessions, fruit growers; Allen Staples, fruit grower; Thomas Westbrook, fruit grower; Joseph Stow, fruit grower. Both James and William Pateman lived at one time in Stow's cottages at Church Lane, Farnborough Village. These cottages were named after Joseph Stow, who was also an overseer at St Giles and a Farnborough Commons Conservator.

Fruit growing was clearly a major industry in Farnborough, and much of this activity was concentrated in and around Lock's Bottom, where James Pateman lived at Tugmutton Common: 'Lock's Bottom is a hamlet [of Farnborough], three quarters of a mile north by west. Here are a Baptist chapel, a police station and the Bromley union workhouse.' It may have been the fruit growing which attracted James and William to Farnborough / Lock's Bottom in the first place. When their father died at Farnborough in 1890 he was described as a greengrocer. James Pateman was variously described as a greengrocer, potato dealer, potato merchant and potato salesman.

'Kent, sir, everyone knows Kent – apples, cherries, hops and women'. So said Mr. Jingle, in *The Pickwick Papers*, by Charles Dickens. Kent, with its hop fields, its apple, cobnuts and cherry orchards, was the garden of England from the time of the Romans. And this is where William and James traveled each summer before returning to Farnborough at the end of the season:

Galer: 'As I pass the blacksmith's forge I hear that metallic sound of a cart wheel being ironed. It is a Gypsy cart. Now this is the high season in the Gypsy world, for the season of picking has started. Pea picking, strawberry picking, soft fruit picking, apple picking and then the great climax of hop picking. Maybe after that a short season of nutting. Well, they will not come back till autumn mists at night and early frosts by morning call them back to the 'Pit' for the winter season. Of course, in my mind I can see that cart traveling along many a Kentish lane, and galloping through many a Kentish village. At night I can see a horse grazing by the side of a caravan, 'resting'; does not that caravan remind you of the traveling days of your life, days and months and years passing by – a moment's pause – a setting sun and then a 'rest', but people who do not vision such things, or ever dream a dream, cannot realize the meaning of life. To them this is Midsummer Madness, and nothing else.'

Cherries: 'If they blow in April, You'll have your fill, But if in May, They'll all go away.' The two wild cherries growing in Kent – the Gean and Dwarf or Wild Cherry – would have been noted by the Romans during their occupation of the county for they cultivated cherries in Italy and in other parts of Europe. It is therefore likely that they introduced varieties to cultivate around their settlements and possibly cross bred them with better examples of the wild cherries to improve the latter – a policy that may have also been practiced by early Kent growers. In the 19th century cherries were grown in Canterbury, Folkestone, Maidstone, the Weald, Gravesend, Swanscombe, Dartford and Crayford to meet the demand from London and northern England markets. Cherry cultivation was labour intensive. Men and women pickers were required at the critical time in the fruit's maturing. Some varieties had trees as high or higher than houses and ladders with 60 or 65 rungs were needed to reach the crop. The cherries were hand picked into kisby baskets worn on the picker's back and they were transferred to half sieve baskets (later chip baskets) to be taken to market by rail or lorry.

Apples: 'Christmas and a little before, The apple goes and not the core; Christmas and a little later, The apple goes and the core comes after'. This Kentish saying is a reminder of the days when apples were so plentiful before Christmas that only the flesh was consumed, but after Christmas there were not so many available and so every bit was eaten – including the core. The Kent fruit orchards were considerably expanded in the 18th century to meet the increasing demand of London's markets. There was a further rapid expansion from 1820 when a tariff was placed on the import of foreign apples which encouraged growers to plant new orchards. At the beginning of the 20th century demand for Kent culinary apples rose and many new orchards were established. The areas most favoured for apples and other fruit formed a band starting out from south-east of London (including Farnborough) and followed the belt of free working loams on the Thanet sands and chalk as far as the Medway valley.

Fruit and nuts: As well as the 'sweet cherry, temperate pippin and golden renate', Henry VIIIs gardener, Richard Harris, planted varieties of pears imported from France at Teynham in 1533 and their cultivation spread to the other fruit growing areas of Kent. The Farleigh Damson appeared in the 1820s and the Diamond (or Black Diamond) Plum and Kentish Bush (also known as Kentish Blue or Waterloo) were introduced in the 1830s. Gooseberries were first recorded in the 1840s and raspberries were raised in the 1870s. Blackcurrants were also grown and strawberries were cultivated in North and East Kent but increasing demand from jam makers brought about the rapid expansion of strawberry growing closer to London, around Swanley and St Mary Cray. One grower in the 1880s had 2000 acres of strawberries. His pickers started work at 3am so the strawberries would arrive at Covent Garden and other markets fresh for the early morning's soft fruit sales. In 1878 Farnborough had 200 acres of land planted with strawberries.

Kentish cobnuts and filberts: The ancestors of Kent's cobnut and filberts were examples of wild hazel, the common cobnut, found in copses, hedgerows and woodland edges, and gathered as a free harvest when ripe. They were later cultivated as a farm crop. Filbert was the name given to nuts which were enclosed by long husks or 'full beards' which clearly projected beyond their outward ends. The nuts were picked in three stages – firsting (in late August), seconding (in late September) and sometimes a thirding, when the bushes were shaken so that any remaining nuts would fall to the ground. Buckets or kisby baskets of the nuts were tipped into hessian sacks or Dutch trays, and taken to the pack house where they were riddled, the empty nuts sorted out, and then tipped into 10lb wooden trays to be weighed and lidded.

Mangolds, white mustard and woad: Some unusual but important crops have been cultivated in the past on Romney Marsh, in the Sandwich area, on the Isle of Thanet, in North Kent, the Isle of Sheppey and the Hundred of Hoo. William Pateman's family came from the Hundred of Hoo and James Pateman was born there, at Cliffe, in 1846. Mangolds, radishes and turnips were grown for the seed they produced not, as now, for their edible roots. So was black mustard which contained up to 22% oil. Rape, now grown for its oil, was then grown as a sheep forage crop, as was white mustard. Lucerne, red and white clover and trefoil were grown as hay or forage crops. Kohl-rabi, known also as the turnip rooted cabbage, was grown like swedes and turnips and used as a cattle and sheep feed. Woad was grown on the poor or chalky soils of West Kent, and turned into a dye, as was the yellow flowered madder.

Peppermint: Crockenhill and Chelsfield are among the areas in Kent where peppermint was cultivated. William and Mercy Pateman were working in the peppermint fields of Crockenhill when their first child, Mary, was born in 1876. The dark green leaved peppermint was usually ready to be harvested in mid August when it was 20 or so inches high. The whole of the plant above ground was harvested by hand using small mint hooks. Harvesting had to be done in dry weather. The peppermint stems were then laid out in long, even rows, to dry. They were turned periodically like hay, to allow the air to dry the plants thoroughly. After two days, if the weather had been fine, the crop was collected into small heaps and allowed to stand for another two days. It would be turned once during that time. When dry and brittle the cut peppermint stems would be ready for distilling.

They would be heaped into one hundredweight bundles and wrapped in open ended hessian bags, tied up and taken to distilleries at Mitcham. One company that used Kent grown peppermint as well as lavender was W.J. Bush of Batsworth Road, Mitcham. It is believed that peppermint as a crop was grown for the first time at Wested Farm, Crockenhill where George Miller planted it in three fields. The crop was sufficiently successful to prompt him to grow more, which he did both at Wested Farm and at Warren Road, Chelsfield.

Lavender: 'Here's flowers for you. Hot lavender, mints, savory, marjoram.' (Shakespeare, *A Winter's Tale*). The Mitcham area of Surrey is traditionally known for the cultivation and use of lavender. Mitcham Common was a traditional stopping place for Gypsies, and William Pateman's father, Robert, was living there at the time of the 1881 Census. Lavender was grown in Kent for local use and to supply the demand from the Mitcham lavender trade. It was grown between Swanley and Crockenhill in large quantities up to the 1930's. William and Mercy Pateman were living and working in the Crockenhill area in the 1870s and 80's. Mercy may have worked on the August lavender harvest. Women did the cutting with sharp, sometimes toothed sickles. The sickle was held in the right hand, while the left hand firmly held a number of lavender spikes. The women wore gloves or had their knuckles bandaged and also wore long sleeved blouses or cardigans to protect their arms from the rough foliage. Although it might seem to be a pleasant task the women had mixed feelings about it. As with hop picking, where the yellow lupuline from the hops cones stains hands and clothing, so with lavender. The scent of the lavender clung to the clothes, hands and hair of the cutters and wherever they went it gave away the fact they were employed in the lavender fields.

The harvested lavender in the Crockenhill and Swanley area was taken to various distilleries in the Mitcham district, one being W.J.Bush who also imported peppermint from Kent. Potter and Moore produced the world famous Mitcham Lavender Water and also supplied oil to other users, including Yardleys. Ray Galer had a dream about lavender:

'It was all the fault of the lavender bush, and you, reader, must blame the bush and not the writer, for it was the smell of the lavender that overcame my brain – and it did its work well, for I was in that state that made me sit down under the bush and dream my dreams – dreams of peaceful days and quiet nights – days when the old High Street went its usual way of a quiet life, when the old Church clock ticked out the hours of peaceful times in a leisurely manner, days when the countryside heard only the call of the reapers and the shouts of children, and of quiet nights, of gentle dreams, of children sleeping a peaceful sleep that comes from the joys of happy days, of old people going to bed without a qualm of fear on their minds. I dreamed of rooms lit up by the glow of a candle or the shine of a lamp, and no blinds drawn down, or shutters put up, of an open sky, of a moon that shone, and stars that glowed and nothing to be frightened of or be fearful about, and thus this lavender lured me on. It made me think of happier times and happier days, and I remembered that as children we knew that it was time to begin to think of that greatest event in the year, a real excitement that only comes to children – 'the going away' for the summer holiday. We knew that it was time to begin to think, for down the road came the Gypsies, and we heard the old, old song of 'Won't you buy my sweet blooming lavender, sixteen good branches for a penny.'

Now I may have misquoted this old London cry, but I still have the lilt of the song in my brain, and I can still see the Gypsies. And this takes me back to those old cries of London, of which I think that this lavender one was the last to fade away. Now I wonder if any kind reader would jolt my memory as to other cries of London which they have heard in their time. Of course there was the man with the barrow of flowers for the garden, the cry of geraniums at four pots a shilling, but this was not a London cry. It should rightly and truly be called a Kentish cry, for the original home of the scarlet geranium was at Swanley, for one Mrs. Henry Cannell 'created' this popular colour there – all true gardeners know the name of Swanley because of this fact. Then again, why has the cry of 'Fresh watercress' passed away? This should be another Kentish cry, for the watercress beds originated at Springhead, near Gravesend. Well, let us get back to the Gypsies, the lavender. North and West Kent, as compared to Mid and East Kent, seem to be the homes or camps of the Gypsies, or those whom we style Gypsies, for there are in reality very few real Gypsies about, and by real I mean those who have Romany blood in their veins. All those who have not Gypsy blood in their veins, are what are termed as 'Gorgios', and a true Romany must not have anything to do with them except for the purpose of buying or selling. Do you remember, reader, George Borrow's 'Lavengro' and 'Romany Rye'? Do you remember Mr. Petulengro and 'There's wind on the heath, brother.' Well, well, see what this lavender is doing to my brain brother. I do not suppose that the Gypsies had any more affection for Kent than they had for any other county in England, but to my mind, it is an interesting thought that their language or their slang vocabulary was called 'canting.'

The original name for Kent is called 'Cantiana' and one of this word's translations is 'free or open'. We still have the old name in 'Canterbury' so I wonder if there is any connection with canting and Cantiana. Of course, one knows that the word canter pertains to horse riding and is derived from the days when Chaucer and his pilgrims cantered along the old Watling Street to Canterbury.

And the lilt of the lavender song on this last day of July brings me to that enchantment of all nomadic open air life, the romance of a caravan life. Every real Gypsy who claims Romany blood owns a caravan. Reader, have you ever felt the impulse to be 'on the road.' If you have, the inside arrangements of a caravan will thrill you, and if it does not thrill you, then you do not hold the romance of 'the road'. At the far end of the house that travels the road, you will find the bedrooms, that is just the big bed or bunk, with its clean and very often highly coloured eiderdown, its spotless sheets and its spotless pillow, for a Gypsy on the road often looks from the outside the very opposite to what he is inside the caravan, when off duty. Then underneath this big bunk is a smaller bunk for the 'childer'. Does the smoke from the chimney entice you – well, just inside the door is the stove, a real coal stove, with its front of brass polished up to the nines. On the mantel-piece above it there are polished brass candlesticks; in the corner there is a corner glass cupboard filled with really good china, for the Gypsy is very particular as to good china, and he certainly has a good knowledge of the value of real china. In the middle of the room there is a table which lets down when not in use. Mind you, I am only giving a description of my friend's caravan – he who claims real Gypsy blood and who can tell you of the Lees and the Smiths and the Pettigroves. But what attracts my Romany friend to me is his knowledge of Kent; its country lanes, its towns, and its villages, are all known to him. He is a map of the county. He is a signpost in every lane. He is a guide in the town, and he can describe each village. He knows just where to be at the right moment, and what to do at each season of the year. A bit of pea picking, a bit of potato pulling, gooseberry picking, the strawberry season, the cherry season.

You will find him just in the right place at the right moment. Then there is the harvest of the fruit. The soft fruit first; he will be near Maidstone and Ashford for this. Then the hard fruit season; this season will find him round Sittingbourne, near Newington, the centre of the orchard land, and then comes the high season of the year – 'the height of the season,' and that, of course, is hop picking season. Kentish hops are known all over the world, and the two great centres of the hop gardens are Canterbury, which is East Kent, or around Paddock Wood, which is Mid Kent. Each centre has different methods of picking. In East Kent one picks into baskets. In Mid Kent one picks into bins. Generally, the Tally, or rate of pay, is five bushels a shilling, and it is really wonderful to watch a Gypsy picking hops. He far outstrips any 'Gorgio' in his picking. My friend prefers the Mid Kent centre, which runs from Tovil to Tonbridge. As he puts it, here are miles and miles of hops – East Farleigh, West Farleigh, Wateringbury, Yalding, Beltring and Paddock Wood. These places or villages are all of them on the banks of the river Medway, and those who do not know this part of Kent have missed one of the most beautiful parts of the county. There is something interesting about each village, and there is some romance in each place which holds the Gypsy picker to the same place year after year. His mother came before him, and her mother before her. Generally in each place there is elected a Queen of the Hopping chosen from the foreign pickers, and he is proud to tell me that his mother was Queen for some years.

This word 'foreign' seems rather strange, but to the picker it simply means a London picker as compared to a home picker. The record books of the hop grower are most picking the hops. This annual intermingling of town and country people had a unique and very enjoyable quality that is fondly remembered by many of those who were involved. *Travellers Remember Hopping Time* (The Romany and Traveller Family History Society, 2003) contains a number of accounts of Gypsy hop picking in Kent.

William Pateman's son, Henry (1880-1961) made oast houses for the hops trade. Oast houses are a great speciality of Kent and East Sussex. They are essentially hot air towers for the rapid drying of hops used to make beer after picking. The base consists of a round or square, brick or stone wall topped by a 'witch's hat' roof with a cowl on the summit that swings in the wind, helping to control the flow of air from the kiln. During the picking season the hops were taken directly from the garden to the oast house where men worked day and night to dry them on floors above the kilns, a task requiring skill and judgement. The hops were then tightly packed into giant sacks called pokes ready for storage and their journey to a brewery. Ray Galer describes an old oast house in St Mary Cray:

'The New Estate was the first hop garden out of London. There is still to be seen a solitary hop vine clinging to the past in some of the gardens. Do you know reader, that the St Mary Cray oast house has become part of a factory. Anyhow, it is still there, and there is to be a new road built by the side of the factory. This road I would term 'Oasthouse Lane'. It would be a very dear name to those who have smelt and tasted the twang of cooking hops and coke and sulphur. I know that all true hop pickers will be with me in this matter. The oast house once stood by the side of a country lane. This country lane is now the arterial road. Thus does time march on, and we with time.

I must look in at my old friend the basket maker, just to remind him that tomorrow will be mid-summer's day and to jog his memory that many a bushel basket will be needed over against the time of hopping in many a Kentish hop garden this coming harvest – he has turned out many a bushel basket in his time as his father did before him. Yes, I must jog his memory, for he is, like everybody else, doing other work. Yet the colour of his mind must give him the vision of many a hop 'Hill' – of crowds of home pickers and 'foreigners' (Londoners) who make the gardens ring with song, of oast houses working all night, the glow of a red charcoal and coke fire, the peculiar twang of heated hops that pervades the whole countryside, for 'hops' are Kent and Kent is Hopland. And hop gardens are not far away from Cray even today. And just to remind you, reader, there is still the remains of the old oast house on the arterial road, which is now a factory; it baked the hops which originally came off the new estate, for many years the first hop garden on leaving London. Well, so much for my friend the basket maker.'

The Tugmutton Gypsies were not the largest or best known Traveller community in south east London. This accolade belonged to the Gypsies of Star Lane, St Mary Cray, which is believed to be the biggest Traveller community in England. The history of the Star Lane Gypsies will be the subject of the third volume of this family history: *Corkes Meadow – the life and times of Noah Pateman and his family.*

2. Bastard Green

- Betsy Pateman (1880-1881)
- Emmie Pateman (1882-1956)

Hasted: 'Farnborough Hall is an estate here which was in early times held by Simon de Chellesfield of Simon de Montford, Earl of Leicester, in the reign of Henry III. John Fleming possessed it in the reign of King Edward I, whose heirs paid aid for it in 1347. At the making the Black Prince a Knight, as one Knight's fee in Farnboro which Simon de Chellesfield before held of Simon de Montford. This estate went soon afterwards by purchase to Pettey and again to Peche in as short a time. From him it descended down to Sir John Peche of Lullingstone in this county, Knight and Baronet, who dying without issue, Elizabeth his sister became his heir and her husband John Hart of the Middle Temple Esquire, Barrister at Law became in her right entitled to it and in his descendants it continued until Percival Hart of Lullingstone Esqr. Leaving an only daughter and heir Anne, she carried it in marriage to her second husband Sir Thomas Dyke of Horeham in Sussex Bart and their only son Sir John Descon Dyke of Lullingstone Bart is the present possessor of Farn Hall and the estate belonging to it.

In a private Act of Parliament passed in the year 1756 for a family settlement of this estate it is thus described: 'All that capital messuage and farm called Farn Hall with its appurts and 350 acres of arable, pasture and wood land in the parish of Farn and all that messuage with its appurts and 175 acres of arable pasture and wood land in the said parish of Farnborough is within the ecclesiastical jurisdiction of the diocese of Rochester and the Deanery of Dartford.' The Church which stands at the South East end of the village is dedicated to St Giles the Abbot (he was a retired man and solitary hermit) on which all the churches dedicated to him are commonly placed at the uttermost part of a town or village, to show that he shunned the commerce and praise of mankind to devote himself in his retirement to work of charity and good deeds among the poor and impotent.

On December 26th 1639 it was so rent and torn by a violent storm of wind that the inhabitants were forced to take it down and rebuild it, as appears, by a brief granted for that purpose dated December 27th in the seventeenth year of King Charles I Anno 1641. The Church of Farn is only a Chapel to the adjoining parish of Chelsfield, the Rector of which is instituted to the Rectory of Chelsfield with the charge of Farn annexed. Adjoining to Keston eastward lies Farnborough, called in the Textus Roffensis Fearnberga. It most probably took its name from the natural disposition of the soil to bear fern the latter syllable berge signifying in old English a little hill an etymology well suiting the situation of the place.

The Manor in the reign of King Edward I was held of Thomas Earl of Lancaster by the eminent family of Grandison, Otte de Grandison made it the principal seat of his residence. He was greatly esteemed by that prince having in his father King Henry the Third's time attended him in the Holy Land. In the eighteenth year of King Edward I he obtained license to hold a market upon a Tuesday here and a fair yearly on the feast of St Giles the Abbot Septr. 1st and had at the same time a grant of free warren in all his demesne lands at Farn.'

James Pateman

James Pateman was born on 17 July 1846 'in a tent on Cooling Common, Cliffe'. His father, Robert Pateman, was described as a labourer. Charles Dickens is associated with several places in the county of Kent where he lived for many years. Some of the places he described in his books were based on places in Kent. One such was the tiny village of Cooling, situated just outside the City of Rochester.

Cooling's history is said to date back to before Saxon times. The parish in which it sits is just over two thousand acres in size and stretches from Lodge Hill near Chattenden in the north to the River Thames which forms its northern boundary. It is near the river that the oldest part of the village lies, including a unique ruined castle and a church. It is believed the word Cooling comes from the old English words 'Cu' meaning 'cow' and 'Ling' meaning a 'pasture' though another theory suggests it was named Cooling because of its somewhat bleak and cold situation. The first theory is probably correct as a Saxon charter calls it 'Cinges Culand' or 'The King's Cow Land.'

As it was primarily a Saxon settlement, it must have been one of the first in the county of Kent. The Saxons first called it 'Culingas', later it was referred to in the eighth century Doomsday Book as 'Coolinge' and a map dating back to 1596 describes it as 'Cowlinge'.

In 1241 the de Cobham family became lords of the manor and the Cobhams held this manor until the late 1600s. In 1381 the third baron, John de Cobham, applied to Richard II to fortify his manor house. The tide used to flow up to the castle then, bringing the risk of attack from the sea, though now there is over two and a half miles between castle and Thames. (A fact realised when in the course of the clearing of "rubbish" away from the walls of the castle in the nineteenth century, a "large vessel was cut through", this apparently being an unidentified wooden ship's hull.)

In 1379 the French had sailed up the river and burnt the villages in the vicinity which concentrated the king's mind to grant John de Cobham his license to build. On completing his castle, outer and inner wards with curtain walls, connected by a drawbridge over a moat, he fixed to the gatehouse a copper tablet that has been restored since and can be seen high up on the east tower. The inscription states:

"Knouwyth that beth and schul be
That I am mad in help of the cuntre
In knowing of whyche thyng
Thys is charter and wytnessyng"

Henceforth the manor house was known as Cooling Castle. The two towered gate house (built by Thomas Comp at a cost of no less than £8) and parts of the curtain wall are all that survive in recognizable form of de Cobham's castle; when visitors see the complete 40ft high impressive gatehouse topped by battlements they sometimes assume it is the castle, but the remains of this are within the gatehouse's entrance across the dried up moat.

When Sir John died in 1408 the house was inherited by his daughter who survived three husbands before she married 'that warrior of renown' Sir John Oldcastle, a Lollard leader and, therefore, a kind of early socialist, believing that church wealth should be distributed among the poor. The Archbishop of Canterbury did not share Sir John's views and a summons for the Squire of Cooling's arrest was delivered to the castle. Sir John escaped but was eventually caught, tried in London, hanged and burned before a large crowd outside St Giles' Hospital in London on Christmas Day 1417.

Sir John is usually supposed to have been the model for Shakespeare's Falstaff. His widow married for the fifth time and in 1554 the castle was captured by Sir Thomas Wyatt. But it was not much used after 1580 and the present house was built in about 1670, on the site of the original Saxon manor. Today the house remains in private occupation. Immediately adjoining it is the sixteenth century tithe barn, a listed building which has been beautifully restored and is now available for functions of all kinds. Part of the building is equipped and licensed for the conduct of weddings.

In 1797 the Kent historian, Edward Hasted wrote of Cooling: 'Cowling is an unfrequented place, the roads of which are deep and miry, and it is as unhealthy as it is unpleasant.' A nineteenth century writer on Cooling recorded that Thomas Murton, a farmer on the Cooling Castle estate, found a use for one part of the castle by annually holding his Harvest Home supper in the castle's former chapel. Here 70 to 80 of his labourers were 'regaled with true olde English hospitality'.

The Church of St James

The charming little church of St James, Cooling, dates mostly from the thirteenth century, though parts of it are Norman, and the tower is fifteenth century. It has a stair turret and fine examples of medieval stone canopied stalls. Built of local ragstone, banded with knapped flints at the base of the tower, much is contemporary with the castle. Inside, however, the chancel has a striking scheme of six arches on each side, sedilia and piscine, all richly carved and dating from about 1260. There is old woodwork, a fine thirteenth century font, some interesting memorials and the vestry walls are covered with cockle shells.

The marshland is just over the wall and the Thames is but nearly two miles distant. Cooling churchyard is about 20 feet above sea level and one can imagine swirling mists over the marsh to the horror of villagers and parents of small children in particular over the centuries. The Comport family are said to have been organizers of smuggling in the area and to have even hidden some of the smuggled goods inside Cooling Church – under the pulpit.

When you enter the churchyard of St James at Cooling you are instantly aware of the deep sense of history associated with it and the church. The churchyard's association, in particular with the novels of Charles Dickens, attract people from all over the world. Many come to see the strange lozenge shaped graves which Dickens described in the opening pages of *Great Expectations*.

The graves Dickens described belonged to members of the Comport family, many of whom lived at Cooling Court and in the manor house built in the ruins of the outer ward of Cooling Castle which they purchased in 1795. Near the south side of the tower by the porch is a headstone with three winged cherub heads at the top. Beside it on the west are three small body stones. These are the graves of Ellen Elizabeth Baker, died 11 August 1853 aged three months; Sarah Anne Baker, died 2 July 1837 aged three months; John Rose Baker, died 9 June 1837 aged one month. They were the children of John Rose Baker and his wife Sarah Anne, daughter of Michael Comport of Decoy House, High Halstow.

The row of ten stones on the east side of the head stone are: William Comport, died 12 May 1771 aged eight months; William Comport, died 7 June 1773 aged seven months; James Comport, died 15 October 1777 aged four months; Frances Comport, died 7 June 1775 aged 17 months; William Comport, died 9 March 1799 aged eight months; Elizabeth Comport, died 5 October 1799 aged three years. These six children were sons and daughters of Michael and Jane Comport of Cooling Court and Cooling Castle. The other four headstones consist of Sarah Elizabeth Comport, died July 1799 aged three months, the daughter of George Comport of Gattons House, Cliffe; Thomas Comport, died November 1800 aged three months, second son of Michael Comport of Decoy House, High Halstow; not identified, but thought to be Mary, eldest daughter of Michael and Jane Comport, born at Cooling Court 17 October 1767.

Though the names on the tombstones are all children of the Comport family what is so tragic is their ages; they were all very young. Unfortunately Cooling at that time was greatly affected by malaria which is transmitted by a strain of mosquito so it is possible they might have succumbed to the disease. At that time no one knew malaria was the result of a mosquito bite, it was believed to have been caused by foul air emitted from the marshes.

Great Expectations

Charles Dickens lived for many years at Gad's Hill Place in the village of Higham just over five miles away and regularly walked through Cooling. The opening chapter of *Great Expectations* features Pip, the narrator, describing the tombstones of his parents and siblings:

'The shape of the letters on my father's grave gave me an odd idea that he was a square, stout dark man with curly hair. From the character and turn of the inscription, 'Also Georgiana Wife of the Above', I drew a childish conclusion that my mother was freckled and sickly. To five little stone lozenges, each about a foot and a half long, which were arranged in a neat row beside their grave and were sacred to the memory of five little brothers of mine – who gave up trying to get a living exceedingly early in that universal struggle – I am indebted for a belief I religiously entertained that they had been born on their backs with their hands in their trouser pockets and had never taken them out in this state of existence.'

Although there is no actual proof that Dickens was describing the churchyard at Cooling most historians believe he was. Even though there are other church yards in the area with similar tombstones it was the description of the surrounding landscape which makes it more than likely that Cooling was the site of 'Pip's graves':

'Ours was the marsh country, down by the river, within, as the river wound, twenty miles of the sea. My first most vivid and broad impression of the identity of things seems to me to have been gained on a memorable raw afternoon towards evening. At such a time I found out for certain, that this bleak place overgrown with nettles was the churchyard;…and that the dark flat wilderness beyond the church yard, intersected with dykes and mounds and gates, with scattered cattle feeding on it, was the marshes; and that the low leaden line beyond was the river; and that the distant savage lair from which the wind was rushing, was the sea."

Charles Dickens' son, Sir Henry Field Dickens was also convinced that his father used Cooling church yard for the scene in *Great Expectations*. In a letter to *The Dickensian* magazine of January 1925 he wrote: '…the church is Cooling Church – Lower Higham is quite out of the question. I know this as an absolute fact, having often walked with my father and we have together looked down upon the little gravestones in Cooling Churchyard.'

Today the area may appear less wild than it would have done when Dickens describes Pip's meeting with the convict, Magwich, but not much has changed. There may be a few more houses and the road is no longer a rutted track but when the sea mists rise and the wind blows the picture appears little different. If more proof be needed, the following account of a visit to Cooling provides it:

'It was in this place that something of Dickens's vivacity can be evoked in an incident one summer's day. As James Field the American publisher recalled Dickens had chosen a good flat gravestone in one corner…he had spread a wide napkin thereon after the fashion of a domestic dinner table, and was rapidly transferring the contents of the hamper to that point. The horrible whimsicality of trying to eat and make merry under these deplorable circumstances, the tragic-comic character of the scene, appeared to take him by surprise. He at once threw himself into it…with fantastic eagerness. It conjures up what Dickens would have called a 'picture' – the church on the edge of the wild marshes, a few cottages and a decayed rectory beside it, the distant sea line, the tall grasses of the marshes with the wind going through them, and here is Dickens, who has so often mimicked the tones of the waiter in his fiction, going through this 'routine' by the very graves of the children of Cooling. If it is reminiscent of anything, it is of the scene in *The Old Curiosity Shop* where Little Nell and her grandfather come across the image of Punch perched cross legged upon a tombstone. It is quintessential Dickens, in fact, this wild humour in a melancholy landscape.'

Even though Cooling Church and its church yard looks very much the same today as it did when Charles Dickens used to visit, Cooling itself has changed. Adjoining the church yard at that time was a row of three small houses known locally as 'The Poor Cottages'. Between them and the school house nearby was a space for a garden in which there was a well. This was presumably for the use of the cottages.

Besides these, on the side of the road, a small forge existed until about 1888. The building in which it was situated was a rough timber shed, the back of which leaned against the wall separating the school from the garden. The smithy belonged to a farmer who lived at the castle and who allowed his neighbours to use it for shoeing their horses and repairing farm implements.

Eventually the forge was torn down and a cottage built on the site. This was named appropriately enough 'The Forge' and its first tenants were a Mr. and Mrs. Bloomfield who came to Cooling in 1863. The Forge and The Poor Cottages were all demolished at the same time and the present row of four brick cottages erected on the site are known as 'Strand Cottages'.

Further along the road is the Old Rectory now converted into flats and then, beyond several houses and bungalows on both sides of the road, there is *The Horseshoe and Castle* public house. A map of 1897 shows a pub on this site. The editor of *The Dickensian* magazine in 1922 described it as a 'typical village inn in all appearances like a doll's house built of wood in a quite plain fashion, lying a little back from the road.' It was also described in *Great Expectations* as *The Jolly Bargeman* where Joe Gargery and Pip used to while away hours in the evening.

The pub is also the scene of many incidents in the story. It was the meeting place of all the men of the village to whom Mr. Wopsle read the news around the fire and where all the village gossip of the village was relayed. It was the inn at which Mr. Jaggers unexpectedly appeared one day enquiring after Pip which ultimately resulted in the change in Pip's fortune.

During the Great War *The Horseshoe and Castle* caught fire. Firemen from Cliffe galloped to the scene but there was not enough water in the nearby pond to save the building which had to be entirely rebuilt. In 1987 the pub was under threat of closure. It was saved following a campaign by Ann Marsh, whose grandmother walked the marshes with Charles Dickens. 'The Shoes' is still a popular pub, and the atmosphere has changed greatly from the days when the rules of the house, dated 1786, stated:

'No thieves, fakirs, rogues or tinkers,
No skulking loafers or flea bitten tramps.
No slap or tickle of the wenches.
No banging of tankards on the tables.
No cockfighting.
Flintlocks, cudgels, daggers and swords to be handed
To the innkeeper for safe keeping'

It is interesting to speculate whether James Pateman or any of his family would have been served in this pub!

Cliffe

James Pateman was baptized with his brother, John (born 1844), on 26 July 1846 at St Helen's church, Cliffe. His father, Robert, was described as a basket maker. Cliffe is on the Hoo Peninsula (between the Thames and the Medway), one of the hidden corners of Kent, often overlooked by travelers visiting the main attractions of the county. It is a largely unspoilt region, with over 155 miles of public rights of way from which to explore this empty landscape, so beloved of Charles Dickens.

Cliffe, now little more than a village, was once an important religious centre and a medieval town of some size. The medieval street pattern can still be traced within the modern settlement. Cliffe stands on a low bluff that slopes gently away to the marshes. Its position between the rivers Thames and Medway, and close proximity to Rochester, Gravesend and London, helped the town to prosper in the early Middle Ages, although its origins are far older. There may have been a settlement here in pre-Roman Britain and it was certainly a place of some importance in Saxon times. Synods (church councils) are thought to have been held at the church between AD700-800. Stephen Langton is also believed by some historians to have drawn up the draft for the Magna Carta in the church rectory.

St Helen's Church was begun about 1260, on the site of a much older predecessor. Its distinctive style, using alternating bands of flint and ragstone, both natural stones to Kent, and its impressive size, gives a hint of the former importance of Cliffe. The town once stood much closer to the sea, as evidenced by the presence of Wharf Lane that now terminates at the marsh edge. The area was also once a popular smuggler's haunt and some of the houses, particularly in Wharf Lane, had deep cellars in which to hide the contraband.

From the twelfth century onwards the marshes were gradually drained and reclaimed by the monks of Christchurch, Canterbury; the Church Commissioners still own large tracts of land in the area. By the mid fourteenth century the present day coastline had been more or less established, leaving Cliffe marooned some distance inland. Since then the sea walls have been progressively extended and heightened, partly to reclaim more land for use as pasture and partly as a sea defense. Some idea of what this landscape might have looked like in the early Middle Ages can be gained by looking out across the flat marshes, interspersed now with drainage ditches and gravel workings, and imagine that all of this was once water, stretching right up to the River Thames on the horizon. In the great floods of 1953 the Thames burst through the sea defenses to reclaim its old domain, giving a glimpse of its medieval grandeur.

In 1520 Cliffe was badly damaged by a disastrous fire, which further hastened the decline of the town. During the late nineteenth and early twentieth centuries, it briefly prospered again with the growth of cement workings and a gunpowder works, but these industries have now also gone into decline to leave Cliffe once more a forgotten back water. In 1860, as a result of a Royal Commission, an artillery fort was built, intended to provide a cross fire with similar forts on the Essex side of the river to protect the lower Thames from a feared French invasion. In 1885 an experimental torpedo station, designed by the inventor Louis Brennan, was constructed in the fort and guns remained in position there until after the Second World War. Sadly, the fort has been neglected and is in dire need of restoration. It stands on private land, but can be clearly seen from the public footpath that runs along the sea wall, as can the launch rails for the torpedoes

James spent his child hood traveling around Kent, Surrey and Middlesex with his family, picking fruit, vegetables and hops and making baskets, skewers and pegs. These journeys took him to Westwood (1851), Burham (1855), Frindsbury (1856), Rochester (1857), St Mary Hoo (1858), Stockbury (1859), Hammersmith (1861) and Bromley (1866).

1871 Census

On 2 April 1871 James Pateman (21, Cliffe, Gypsy) was living with his family in an old stable on a brick field at Becks Lane, Beckenham, Kent. Sometime after 1871 James left his family, 'married' Jane Reynolds (for more information about Jane and her family, see Chapter 6 – Fellow Travellers) and moved from Beckenham to St Mary Cray in Kent.

James and Jane had eighteen children between 1880 and 1904: Betsy (1880), Emmie (1882), Phyllis (1883), Hannah (1884), Robert (1885), Mary Ann (1886), Charlotte (1887), Phoebe (1889), Jane (1890), Celia (1892), John (1893), Polly (1894), Betsy (1896), Elvy (1897), George (1899), Daisy (1901), Rose (1903), William (1904).

After James moved to Farnborough in 1881 he lived the rest of his life in this area. His address was variously described as: Farnborough (1881); Bastard Green (1881); Tugmutton (1882); Stone's Cottages (1886); Locks Bottom (1893); Starts Hill (1894); Willow Walk (1900); 5 Tugmutton (1901); Wellbrook Road (1901); Willow Lane (1902); 5 Willow Walk (1912).

Farnborough is a generic name for the whole area of Farnborough Village and Locks Bottom (a hamlet of Farnborough Village). Stones Cottages (Stow's Cottages) are in Farnborough Village. Bastard Green is adjacent to Tugmutton (Common), Start's Hill and Wellbrook Road. Willow Walk (Lane) runs along the edge of Tugmutton Common. 5 Tugmutton is the same address as 5 Willow Walk.

James Pateman was described as: Gypsy (1871); Hawker (1880); labourer (1881); bricklayer's labourer (1882); builder's labourer (1886); greengrocer (1887); Pedlar (1889); potato dealer (1891); general labourer (1892); general Hawker (1893); potato merchant (1922); potato salesman (1928); salesman (1928); general dealer (1929).

From this we can surmise that James carried out a number of occupations which can be categorized as follows:

Gypsy, Hawker, Pedlar, general Hawker: this was when James was living the life of a Gypsy, traveling around Kent and selling Gypsy crafts such as pegs, wooden flowers and skewers.

Labourer, bricklayer's labourer, builder's labourer, general labourer: this was when James was leading a more settled life – in the winter months at least – at Farnborough and offering his services to local builders. His work as a bricklayer's labourer provides a link with the many connections between bricks and the Pateman family (see *Hoo, Hops and Hods*)

Greengrocer, potato dealer, potato merchant, potato salesman, salesman, general dealer: this was when James was fully settled in Farnborough and ran an established business selling fruit and vegetables from a cart to local residents. His father, Robert Pateman, was also a greengrocer (1890).

James Pateman died on 29 May 1926 at 5 Willow Walk, Farnborough. He was a 79 year old general labourer. He died of "senile decay" and the informant was 'F.

Pankhurst, son in law, present at the death, 5 Willow Walk, Farnborough.' This was Frederick Pankhurst, the husband of Phoebe Pateman. James was buried on 5 June 1926 at St Giles Churchyard, Farnborough, in the same grave as his father, Robert Pateman (1890) and his son George Pateman (1921).

Betsy Pateman (1880-1881)

Betsy Pateman was born on 22 November 1880 at Star Lane, St Pauls Cray. Her father was a "Hawker" and the informant was "Jane Pateman, mother, Star Lane"

Star Lane is actually in St Mary Cray. The local Gypsy population is believed to be the largest in England. Gypsies have been living in St Mary Cray for over 130 years. There is a photograph of a bender tent at St Mary Cray, dated 1870. When Corke's Meadow (near Sevenoaks Way Gas Works) was cleared for development, many of the displaced families were re-housed in the Star Lane area.

Ray Galer was the vicar of St Mary's church, St Mary Cray, and he befriended the Star Lane Gypsy community. Here he describes where he would like to travel to in a Gypsy vardo:

'I was going along the High Street towards the old Church when to my keen and delighted eyes I saw a caravan all newly painted up. The red was so red and the gold was so gold and it was ready harnessed to start on the road – the open road to land of romance whither the old horse will lead it. Its interior looked so snug – there was the stove, shining in brass – there was the bed made up in the bunk with a quilt the colour of the wild flowers of the field, and there was I, ready to jump on board and let the old horse take it, or me, wherever we desired to go. Yes, I wanted the wind and the heath, the hills and the dales, the hops, the apple trees, the woods and the clothes pegs, the meal by the hedge and the evening full of stars, the silence of the night out in the open, when birds, and beasts and flowers have gone to sleep – and one learns far more in the silence of the night than in the bustle and noise of the day.

Once upon a time there was a poor Oxford scholar, who, tired of waiting for preferment which never came his way, and tired of the promises of friends at Oxford which came to nothing, saw a company of Gypsies pass by with their caravans and on the impulse of the open road, left the City of Spires and Dreams for the wind and the heath, all promises thrown to the wind, all conventionalities scattered, for to his mind he had found his heart's desire – and those who have read the poem of the Scholar Gypsy by Mathew Arnold, realize the power of attraction in a caravan, an old horse, and the open road before one.

Naturally, this new caravan made me envy the Oxford Scholar and the call of the open road – my mind was full of it - and when the man in charge of the horse asked if I would buy it, here was my dream come true, here was my forgetfulness of life's worries, and my absent mindedness about to be really on the move and on the road.

Where would I go? There were so many roads I wanted to go on at once. Should I take the road past the oast houses and put up the caravan by the side of the hop garden? I could smell the sulphur of the baking hops; I could feel the tang in the air as I finished another day's hopping. Would the tally still be five bushels a shilling?

Would the measurer's hand go heavy? Would my hops be clean enough for the poke? And once again could I smell the frying of the herrings out in the open fields when picking had been called off for the day. Yes, I would take the road to Paddock Wood, to Wateringby, to the Farleighs. I would go there through the old county town of Maidstone, and I would have a goodly company on the road, for the cry of the hops has gone forth and many are answering that call.

And yet, there was another road I would take – the road across the heath where, sitting by the roadside, my pile of clothes pegs would mount up, provided I had enough old tins to make the bands – and now is the time for clothes props. Yes, I would make my way across Coxheath and go down to sell my wares in the villages of the Weald.

It was so difficult for me to choose. I would take the road via Farnborough, once famous for its rushes - the church still has its annual rush sermon – and I would turn out those wicker chairs which hang on the outside of caravans. No doubt, my friend the basket maker, could give me a tip or two as to what kind of rush I should use.

Then suddenly it took me – the old road across Romney Marsh, past Dymchurch, past old Romney, and here I would turn the remains of the fleece of the sheep which also adorn the outside of my caravan, and many a cottage hearth here in the marsh. So here would my caravan halt amidst the mists of old smuggling days, so here would I weave my fleece as well as the fancies of my mind.

Another road! But my forgetfulness and my absent- mindedness came to a sudden end by the man demanding the price I was to pay for the caravan, so I came down to earth with a bump – and to modern ways of life, for I was due at the old church in a very little while – but I was there in time, alive and alert for my work

'You might think that I made this song,
for joy of song as I strode along, one
day between Kentish lanes, slashing
at scarlet hips and haws, but thinking, so you
nothing know, of children taken unawares,
of tinkers' tents, among the gorse, the
poor lean goat, the hobbled horse,
and painted vans for country fairs.'

Anyway, I was up to time and alert for work. But I do know that I went with a lighter tread and a sweeter mind after my encounter with the man who wanted me to buy the newly painted caravan of red and gold, with the horse in the shafts ready to start on the road'.

Galer mentioned Farnborough, and there were connections between the Gypsy communities of St Mary Cray and Farnborough. Today a bus service – the R4 – connects the two historical Gypsy communities of Farnborough and St Mary Cray.

1881 Census

Sometime after Betsy was born in November 1880, James moved from St Mary Cray to Farnborough in Kent. On 3 April 1881 James Pateman (29, bricklayer's labourer,

Cliffe) was living at Bastard Green, Farnborough, Kent, with his wife, Jane Reynolds (20, St Mary Cray) and their daughter Betsy (4 months, St Mary Cray). "Bastard Green" was in fact "Broadstreet Green", also known as Brasted Green and Broad Green. This piece of land was adjacent to Pickington's Lane (also known as Piggendens Lane, Croydon Road and Orpington Lane) though its true old name is that of Piggerton Lane, after a farm of that name near the *Black Horse*. Today it is known as Crofton Lane.

John Reynolds (brother of Jane) was also living at Bastard Green with his wife and seven children. John Pateman (older brother of James) was lodging in Orpington Lane. William Pateman (younger brother of James) was living in a van on the side of Orpington Lane with his wife Mercy Reynolds (sister of Jane) and their two children. George Reynolds (brother of Jane) was living in a van in Piggendens Lane with his wife, Mary Pateman (sister of James) and his four children.

So here we have the start of a Gypsy community in Farnborough consisting of members of the Pateman and Reynolds families who had settled in this area of north west Kent / south east London. They used Farnborough as a winter base where they could make and sell their wares – pegs, skewers, wooden flowers – and offer their services – chair repairing and basket making. When the spring came they would set off on their travels again to Kent for the vegetable, fruit and hop picking.

Also living at Bastard Green were Thomas Weatherley*, John Lockyer, William Mitchell*, James Cutbush, Charles Luis, George Clark, Robert Gregory*, George Bird and Jonathan Bird*. Those with an asterisk had also been living at Bastard Green at the time of the 1871 census: Thomas Weatherley*, Richard Johnson, George Steers, David Bridger, William Mitchell*, Sarah Weatherley, Henry Clark, Sarah Messenger, Edward Friend, Robert Gregory*, William Poynter and Jonathan Bird*.

Broadsteet Green is in the hamlet of Locks Bottom, Farnborough. Researchers cannot agree on how Locks Bottom got its name. There are a number of theories as to who it was named after: J. Lock, an overseer at St Giles church; a blacksmith whose forge was built opposite the *Black Horse*; John Locke Lovibond; the Lock Up (i.e. police station); the lock of a toll gate. None of these have been proven and the mystery remains.

Less mysterious is the derivation of nearby Pratts Bottom, which was named after the family of Stephen Pratt (1332). The name of Bottom (which means lower) appears in many places in the UK such as: Ramsbottom (Yorkshire), Wray with Bottom (North Lancashire), Bottom Boat (Yorkshire), Bottom Craig (Scotland), Bottomstead (Berkshire) and Bottom Net (Cornwall).

Betsy Pateman died on 13 November 1881 at Tugmutton, Farnborough, aged 12 months. She died of 'convulsions exhaustion', which lasted for five days. She was described as the daughter of James Pateman, a labourer. The death certificate was signed with 'the mark of Jane Pateman, mother, present at the death, Tugmutton, Farnborough'. Betsy was buried on 19 November 1881 at St Giles, Farnborough.

St Giles the Abbott, Farnborough

Mr Wilson, M.A., F.S.A, in the *Parish Registers of Farnborough* gives 'Notes extracted from the registers of Rochester, Lambeth &c.':

'Farnborough paid sixpence chrism fee to the see of Rochester as a chapel according to Textus Roffensis. It was a chapel of Chelsfield, from which it was served in the time of Bishop Longdon, 1430. But in 1385 we find in Archbishop Courtenaye's register, folio 350, John de Dounstone styled Perpetual Vicar of Farnborough'.

There is no record that will give an idea of the age of the Yew in front of the Church. The Yew in Orpington church yard was planted in 1630, so probably the Farnborough Churchyard yew was planted around the same time, possibly in 1639 to commemorate the rebuilding of the Nave in that year.

The church was rebuilt in 1639 wholly of flint. If the walls of the Church are examined it will be seen that the North Wall of the transept is much older than the other, and a different class of work, and contains some stone intermixed with the flints; this stone may have been some of the sound material saved from an old edifice; the wall with its Tudor window is the fifteenth century work. The whole of the glass now in the transept window is not the original glass. A small thief got through the window and broke open the alms box, in which, as usual, there was only a trifle. The glass was replaced and fairly well matched; but it is easy to distinguish the old and new glass by looking at the centre of the flowers, the new glass is much clearer. The glass in the Church windows was frequently broken by boys throwing stones, and the accounts show heavy expenditure on replacing glass.

The present gallery, and one above it, was erected in 1723. The steeple was blown down in 1724, when a great storm passed over part of Kent, and in 1791 a charge was made for taking down the weather cock, painting, gilding and replacing it. In 1828 the steeple was slated, before this it was covered with oak shingles. There are no records to show how the steeple was destroyed in or about 1838, but from information obtained from villagers it was destroyed by lightning, and the following resolution shows the tower was badly damaged, which points to lightning, for had it been wind it would probably have been blown down. The steeple is not mentioned. 'Agreed to rebuild and resolved to rebuild to a reduced size of ten feet square in the clear', and in 1838 the tower was rebuilt.

The Vestry Room was rebuilt in 1838 and the present entrance into it made. The old doorway leading into the Church from the Vestry was built up. In the upper gallery the musicians sat, and in 1842 an organ was placed there. The North side of the Church was re-tiled in 1844, and the South side some years later. In 1845 the organ was removed from the upper to the lower gallery and the upper gallery dismantled, and to compensate for loss of sittings the old pews on the South side were remodeled, and a few years later those on the North side of the aisle.

St Giles has seen more big occasions than many village churches, due to the close proximity of two wealthy families: the Lubbocks and the Aveburys of High Elms and the Fox's of the brewery. From 1875 we have a good description of one such occasion, the marriage of Helen Fox. Many hours before the ceremony, villagers of all the surrounding places began flocking in by cart and on foot to see the elaborately dressed society guests arrive. Each side of the main path, Sunday School children formed a guard of honour, carrying posies of flowers to throw at the feet of the bride, who had been their teacher. Typically the Fox family did not forget the workers who underlay their wealth; on the evening of the next day, their entire workforce plus the men's wives were entertained to supper.

The Revd. George William Hingston became Rector of St. Giles in 1876 and over the next few years many changes were to take place. In 1885 Frederick Jessop Kelly became the Rector of St Giles. In 1885 Mr. John Fox offered St Giles church a new organ with the proviso that the congregation provide a suitable chamber in which to house it. The offer was taken up promptly, and by 1886 the Diocese Architect Joseph Clarke had been appointed to undertake the work. By the time work commenced, the brief had been extended to include the restoration of the chancel, a project which produced the Eastern arrangement that exists today. Mr. Fox was one of the generous landowners in Farnborough with deep concerns for both the village and its people.

The Parish Vestry consisting of the Rector, Churchwardens and Overseers, who had to carry out all the civil duties in the parish, such as raising local taxes, looking after the poor and repairing the roads, was replaced, under an Act of Parliament in 1894, by an elected (Civil) Parish Council whose area of administration was the same as the Ecclesiastical Parish. In the case of Farnborough, this Civil Parish became combined with other Civil Parishes to form Orpington Urban District Council, later to become part of the London Borough of Bromley.

New windows were placed in the South wall of the Church in 1894, the old windows having been blown in during a storm. Lord Avebury, Messrs Fox and Sons, Mr. Bealby and friends each gave a window, and the other was paid for by subscriptions. Graves Lombard became the Rector of St Giles in 1898.

The Vestry was re-tiled in 1901. The Choir Vestry was built in 1903. Ebenezer Joseph Welch became the Rector of St Giles in 1904. A postcard of the church in 1907 shows no sign yet of the beautiful grove of trees that were destroyed by the hurricane in 1987. Gas radiators were fixed in the church in 1908 to act as auxiliaries to the old furnace. In 1908 the large bell was re-cast by Messrs. Gillett and Johnson, of Croydon, and made about 2 cwts. heavier. The date on the old bell was 1667, and was made by John Hodson. The small bell was made in 1664 and when it became cracked was put in the Church Porch; this small bell in the accounts is called 'tinker bell'. There are signs in the oak beams in the belfry roof that several bells were fixed there at some time before the tower was rebuilt in 1838; but they are not mentioned in any of the available records, and in any case only two bells have been used for about the last 300 years, for in the accounts are the following entries: '1718 mending the bell wheel. 1764 paid for a bell rope and grave, and tinker ropes'. In Edward VI's valuation we read: 'Item iii bells sated in brass in the steeple.'

The wooden chest in which the parish records were kept is made of fir, the inside is in very good order; but the outside has been badly damaged by insects. The chest is four feet, six inches long, seventeen inches wide and eighteen inches deep; there is nothing to show the age of this chest; but in 1790 it was broken into by robbers and slightly damaged near the two locks by the instruments used in forcing it open. Nothing appears to have been taken from the chest, but a few things were stolen from the Chancel, or Vestry. The chest contained old account books and a lot of Indentures, Securities for people coming into the village, License and Faculty, Tithe Maps in locked tin case, and a large quantity of miscellaneous papers.

The beautiful parish church of St. Giles was testimony to the hold which religion still had over some of its parishioners. The church played an important social role in various ways. It was a place where squalid home conditions could be forgotten for a short while during a service of worship and music. The Beulah Baptist Chapel was in Wellbrook Road; the Rev. Isaac Ballard was its founder, and he was the pastor for 35 years until his death in 1899. There was also a Mission Hall at Green Street Green. It was estimated that less than a third of the village people attended a religious service. Sunday schools for the children were popular and were conducted usually by well-meaning young ladies from local well- to-do families.

The ancient St Giles Fair, which dates back to 1292, is still held in the field behind the church in July, one of the happiest days of the local year. The interesting Rush Sermon is still regularly preached on the uncertainty of life. This was ordered after a local drunkard who was locked out by his angry wife, tottered off towards Tubbenden and staggered into a rush fringed pond to drown.

The churchyard

A sketch plan of the churchyard shows its original extent, with 'quick hedges' erected in 1856, 'iron standards and wire fences erected in 1885, 'chalk pit filled up 1909', and 'Lord Avebury's Plantation'. Another sketch map (on the church website) shows how land was added to the original church yard in 1854, 1885, 1935 and 1995. The Churchyard was enlarged by a quarter of an acre being attached on the West side in 1854. Five pounds was paid for trenching and planting the quick hedges along the West and North boundaries in 1856.

A new iron gate and unclimbable fence was erected in 1908 at the East End of the new portion of the Churchyard. The old chalk pit at the East end was filled up in 1909 with soil excavated for the sewer in the Gladstone and side road: it was a great help to the contractor to find a place so near to shoot the spare soil, and it was an advantage to have the hole filled up, and dressed off without cost. The oldest portion of the graveyard is probably the part east of the Chancel. When the foundations were being excavated for the new chancel the end of a lead coffin was seen, and it was just out of the line of excavation; there are no memorial stones on the site, probably they have been removed.

A list of families having memorials in the Church or Churchyard can be found in Blandord (1913). There are some old grave stones in the Chancel under the choir back seats on both sides, these memorial stones are probably those that were on the site of the enlarged portion of the Chancel; only a portion of these stones are visible; to see the other portion it would be necessary to remove part of the wood block floor. The age of the oldest person buried in the Church or Churchyard appears to be 96 (grave no. 79). The oldest memorial is to Edmund Pike in the aisle – no. 168 – and the date of this is 1624, but the registers give it as 1625. The oldest in the Churchyard is no. 172, year 1725.

A team of local historians recorded all the tombstones in the churchyard where the person died before 1900 – with a very few exceptions:

'When we set out to record the tombstones in Farnborough churchyard we thought it would be a simple straightforward task easily accomplished within a few days. In fact it took several weeks, although admittedly we were only able to spend a few hours on it each week.

It turned out to be most fascinating and interesting. The permission of the Rector was sought and given, and so armed with a suitable notebook we arrived at the church yard. Fortunately it had been possible to obtain a plan and a most helpful start from J. Harland Blandford's book on Farnborough which was published in 1913. In this book he identifies the memorial stones and gives a list of names, but some of these names have now faded and it is not possible to obtain any useful information about them. A simple list of names such as is contained in this book is really of no great use to either local historians or to genealogists.

The question of whether copying the church registers would be more useful than copying the inscriptions on tombstones, was considered. The position is that the church registers are preserved. The old ones for Farnborough are at present in the County Archives Office, Maidstone, and are available for inspection by interested persons, and it is hoped will be available in the future [these are now available at the Local History Library in Bromley]. The inscriptions on the tomb stones often contain more information about the deceased and his relatives than is contained in the registers, and it is this additional information which is so important to local historians and genealogists. These inscriptions are fading – even now it is not possible to decipher them all. In too short a time many will have gone – the tombstones perhaps removed or fallen and the wording gone for ever. In the circumstances it was decided to proceed with the recording of the older inscriptions.

We decided to start on one side of the church, and eventually armed with brushes, rags, buckets and pads of paper, the real job started. It was perhaps unfortunate that we started with some of the older tombstones, but after much rubbing, scraping and dodging about to get the sun's light at the right angle, we were able to record most of them. A surprising thing was that often we could read the letters on the older stones immediately after they had been cleaned, but within a second or two, the letters could no longer be read without further cleaning, when the letters would again become legible for a second or two. One, a flat stone, defied all our efforts. We spent a lot of time on this, and could pick out various letters, but the words remained illegible.

There is a mass of interesting and useful (and sometimes surprising) information contained in these inscriptions. That life can be short, even a hundred years ago, is clearly indicated by the number of children whose names we have recorded. A few people were long lived – Frances Bennett lived to 92 and Barbara Woodhams achieved 94 years. In addition to the range of the life's span there are tombstones recording those who have trod the paths of glory – General Sir John Floyd, Colonel of the 8th Dragoons and Governor of Gravesend and Tilbury forts; Walter St. John Fox, O.B.E., no doubt connected with the local brewery family and Commandant of the Metropolitan Special Constabulary, and others. How sad it is to learn that Edward Jones, aged 26, had only two months of holy wedlock. Jones was a common local name and we have recorded information about 18 of them. They are surpassed however by the Stows, for we recorded 20 of them. Mary Stow who died in 1748 left a husband and seven children, all of whom are named on the stone. Thomas Stow who died 27 years later is recorded as having left 3 sons and 4 daughters. The stone recording the death of Lieutenant William Hopson Player has never been completed and his date of death and his age seem to have been left blank.

Some of the people lived at Farnborough for many years and must have loved the place, and it is hoped, its people. William Richardson who died in 1836, was clerk of this parish for many years, and the Revd. Kelly was vicar of the parish for 14 years. Others perhaps retired here to spend the last years of their life in the peace and quiet of a country village. Thomas Carpenter, late of Scotland Yard; James William Carvill, surgeon; Simon Temple of Middle Temple, whose epitaph 'In honest men is the noblest work of God' must surely be the most sincere. One can only hope that the founder of the local Baptist church was quite happy to be buried in a Church of England church yard.

It is possible to identify places in the area Eg. Denbarn Farm, Chalk Farm, and Petleys. Also it is possible to identify two residents of Farnborough Hall; Frederick W. Smith who died in 1785 and William Stow who died in 1865. The Avebury / Lubbock memorials were a great shock. Some of the Lubbock family are buried in the church yard, and their memorials are in good condition, but the special or private burial ground of Lord Avebury and others of the Lubbock family, a short distance away from the church yard is in a deplorable condition. It is a great pity that the Lubbock family or Bromley Council cannot do something to restore to their rightful grandeur and dignity, the memorials to such a notable and famous local family.

Although it did not come within our 'time limit' terms of reference, we were most impressed with the beautiful, artistic, and also rather touching, memorial to Vernon March and his parents. This great artist has perhaps been rewarded by having such a memorial in the church yard. He may have designed it himself. We only took a spade in the church yard once. We expected a great deal of interest in our activities on this occasion, but we had no more than usual. Our intention was to raise a stone which was flat on the ground, but after cleaning it, we found the wording was on the side which was uppermost, so the spade was not used and was returned to the boot of the car. Passers by took a polite interest in our work and most expressed their approval of our intention to record the wording on the stones, especially when it was pointed out that so much of the wording was fading and would in a few years be illegible. One woman connected with the church was more than interested and turned out to have a great fund of local history information and told us anecdotes about some of the people registered on the tombstones, as she knew their descendents who still live in the village.

One interesting occasion we witnessed from a distance, was the burial of a Gypsy. We were impressed not only by the large number of wreaths and sprays, but also by the size of the crowd attending the funeral. We also noticed that someone places fresh flowers on graves which have no tombstones.'

There are many Gypsies buried at St Giles. One of the main sights of the graveyard is the elaborate gravestone of the Boswells, Gypsy 'royalty' whose extraordinary funerals remain legendary. Among them was Urania Boswell (Gypsy Lee), 'Queen' of Kent's Romanies and head of the Lee-Boswell clans. In 1933 her funeral was reported in the *Kentish Times*, the national *Times* newspaper and on a *Pathe* news reel. 15,000 spectators and mourners lined the route from dawn to see her wonderful ceremonial hearse drawn by six black horses slowly drive from the thatched cottage where she had lived for forty years. Liveried coachmen and outriders made an almost aristocratic occasion of the event. It is said that the crowd was so hushed that, when the coffin was carried out, an audible swish of the air was heard, as thousands of hats and caps were doffed at once. As the two hundred family and Gypsy mourners moved off, the onlookers tagged on to form a huge procession. Also buried at St Giles are Urania's husband, Levi Boswell (1924) and their children: Levi junior (1934), Kenzie (1949) and Percy Herbert (1947). It is said that their daughter, Norah Rose (1934), was buried quite literally on the 'other side of the hedge'" because she married a Gorgio. For a full account of the Boswell family see Chapter Seven.

Also buried in the church yard are: Mary Beatrice Stow (1925-2000), Charles Edward Stow (1921-2000), Eliza Coates (died 13 September 1951, aged 89), Albert Lee (died 20 March 1947, aged 65) and Matilda Lee (died 3 April 1955 aged 73).

Emmie Pateman (1882-1956)

Emmie Pateman (1882-1956) = William Fenton (1879-1927)
- James
- William
- Mary
- George
- William

Emmie Pateman was born at Tugmutton on 20 March 1882. Her father was a 'bricklayer's labourer' and the informant was 'Jane Pateman, mother, Tugmutton'.

Within the hamlet of Locks Bottom, Farnborough, there is Tugmutton Common. The name is derived from the English village green game of tying a leg of mutton on a high branch or pole, and getting contestants to jump to try and tug it down. It was also known as Leg of Mutton Common because it was shaped like a leg of lamb. The distinctive contours of Tugmutton Common can be clearly seen from Ordnance Survey Maps of 1909 and 1933 and from aerial photographs. These also show the cottages in Willow Walk where James Pateman, John Reynolds, Levi Boswell and the rest of the Tugmutton Gypsies lived.

On 27 August 1904 Emmie Pateman (23, spinster, Farnborough, father - James Pateman, labourer) married William Fenton (25, bachelor, blacksmith, Farnborough, father - Henry Fenton, chimney sweep) at St Giles, Farnborough. One of the witnesses was Mary Ann Fenton, William's brother. His mother's name was Mary.

There was an army barracks at Farnborough at the turn of the century. William Fenton was a blacksmith who came down from Nottingham to work for the army, and that is how he met Emmie Pateman. She was living with her family at a cottage in Willow Walk.

They had five children: James, William, Mary, George and William. James died aged two and a half years just a few days after the first William was born; because Emmie was so shocked and upset it affected the new baby who died at ten days old. So there was a double funeral. William was never christened which is probably why Emmie used the name again for her last child.

Mary Fenton married Ernest Copus and they had two children, Joan and John. Joan married Roy Bright.

Emily Fenton died on 18 February 1956 aged 73 at 67 Sangley Road, Catford. She was the widow of William Fenton, farrier. The cause of death was congestive cardiac failure, bronchopneumonia and chronic bronchitis. The informant was G. Fenton, son, 27 Brookbank Road, SE12. This was George Fenton. Emily was buried with her husband William Fenton in Farnborough Churchyard. Joan Bright remembers this quite clearly as it was the first funeral she had ever been to.

William Fenton married Lily and they had two children, Mildred and Patricia. George Fenton married Ivy Watson and they had two children, Carole and Colin. Colin Fenton sent me a photograph of William Fenton working in his forge and this information:

'Emmie lived with William next to the Forge in Sangley Road, Catford. My father George worked in Sangley Road, so he was able to call in and see Emmie every day, even though he had to cycle from Lewisham to Catford and back. Mary and her husband also lived in Sangley Road and would see Emmie frequently. William, the youngest son, lived in Balham, moved to Crawley and then emigrated in 1956 to Australia.'

Colin visited Farnborough Churchyard where he found the grave of William Fenton (died 1927, aged 47) and Emily Fenton (died 18 February 1956, aged 73). 'I then got directions from a local chap to Tugmutton Common at Starts Hill, just past the Hospital. I parked and walked over to a very nice cottage with a wishing well in the garden and I spoke to a man who was in the garden. He was a mine of information and a Gypsy himself who had owned a lot of land which he had sold for housing etc. He was seventy years old and was happy to talk about the old days. He had attended Gypsy funerals and said two Gypsy princes had lived in the cottage (they were both cripples). The cottage used to be thatched but is now roofed with tiles. He confirmed that we were on Tugmutton Common and he had lived there all his life. The actual cottage is next to a firm of cabinet makers.'

Tilly Rabbeth

The Gypsy that Colin spoke to was George Rabbeth who lives at 7 Willow Walk, also known as Gypsy Cottage. This was the former home of Urania and Levi Boswell and the 'Gypsy princes' were their sons, Kenza and Percy. George was the son of Tilly Rabbeth, who was Urania Boswell's housekeeper. She travelled with Urania and cared for her after Levi died. Tilly led the Boswell's donkeys from Farnborough to Blackheath via Bromley and Lewisham, and home again to Farnborough every day.

Dr Dawson joined the Crofton Road practice in 1953. He had a number of patients among the Tugmutton Gypsy community, including Tilly Rabbeth, who he met in 1955: 'I visited her to treat an ulcer that had spread all around her ankle. It was caused by an infected wound acquired while hop picking. Tilly went hop picking in Kent to the same farm each year. I got the ulcer down to a manageable size but it never fully healed. Tilly believed that if it healed she would die. Tilly believed in God but did not go to church. She asked to be buried at Farnborough church where the soil was good and she would last longer in the ground.' Dr Dawson gave me a photo of 'Aunt Tilly': 'It was taken by my wife in 1957 when Tilly was sitting in her downstairs room (Tilly did not go upstairs) just inside the front door of the cottage. She was a great character and a lovely person to talk to or just let her talk of days past. I had a great respect for her.' She died in 1973, but Dr Dawson has many fond memories of her:

'My practice covered the area from Orpington Station to Farnborough Village and Tubbenden Lane, but also included patients from Keston and Downe. My patients were a cross section, from the very poor to the very rich. I would drink tea from a chipped enamel mug at Tilly's and then go straight to a mansion in Farnborough Park and drink tea from a silver tea pot poured into bone china cups. Aunt Tilly's family were more interesting than the rich patients. I would visit Tilly every fortnight on a Tuesday afternoon for a cup of tea, until the health inspector told me that the toilet pit was next to the well. At Christmas Tilly laced my tea with rum. All of Tilly's family from Farnborough Village would be present when I called. They were all inter related and respected her. They would chat with me and exchange views. 7 Willow Walk was like a clinic, where people would ask me for help and advice. They did not have their own doctors. I could leave my wallet or my medical bag at Tilly's cottage and she would guard it with her life and let no one touch it.

My partners could not believe I went there. I thought they were a marvelous family and I would have hidden there if I was in trouble with the law. Tilly had an accent but not much Romany. She received no education and could not read or write. She would smack her children and take a chicken which ran in front of her path. Tilly did not travel. She did not pay into the DSS but received a reduced pension. She sold Christmas wreaths which she made by recycling old wreaths from graves.

When Tilly's husband died she became head of the family. Her youngest son, Scott, was still living with her. Her other son George, who ran a garage, installed electricity in his garage in the yard and ran a wire to Tilly's house. When Tilly got electricity (she had oil lamps before) and a television it was not good for her. She was upset by the violence. Tilly gave me a Hatcham Dairy Farm brass churn with the Royal coat of arms on it. It was on Urania Boswell's caravan when Edward VII had his fortune told. She gave it to me wrapped up in a pillow case made from cloths which they covered the donkeys with.

When I needed some wood for a fence I asked Tilly's youngest son. I knew that the Rabbeth family did fencing. I asked them for wood and the son said, yes, and put some wood in my garden. I paid him and the son said 'They ain't knocked off but don't tell anyone where you got them'. I hid the wood in my shed and creosoted it straight away. The Bedfords did some fencing at my surgery, without estimates or receipts. They did it quickly and well and it lasted twenty years.

One day Tilly was dressed up in a red blouse, bosom up, black skirt. The district nurse, sister Wood, asked her 'Why are you dressing up?' Tilly would not answer. 'Is it because the doctor is coming?' the nurse asked. 'No', Tilly said. 'Have you got clean drawers on?' the nurse enquired, to which Tilly replied 'I ain't had my drawers down for years for any man and I'm not about to now for the doctor either".

When I was in hospital they tried to get Tilly to visit and say she was my mother. It did not happen but Tilly would have played the part. Tilly would not go into hospital.' Matilda (Tilly) Rabbeth died on 27 February 1973, aged 80 years. She was buried at St Giles, Farnborough. Also buried at St Giles are her husband, Samuel Rabbeth (died 11 April 1933, aged 44) and two of her children: Matilda Rabbeth (died 19 September 1930, aged 10) and Elizabeth Rabbeth (died 11 August 1926, aged 14 months).

Dr Dawson's father was a Baptist minister in Hemel Hempstead: 'As a child I visited all kinds of people with him and became at ease with everyone. My father did not preach to people but just made suggestions. Public school made me a snob, but two years on the lower deck of a war ship was a better education, and I learnt to get on with all sorts. As a magistrate I wanted to be able to tell working class people how to pay their fines by using strong language – the language they understood - rather than give them enforcement notices which they could not read

I went to Corke's pit (a large Gypsy encampment in St Mary Cray) when I was standing in for some other doctors. Doctors, mid wives and district nurses were well received but the Gypsies were suspicious of everyone else. I was met at the entrance and asked who I was visiting and why. I was then taken to the caravan. I also visited Star Lane.

I delivered a baby in a horse drawn vardo in Downe. The grandmother boiled water by the door while the District Nurse stood in the centre of the van and I was by the bedside. We formed a chain gang for the hot water. The child's father picked me some strawberries as a gift. I visited every day. The family returned each year to pick strawberries at the same farm until one of their children (who suffered from Downs Syndrome) died in Farnborough Hospital. They would let me know when they were in the area and I would sit around their fire and drink tea.

A young girl (a distant niece?) by the name of Bedford lived in a converted bus in Boswell's Yard. She went to Newstead Wood school and could have become a nurse or a doctor with my support. But she moved with her family to a caravan in Cambridgeshire and the opportunity was lost.

The Patemans lived in Denmark Cottages – they used the F word very often. I gave Mrs. Pateman some pills for congestive cardiac failure. I wrote out detailed instructions saying when to take each pill. The next week Mr. Pateman arrived in the surgery shouting and swearing. My partner, a Baptist minister, wanted him taken off the surgery list. I intervened and went with Mr. Pateman to see his wife. She had not been taking the tablets because she could not read and write. Using four letter words I told her what to do with each pill. When I called back she was a different person, the pills were working.'

3. Tugmutton Common

- Phillis Pateman (1883-1902)
- Hannah Pateman (1884)
- Robert Pateman (1885-1960)
- Mary Ann Pateman (1886-?)
- Charlotte Pateman (1887-?)
- Phoebe Pateman (1889-?)
- Jane Pateman (1890-?)
- Celia Pateman (1892-1894)
- John Pateman (1893-1900)
- Polly Pateman (1894-1900)

Phillis Pateman (1883-1902)

Phillis Pateman was born on 21 April 1883 at Tugmutton. Her father was a labourer. The informant was 'Jane Pateman, mother, Tugmutton'.

John Pateman (James's older brother, born 1844 at Cliffe; John and James were baptized together at Cliffe in 1846) died on 26 June 1883 at Broad Street Green, Farnborough, aged 38 years. John was a labourer and he died of 'prostatic disease and retention, exhaustion'. The informant was 'George Reynolds, brother in law, present at the death, Broad St Green, Farnborough'. George was the husband of Mary Pateman (sister of James and John).

John had moved to Farnborough at the same time as his brothers James and William. They had got married to the Reynolds sisters (Jane and Mercy) but John had remained single and at the time of the 1881 census John (34, agricultural labourer) was lodging at the home of Robert Rudd in Orpington Lane. John was buried at St Giles on 28 June 1883.

Phillis went into domestic service and in the 1901 census she was living at No. 2 Wellclose Villas in Farnborough. She was working for William Plumbridge (fruit grower) who had a wife and three children. Phyllis was described as a 'general servant (domestic), Kent, Farnborough'".

The Victorian Domestic Servant

In 1851 there had been over a million servants in Britain, making domestic science the second largest occupation after agricultural work. Not only were a vast number of people thus employed, but the range of households in which servants were to be found was very wide indeed – from aristocrats who employed literally hundreds of servants to lower middle class families who employed a single maid-of-all-work. An example of the latter was the Plumbridge household and Phillis Pateman.

Writing in 1901 the social investigator Benjamin Seebohm Rowntree suggested that the keeping of servants marked the dividing line between the middle and the working class, but this view neglected the fact that many artisans and other members of the working class employed domestic help (to act as child minders, wash clothes or do 'the rough'), and that even some of these servants lived in.

The size of servant establishment depended on the size of a person's income. J.H. Walsh's *A Manual of Domestic Economy* (1857) suggested that a household income of £250 would only provide for 'a maid-of-all-work, aided in some cases by a girl, or in others, by the younger members of the family.'

Between 1881 and 1901 the percentage of girls between fifteen and nineteen in domestic service fell by 7.3 per cent ; but the percentage of women over forty five rose by twenty per cent – a reflection of the fact that alternative employment was beginning to attract younger women.

In the nineteenth century most domestic servants were of humble origin and from a rural background, for country boys and girls were considered more tractable and industrious than their urban counterparts. The first rung of a life of domestic service might well be a place in a local household, and here personal recommendation or knowledge of the applicant's family was crucial. It is possible, therefore, that William Plumbridge knew the Pateman family.

Those who could not afford to employ a footman or who needed extra help for special occasions, could always engage a temporary man to wait at table. Greengrocers seem often to have fulfilled this role. Perhaps this is how William Plumbridge met James Pateman? Alternatively, Phillis may have secured her employment via one of the servant registries which existed in most large towns.

Domestic servants were usually interviewed, either by the employers or their staff. There was a high turnover of domestic staff. Sometimes servants moved because of disagreements with their employer; in other instances it was in order to secure a promotion. Whatever the reason the servant needed to take a good 'character' or reference, which gave the employer considerable power over their staff. Pay and conditions varied according to gender, location, size of establishment and physique. On top of monetary wages, servants also enjoyed perks, including the value of food and accommodation for those who lived in. A lady's maid might inherit her mistress's cast off clothing, or even her whole wardrobe if she died. Servants ate well and enjoyed more meat than most working class people. Their rooms were often sparsely furnished.

Servants were never allowed to forget their dependence and were often treated like children or even animals. They were subjected to discipline and weighed down with petty rules – especially in the case of girls and young women. Visitors were discouraged. Servants resented this lack of freedom and this is why many of them left domestic service.

Housemaids were meant to be invisible, and all cleaning jobs had to be performed either before the family got up or while they were absent. So much work had to be done before the family was up and about that housemaids were obliged to rise very early. The first task of the housemaid in winter was to open all the downstairs shutters and take up the hearth rugs in the rooms that she was going to clean before breakfast. She would then start with the breakfast room, sweeping the dust towards the fireplace.

On a cloth placed over the carpet she would place her box, into the bottom part of which she put the cinders (to be recycled in the kitchen or laundry) and in the top of which she kept the brushes, blacklead, emery paper and cloths needed to clean the grate.

Fire lighting was an art and an experienced housemaid was expected to manage the task using no more than seven pieces of wood. Maintaining the fires was also a test of strength in terms of carrying scuttles full of coal. The fires gave out warmth, but they also gave out dust and dirt, and it was the housemaid's task to wage war against them, usually without any mechanical aid. Carpets were swept with a brush sometimes after damp tea leaves had been scattered on the floor to take up the dust.

The hey day of domestic service was the 1870's and by the time that Phillis became a servant a number of tasks previously carried out by housemaids had either become mechanized or had been relocated outside the home Eg laundry. The Great War set the seal on this process of change.

Phillis died on 22 April 1902 aged 20 at Willow Lane, Farnborough. On her death certificate her name was spelt 'Phyllis'. Her father was a general labourer and the cause of death was acute nephritis. The informant was J. Pateman, father, present at the death, Willow Lane. Phillis was buried on 28 April 1902 at St Giles. Her mother, Jane Reynolds, was buried in the same grave in 1939.

Hannah Pateman (1884)

Hannah Pateman was born on 28 April 1884 at Tugmutton. Her father was a labourer and the informant was 'Jane Pateman, mother, Tugmutton'. Hannah died on 7 September 1884, aged four months, at Crowhurst Farm, East Peckham, Kent. The cause of death was convulsions. The informant was James Pateman, general labourer, present at the death, Farnborough, Kent. If James was present at the death in Farnborough, it is not clear why the death was registered at East Peckham, Malling. The family could have been in this area for hop picking or other agricultural work.

Farnborough in 1885

The Oak Brewery was founded in 1836 by John Fox of Oak House, Farnborough. In 1885 it was still owned by the Fox family. The brewery was in Green Street Green in the High Street. Previously for over a century beer had been brewed in a small house attached to a farm of nearly 200 acres in the midst of park like meadows. The quality of the beer was so high that local demand grew and led to the formation of the business. The brewery produced some of the finest ales in the London area, and the high quality was attributed to the excellent standard of the brewing and the purity of the local water, which came from a well on the premises. Eight types of beer were produced, the best known being F.A. or Farnborough Ale, which was described as 'Bright, Sparkling and Nutritious'. At the brewery there were industrial shops and a saw mill, where the drays, vans and barrels were made. Ten drays were in regular use delivering beer, and there were 50 horses, together with a blacksmith's forge and a horse hospital. A total of 110 men were employed and the Fox family provided 30 cottages and three residences for their staff. This brewery and Farnborough Ales came to an end on 15 July 1909.

When in September of each year the Friendly Societies - the Court of Lord Farnborough - celebrated their anniversaries, they met at the *New Inn*. A procession was formed and, led by a band, they paraded through the village and visited the residences of local notable people. This was followed by a dinner at the *New Inn*. It was reported in 1885 that the Farnborough branch of the Foresters had 150 members and its funds were about £1,000. Many of the new members were young men. After the dinner, a village fete was held with sports and various entertainments. St Giles Fair was a great day for the villagers.

Cricket was a very popular sport. One match, typical of many, was Married men versus Single, in a meadow lent by Robert Sessions. After the match, which the married men won, there was a supper at the *New Inn*, followed by songs etc. At the back of the Oak Brewery was a cricket pitch for the use of the men who worked there. A bazaar and exhibition was held in the schoolroom of the Beulah Baptist chapel. Examples of silk work, several hundred years old, were lent by the Stow family. The flags of England, worked in coloured threads by sailors while at sea, were exhibited along with a picture scratched on an ordinary wine bottle and the Lord's Prayer engraved on a shell. Hiriam Ballard exhibited a reed organ 'f excellent tone' which he had made. This exhibit also won a special prize at the Bromley Industrial Exhibition.

Extraordinary tithes were at this time payable on fruit, hop and market garden ground. This was strongly objected to locally and in February 1885, an indignation meeting of the Anti-Extraordinary Tithes Association was held locally. There was a large attendance and it was decided that these extra tithes were an impediment to agriculture, hampered new cultivation and should be abolished. Mr. Stow, a local fruit grower, had refused to pay the extra tithe and a Berkshire sow of his was to be sold to pay the amount due. Mr. Stow tried to push one of the agents who came to sell the sow into a pond of liquid manure. The agent went for the police and when they returned they found that a wagon had been drawn across the path blocking the farm entrance. They were bespattered with mud and filth, were compelled to withdraw and were hooted out of the village. In 1885, Farnborough was very much an independent and self-contained village.

Robert Pateman (1885-1960)

Robert Pateman (1885-1960) = Phyllis Rose Lockyer (1887-1967)
- Robert Henry (1911-1990)
- Phyllis Daisy (1914-1918)
- William George (1924-?)

Robert Pateman was born on 30 May 1885 at Tugmutton. His father was a bricklayer's labourer and the informant was 'Jane Pateman, mother, Tugmutton'.

In the 1901 census Robert (16) was described as a 'greengrocer's apprentice'. He was following in his father's footsteps, but he later became a labourer / general labourer and nursery gardener / nurseryman.

On 27 August 1910 Robert Pateman (24, bachelor, labourer, Willow Walk, father - James Pateman, greengrocer) married Phyllis Rose Lockyer (23, spinster, Willow Walk, father - Henry Lockyer, labourer) at St Giles.

Phyllis was the daughter of Henry Lockyer. In the 1891 census Henry (45, widower, general labourer, Farnborough) was living at 50 High Road, Farnborough with his four children: George (20, general labourer, Farnborough), Amy (15, Farnborough), Henry (5, Farnborough) and Phyllis (4, Farnborough). Phyllis's mother must have died some time between 1887 and 1891. In 1910 and 1911 Henry Lockyer was living at Willow Walk, Tugmutton. In 1914 Henry Lockyer was living at 9 Pitt Road.

There were two other Lockyer families living in Farnborough in 1891: William Lockyer (30, general labourer, Farnborough) was living at 48 High Road with his wife Emma (28, Lincolnshire) and their two children, Minnie (3, Farnborough) and Bertram (1, Farnborough). In 1902 William Lockyer was living at 6 Isard's Cottages. In 1914 William Lockyer was living at 4 Orchard Road.

George Lockyer (40, labourer, Farnborough) was living at 15 High Road with his wife Emma (28, ?) and their four children William (9, Farnborough), Elizabeth (8, Farnborough), Mabel (6, Farnborough) and Hilda (2, Farnborough).

It is possible that Henry, William and George Lockyer were brothers. In 1881 another possible brother, John Lockyer, (34, labourer, Farnborough) was living at Bastard Green with his wife and three children.

In 1911 Robert Pateman was living at Willow Walk. His first child, Robert Henry, was born on 27 January 1911 at 9 Willow Walk. Robert was a nursery gardener. Robert Henry was baptized at St Giles on 20 December 1911.

In 1913 Robert moved to 1 Colegate Cottages where Phyllis Daisy was born on 11 October 1914. Robert was still a nursery man. Phyllis Daisy was baptized on 28 November 1914 at St Giles. There is a photograph of Colegate Cottages with a woman and boy, presumably mother and son, standing in the front garden. There is a communal passageway to the small back yards. The photograph is captioned 'Rye &?', Crofton Road (Colegate Cottages).

During the Great War Robert joined the Army and there is a photograph of him in his uniform. Having survived the war, Robert suffered a tragedy when his daughter, Phyllis Daisy, died on 17 November 1918 aged four years at 1 Colegate Cottages, Locksbottom, Farnborough. Her father was a gunner in the Royal Field Artillery and agricultural labourer. The cause of death was influenza and broncho pneumonia. She was a victim of the Spanish Flu which swept around the globe and killed more people than the Great War. The informant was P. Pateman, mother, present at the death, 1 Colegate Cottages. It is possible that Robert was not home in time for her funeral on 23 November 1918 at St Giles as this was just 12 days after the Armistice.

Robert is said to have been badly affected by the War and the loss of his daughter. This may explain why his next child, William George was not born until 14 October 1924 at 1 Colegate Cottages. Robert was a general labourer. William was baptized on 30 November 1924 at St Giles.

On 30 July 1938 Robert Henry Pateman (28, bachelor, chauffeur / commercial service, Colegate Cottages, Crofton Road, Farnborough, father – Robert Pateman, nurseryman) married Doris May Rushbrook (33, spinster, domestic servant, 4 Croft Road, Bromley, father – William Rushbrook, farm worker) at Bromley Registry Office.

Doris May Rushbrook was born on 20 September 1904 at Mildenhall, Suffolk. Her father was an agricultural labourer and her mother was Emily Rushbrook formerly Moss.

Robert Pateman died on 4 April 1960 aged 74 at Farnborough Hospital. He was a retired nurseryman of Blackhorse Cottages, 320 Crofton Road, Orpington. The cause of death was congestive cardiac failure, bronchitis and emphysema. The informant was R.H. Pateman, son, 78 Crown Lane, Bromley. This was Robert Henry Pateman. 324, 322 and 320 Crofton Road were also known as 1, 2 and 3 Blackhorse Cottages. They had this name because they were next to the *Black Horse* public house. No 3, where Robert lived, was directly next to the pub. An undated photograph shows these splendid weather boarded cottages with uneven slate roofs, low door ways and upstairs rooms built into the roof space with dormer windows. They were demolished to make space for a supermarket car park. Robert was buried on 9 April 1960 at St Giles.

Phyllis Rose Pateman died on 29 September 1967 aged 80 years at Oakwood Hospital, Maidstone. She was decried on her death certificate as 'Phyllis Rose Pateman, otherwise Phillis Rose Pateman, widow of Robert Pateman, a nurseryman (retired)'. The cause of death was coronoary thrombosis and the informant was 'R.H. Pateman, son, Link Way, Bromley, Kent'. This was Robert Henry Pateman. Phyliss Rose was buried in the same grave as her husband at St Giles.

Doris May Pateman died on 13 December 1982 aged 78 at Farnborough Hospital. She was the wife of Robert Henry Pateman, patrol man, retired, of 18 Link Way, Bromley. The cause of death was carcinoma of the pancreas, obstructive jaundice, terminal case. The informant was Robert Henry Pateman, widower of the deceased. Doris May was cremated on 20 December 1982 at Beckenham Cemetery.

Robert Henry Pateman died on 22 February 1990, aged 79, at Bromley Hospital. The cause of death was myocardial infarction. Robert was a security officer (retired) of 18 Link Way, Bromley. The informant was John Luther Richards, 'causing the body to be cremated', 31 Cowper Road, Bromley. Robert Henry was cremated on 2 March 1990 at Beckenham Cemetery.

Mary Ann Pateman (1886-?)

Mary Ann Pateman (1886-?) = William Loft (1890-?)
- Robert
- William

Mary Ann Pateman was born in 'Stone's Cottages' Farnborough on 17 July 1886. Her father was a builder's labourer. The informant was 'Jane Pateman, mother, Cobham, Kent, as per declaration dated 27th August 1886'.

There are two interesting features about this birth certificate. The first is that Mary Ann, unlike most of her siblings, was not born at Tugmutton. She was born at 'Stone's Cottages', which could be a reference to Stow's Cottages in Farnborough, named after J.W. Stow a local fruit grower. William Pateman (brother of James) lived at Stow's Cottages from 1890 until 1901. Why did James move from Tugmutton Common, Locks Bottom, to Stow Cottages, Farnborough for the birth of Mary Ann? Perhaps he was turned off of Tugmutton Common but, as we shall see, the Farnborough Common Conservators were not appointed until 16 June 1887.

The second mystery is the location of Jane Pateman, who was in Farnborough for the birth of Mary Ann on 17 July 1886, but who then moved to Cobham, Kent 'as per declaration dated 27th August 1886'. What was Jane doing in Cobham and why did she give this as her residence six weeks after the birth of Mary Ann? Was she working in Cobham or visiting relatives? And was the declaration necessary to ensure that the baby was registered within the legal deadline? Mary Ann's birth was registered on 7 September 1886.

On 30 October 1915 Mary Ann Pateman (29, spinster, 5 Willow Walk, father - James Pateman, greengrocer) married William Loft (25, bachelor, paper maker, 5 Willow Walk, father - William Loft, deceased, fish monger) at St Giles.

They had two children, Robert and William (Billy). Billy had four children: Margaret, Sandra, Susan and Peter. Peter Loft was my childhood friend. We went to the same primary school and our mothers both worked at the Morphy Richards factory in Cray Avenue. We got married about the same time and we both had two children of the same age: my son Joe went to school with James Loft; and my daughter Saskia was friends with Callum Loft.

Myself and Peter Loft lived in the same street (32 and 24 Petten Grove respectively) for 47 years and yet it was not until I started researching my family history that I discovered that Peter's grandfather, William Loft, was married to Mary Ann Pateman. Shortly after this discovery I moved to Lincolnshire. We do not know when Mary Ann Pateman died or where she is buried.

Farnborough Common Protection Committee

The Farnborough Parish Vestry Accounts indicate that there had been concerns about the Farnborough Commons for some time. In 1868, for example, it was noted 'That all persons found digging and conveying gravel, turf or other soil out of the Parish, or improperly encroaching on vacant spaces within the Parish. The Parish Officers be instructed to prosecute for such offence and the overseer be instructed to prepare the Notice Boards to the above effect.' No doubt Gypsies were amongst those who improperly encroached on vacant spaces within the Parish.

At the same meeting it was also noted 'That Mr. Thos. Fox be requested to bring under the notice of the Highway Board the condition of the Lane between

Farnborough and Orpington Railway Station, with a view to the widening and otherwise improving of the said Lane, and to the dangerous condition of the gravel pits situate at Green Street Green'. Mr. T. Fox was to become a member of the Farnborough Common Protection Committee and the Board of Farnborough Common Conservators. The Lane between Farnborough and Orpington was known as Orpington Lane and William Pateman was living there in a van in 1881. The gravel pits at Green Street Green were later enclosed.

These gravel pits were also discussed when the Vestry met at its new location in the School Room at Farnborough Board School on 19 February 1874: 'The attention of the Vestry having been called to the fact that the Highway Board proposed to dig gravel on the portion of Green Street Green Common within the Parish of Farnborough, it was resolved that the Chairman of this Vestry Meeting forward to the Highway Board a formal protest against further removal from the Parish of Road Metal, Gravel, etc from the gravel pits in or upon the Common, and Waste lands within said Parish. That the attention of the Parish Officers be called to the encroachments on the Farnborough Common and the Parish Waste Lands.' So the concern of the Vestry was two fold – to preserve the natural resources (gravel) of the Parish and to prevent encroachments (by Gypsies and others) onto the Commons and waste lands.

In 1887 it was decided that these issues should be dealt with by a special committee: 'At a special vestry meeting held at the Board School in Farnborough on 16 June 1887 it was unanimously resolved that a committee consisting of the parochial officers and such other members as the vestry deemed it expedient to elect, should be appointed to take such steps as might be necessary for the protection of the common land of the parish'.

Those present included : Parochial Officers (church wardens) – T.H. Fox; H. C. Cheel ; (overseers) – J. W. Stow ; H. N. Penfold; Elected Members - W. St. J. Fox; J. Griffin; W. Hughes; R. Sessions.

Henry Charles Cheel was a baker; Joseph Stow was a fruit grower; Henry Nathaniel Penfold was a beer retailer; Robert Sessions was the publican at the *White Lion*, Lock's Bottom; the two members of the Fox family were related to John Fox and Sons, brewers and maltsters, Oak Brewery, Green Street Green:

'Green Street Green is a hamlet, partly in this parish [Farnborough] and partly in Chelsfield, one mile south-by-east from Farnborough, about one mile south from Orpington railway station, in Orpington postal delivery. Here is an extensive brewery.' (*Post Office Directory*, 1878).

This group of local businessmen formed themselves into the Farnborough Commons Protection Committee. Their first meeting was held at the Board School on 17 June 1887 at 6pm. J. H Fox was elected as the Chairman and A. H. Palmer was appointed as Honorary Secretary.

'The Honorary Secretary received a report upon the condition of Farnborough Common at the present time mentioning among other things the presence of a large heap of poles, many hundreds of loads of flints, a large heap of earth closed sewage and two manure middens. Besides these things, the common was covered with dirty straw, old rags and the debris left by a succession of Gypsy encampments.

Mr. Penfold spoke in favour of forming a ditch and bank round the frontage of the Common with gates etc. so that no vans could be drawn upon it. The Secretary said he intended writing to the Chief Commissioner of Police with regard to the indecency occurring in the Gypsy camp. After some further discussion it was determined that the overseers should post notices upon the commons on the evening of the 18 June to the effect that if any persons were found camping on the same after twelve noon on the following Monday they would be forcibly removed by the overseers and police.'

A letter was written to Mr. Birkett of the Commons Preservation Society containing a list of questions including: 'What are the Parliamentary and other expenses of placing the Commons under an existing or special act and finally under a Board of Conservators? If Gypsies or other non parishioners pitch upon the Common or waste land at the road side and turn their cattle out to graze (attended) have the freeholders or ratepayers right of action against them? What is the shortest and best mode of procedure to eject these trespassers?'

M.r Birkett replied to these questions in a letter from 4 Lincoln's Inn Fields, London, on 22 June 1887: 'The Common lands in Farnborough Parish appear to be within the area of the Metropolitan Police District and are, therefore, technically speaking, Metropolitan Commons within the meaning of the Metropolitan Commons Act of 1866. A scheme for managing them can be obtained and confirmed by Act of Parliament at comparatively speaking a small cost.

The acts of trespass which you describe as your chief causes of action are precisely those acts which the Metropolitan Commons Act was designed to put an end to, and, when once you have such a Scheme as the Act contemplates, you will have no further difficulty with Gypsies or any other persons trespassing on the Commons.

The police have no jurisdiction until the vans are drawn upon the highway, then the police can insist upon their being removed; but the difficulty which seems to present itself to me is that, if you cannot find the Lord of the Manor, I do not know who would be the proper person to draw the vans off.. I think however that if you will tell me the name of the manor of which a court baron was held in 1852 I shall have no difficulty in finding out who is the lord.'

Mr. Birkett further advised the Committee that 'It is invariably a waste of money to take action against Gypsies. If however you know who are the Commoners entitled to depasture the waste, it is competent for them to require the Lord of the Manor or his Bailiff to pound the cattle not properly turned out to graze. The shortest and best mode of ejecting the trespassers are for the proper persons to draw the vans off on to the road and to pound the cattle and horses depasturing there.'

This letter was discussed at the next meeting of the Farnborough Commons Protection Committee, held at the Board School on 24 June at 9pm and it was proposed that 'The necessary steps be taken to place Farnborough Commons under the Metropolitan Commons Preservation Act.' The cost of the scheme was reckoned to be no more than £150. In order to guarantee these costs the Committee Chairman, J.H. Fox, offered to contribute £25. Mr. Hughes, Walter Fox and H. Wilson each volunteered to do the same. On the 25 June Sir John Lubbock offered to contribute and it was decided that the five guarantors would put up £20 each. Mr. Birkett was invited to their next meeting.

At this meeting on 8 July 'a twenty five inch ordnance map of that portion of the parish, containing the Commons proposed to be dealt with was laid on the table; the Commons being coloured green'. Mr. Birkett, acting as Solicitor to the Committee, presented them with a 'memorial' to sign. Mr Birkett then 'handed copies of the draft scheme to the members, read the same, and explained it clause by clause.' Some corrections having been made it was agreed that the draft scheme 'be forwarded to the Land Commissioners with the memorial'. It was further agreed that 'those present do form the first Conservators, eight in number: J. H. Fox, Walter Fox, J. Griffin, W. Hughes, H.N. Penfold, A.H. Palmer, J.W. Stow and H. Wilson.'

The Committee asked Mr. Birkett how much the scheme would cost and 'he replied that the cost of the proceedings was largely influenced by the amount of opposition met with.' After some further discussion it was agreed 'That an executive Committee consisting of the Chairman (J. H. Fox), the Secretary (A.H. Palmer) and Mr. Stow (J.H.) be formed.'

On 21 July Mr. Birkett advised the Committee that the fees charged by the Land Commissioners in the Chislehurst Commons case amounted to £79. On 22 July it was suggested that 'Mr. George Giles and Mr. Weatherley as being important freeholders and therefore particularly eligible for the purpose of signing the memorial'. The Giles family included Charles (grocer and fruit grower) and Thomas (fruit grower and gardener). James Weatherley was the landlord of the *New Inn* in Farnborough Village.

On 4 August the memorial was signed by Sir John Lubbock, Mr. Weatherley and George Giles. On 2 September a search was made of 'the Vestry Minute book of the parish of Farnborough from 1718 to 1887 and relating to the Commons therein; a search from which the conclusion may be drawn that since the year 1843 the Vestry has been the sole authority acting with regard to the said Commons, but no allusions to any Lord of the Manor.' The conclusion was drawn that a lease had been granted by the steward of the manor in 1843 to the church wardens.

Charlotte Pateman (1887-?)

Charlotte Pateman (1887-?) = James Bassett (1886-?)
- Pauline
- George

Charlotte Pateman was born at Tugmutton on 19 September 1887. Her father was a greengrocer and the informant was 'Jane Pateman, mother, Tugmutton'. Whatever her business in Cobham had been in August 1886, Jane Pateman was now back in Farnborough.

On 29 January 1910 Charlotte Pateman (22, spinster, Tugmutton, father - James Pateman, greengrocer) married James Bassett (24, bachelor, labourer, 5 Kingsley Road, Chelsfield, father - Edward Bassett, labourer) at St Giles.

Charlotte and James had two children, Pauline and George. We do not know when Charlotte Pateman died or where she is buried.

Farnborough Commons Conservators

On 2 October 1887 the Farnborough Commons Protection Committee received a letter informing them that the Land Commissioners would advertise the draft scheme on receipt of £50. J.H. Fox, W.S. Fox, Sir John Lubbock, W. Hughes and H. Wilson put up £10 each. On 11 October it was proposed that the scheme be advertised in Farnborough Village Post Office (in Church Lane), the *New Inn* and in the *District Times*, *Bromley Telegraph* and *Bromley Journal*.

On 12 October 1887 the Committee informed Mr. Birkett that 'The manor of Farnborough included the townships of Farnborough, Chelsfield, Lullingstone, West Wickham, Paul's Cray and Keston. The last Court Baron of which there is any record was held by William Grimwood Taylor, deputy steward of Benjamin Badger (The Lord) at the George Inn 23 June 1852.' This information was inscribed at the front of the Committee's Minute Book.

On 13 October 1887 the Committee received 'a packet of notices and 50 copies of the scheme. The former to be distributed and posted in all the parishes concerned (sites to be noted). The latter to be given to any person who applies and to each of the memorialists. Also that a copy be deposited at the Post Office.' On 14 October 1887 notices were posted 'on the church and chapel doors in the parishes of Farnborough, Chelsfield, Cudham and Orpington and other public places so as to ensure free publicity. The Commissioners will arrange for the necessary advertisements and will communicate with the local authorities of the respective parishes. The total number of notices posted was 150 and the Post Mistress (Miss Harriet Baldwin) was given a gratuity of ten shillings for displaying the draft scheme.

On 21 November 1887 it was agreed that 'the Chelsfield portion of Green Street Green to be included in the scheme and also if possible the Green at Pratt's Bottom.' The vestry at Orpington was also keen for common land in their parish to be included – 'Grumping Common, Darrick Common, Sparrow Common, Broom Hill Common, Skeet Hill and the Gravel Pits. A Supplemental Scheme including any or all of these or Keston Common or Leaves Green may be granted by the Land Commissioners at any future time, as was done in the case of some common land in the parish of St Paul's Cray which by Supplemental Scheme was added to the old Chislehurst scheme'.

The scheme did not stop people from using the common: 'All legal common rights will be reserved by the scheme. Encroachment only will be stopped. No power is usurped by the conservators but all power, whether of contributing towards the funds of maintenance or of electing conservators, and hence the power of maintaining all common rights, rests with the vestry. The cost of maintenance is a purely voluntary matter. A resolution may be passed in the ordinary way by the Vestry every year that so much of the Poor Rate be devoted to the disposal of the Conservators for the maintenance of the Commons. The question of representation on the Board of Conservators is one which the Land Commissioners decide.' Some practices on the Commons could continue, such as depositing manure, but this would now be charged for at a rate of 'say 6d or so for a year or two at a time, the term renewable at discretion.'

On 25 November 1887 the Orpington Vestry voted to include its Commons in the Farnborough scheme. On 13 December an objection to the scheme was received from Mrs. Mills: 'I beg to state I have put dung and other things on a spot in Leaves Green undisputed for about 30 years. When I bought the property I bought the common rights which it states on my title deeds. I am against the Conservators having the right to turn me off.'

This is a reference to the fact that common rights normally belonged, not to persons, but to the property that those persons occupied, cottage, house, or even a field in rare cases. Occasionally, when such properties fell vacant they were never re-let, and if these were not owned by the Manorial Landowner they were purchased, and in both cases the buildings were razed, thus extinguishing the rights by creeping removal. Rights were actually attached to the hearth, which is why so many cottages that fell down naturally, often had the hearth and a bit of chimney preserved so that the rights would not be lost.

The Committee decided that 'all rights, that is legal rights, are especially reserved by the Act and therefore Mrs. Mills can have no cause for complaint.' On 19 December 1887 the Committee was informed that the Enclosure scheme would be approved at once provided that they received a letter from the Lord of the Manor stating that he approved the scheme. The Committee claimed that the Lordship of the Manor had ceased to exist. On 20 December Lord Derby wrote that although he was in favour of the scheme as a whole he objected to there being no clause giving owners of lands adjoining the commons a right of access from such lands to the public roads. The Land Commissioners agreed to insert a clause in the scheme to this effect.

On 22 December Sir John Lubbock joined the Committee and the scheme was certified on 30 December 1887. Notices were posted in the village and plans were deposited at the Post Office on 20 January 1888. The rateable value of Farnborough Parish, according to a new valuation in 1888, was £9085. On 8 March 1888 the Farnborough scheme was mentioned in the annual report of the Land Commissioners to Parliament. The Bill was introduced into the Commons on 26 March and by 12 June that Bill had passed through all its stages and was ready for the Royal Assent.

The Farnborough Commons Protection Committee met at the Board School on 28 June 1888. Mr. Stow claimed that a plot of land in his possession by the reed pond at Tugmutton had been included in the scheme without his knowledge or consent. The Committee agreed to write to their Solicitors and request that this piece of land be removed from the scheme. The Committee agreed to base their Bye Laws on those used for Chislehurst Common. It was also agreed to appoint a Common Ranger.

The first meeting of the Farnborough Commons Conservators was held at the Board School on 9 July 1888. Hamilton Fox was elected as Chairman and Walter Fox was elected as Vice Chairman. At their next meeting on 5 November, Mr. Wilson was elected as Secretary. The Conservators agreed some minor amendments to their Bye Laws which were suggested by the Local Government Board. These Bye Laws were then deposited in the Post Office and advertised in the *Daily Telegraph* and *District Times.* The Bye Laws were confirmed by the Local Government Board on 31 December 1888.

On 10 January 1889 the Conservators agreed to ask Sir John Lubbock for 9 larch poles on which the Bye Laws could be posted on the Commons. Notice was given to the owners of flints, hop poles, manure and other rubbish on the Commons, to remove them within one calendar month, failing which the Bye Laws would be applied. The Conservators requested 'the Vestry, as soon as possible, to levy a rate of one penny in the pound per annum to defray the necessary expenses of putting the Commons under the Metropolitan Commons Act.' This was agreed by the Vestry on 28 March.
On 9 April 1889 the Clerk reported that copies of the Bye Laws had been put up, 'one on the Hill, one by the *Rose and Crown*, 2 on Green St Green, one on Leach's Green, one on Broad St Green, 3 on Farnborough Common'. The Clerk reported that he had served notices on the owners of flints etc and that they were being removed. He also reported that 'he had written to the Chief Commissioner of Police and had received a reply through Inspector Reilly to the effect that the police would not make the first move or interfere with trespassers but they would always support an official of the Conservators if he took the first step. He reported that he had banked up the common at the places where vans were drawn on and had also begun to take off the flints and make the Common tidy.'

The Conservators considered a letter from W. Hubbard of Bromley asking leave to make a footpath across Broad St Green to the Primitive Methodist Chapel recently built on the border of the Common. The Conservators agreed to improve the existing path. They also agreed a proposal from W. Simmonds to level and lay down a portion of Broad St Green as a cricket ground for a club of boys in the parish of which he was Treasurer. Mr. Roberts was appointed Commons Ranger 'at a salary of £12 a year in addition to any fines he has the means of inflicting'.

Phoebe Pateman (1889-?)

Phoebe Pateman (1889-?) = Frederick Pankhurst (1893-?)
- Robert
- Frederick

Phoebe Pateman was born at Tugmutton on 16 April 1889. Her father was a pedlar and the informant was 'Jane Pateman, mother, Tuggmuton'.

The fifth meeting of the Farnborough Commons Conservators was held on 6 November 1889. A letter was read from the Rev. F Kelly with reference to cutting turf for covering graves in the churchyard. Mr. Plumbridge attended to ask whether it was the intention of the Board to enforce the Bye Laws as Mr. Latter was cutting turf from Broad St Green in spite of warnings. The Board put this in the hands of their solicitors. At their next meeting on 27 November 1889 it was reported that, in order to avoid legal action, Mr. Latter had paid one pound in compensation for damaging the

Common and withdrew all claims for cutting turf. Rev. Kelly's request to cut turf was declined. The Board sanctioned the digging of several trenches at various spots on Green St Green to prevent people making cart roads across the Green.

At their seventh meeting on 9 April 1890 'a conversation followed touching upon some sheds at Tugmutton which the Board ordered the Ranger to have removed unless the occupiers did so of their own accord after having had due notice. The Ranger attended the meeting and said that on the whole the notices he had served on various parties had been most effective.' He was instructed to give Mr. Gill three months notice to remove his flints from Farnborough Common.

Phoebe Pateman moved to New Road, Orpington. On 26 December 1914 Phoebe Pateman (23, spinster, New Road, Orpington, father - James Pateman, greengrocer) married Frederick Pankhurst (21, bachelor, fireman, 12 Viaduct Cottages, St Mary Cray, father - John Pankhurst, platelayer) at All Saints Parish Church, Orpington. The witnesses were Robert Pateman and Mary Ann Pateman.

The wedding took place on 26 December, possibly a Gypsy custom and a day which will occur again in this family history. England was at war with Germany but neither Frederick nor Robert had yet been called to the colours. Frederick Pankhurst was a fireman, which may have been a reserved occupation, and worked on the steam locomotives which hurtled between London and the Kent coast, via St Mary Cray.

Frederick lived in Viaduct Cottages, St Mary Cray. The tall railway viaduct of nine arches, which still dominates St Mary Cray High Street, was built in 1858 to carry the line linking the Chatham and Dover routes to London. Priscilla, Daniel and Betsy Coates (see Chapter 6 – Fellow Travellers) were living at Viaduct Cottages in 1920. A photograph c1950 shows the demolition of Viaduct Cottages. The old Engine House dated 1830 is in the foreground.

Phoebe lived at 5 New Road, Orpington. These houses are still standing and one of them has etched into its brickwork 'Cabul Cottages, 1881', giving their original name and date of construction. There was once a brewery in New Road serving the nearby *Cricketers* public house.

The location for Pateman family baptisms, marriages and burials shifted from St Giles, Farnborough, to All Saints, Orpington. Several members of the Pateman family moved from Farnborough to Orpington and the Crays just before the Great War. George Pateman was living at 5 New Road in 1921 and William Pateman lived at nearby Chislehurst Road until his death in 1921. His widow, Mercy Pateman, lived at 61 Chislehurst Road until she died in 1940. The Pankhursts had a yard at Fordcroft, St Mary Cray, close to the scrapyard belonging to Henry Pateman in Poverest Road. The Whiffens had a gardening business in Bridge Road.

Phoebe and Frederick had two children, Robert and Frederick. There is a posed photograph of Phoebe Pankhurst, seated in a chair with an open book on her lap, wearing a long dress and with a severe hair style and expression.

We do not know when Phoebe Pateman died or where she is buried.

Jane Pateman (1890-?)

Jane Pateman (1890-?) = James New (1891-?)
- George
- James

Jane Pateman was born at Tugmutton on 4 August 1890. Her father was a greengrocer and the informant was 'Jane Pateman, mother, Tugmutton'. The 1890 *Strong's Directory of Farnborough* lists James Pateman as living at Tugmutton, Farnborough.

An entry in the Farnborough Parish Vestry Accounts for 1890 notes 'That Mr. Stow, Mr. T.Hamilton Fox and Mr. Joseph Griffin be re-elected Conservators of the Commons of Farnborough in accordance with the provisions of the Scheme for the management of such Commons certified by the Land Commissioners of England, and Farnborough Commons Scheme. Confirmation Act 1888. That a rate of one penny in the pound be levied for the purpose of providing for the expenses for the current year of the Farnborough Commons Preservation Act'.

At a meeting of the Farnborough Commons Conservators on 25 September 1890, W. Stow reported that the sheds at Tugmutton were gone. W. Wilson reported that the last of Gill's flints were removed on 9 August. The Conservators met with W. Ruck the County Surveyor on 29 September and 'pointed out to him four places for the deposit of road metal and scrapings namely Farnborough Common between the 35th and 36th telegraph posts; below W. Kelly's; on Green St Green at the west end of the gravel pit, and at the corner of Chelsfield Lane.'

On 13 February 1891 the Clerk reported that 'an earthenware tube drain had been placed in the watercourse on Leach's Green and that the surveyor asked for leave to take the lump on the green under Capt. Waring's hedge to fill in above this drain'. The clerk reported that the edge of the gravel pit on Farnborough Common was getting dangerously near the road. The Ranger was instructed to warn all persons getting gravel not to work nearer than 15 feet from the ditch. An offer by Lord Derby to plant some ornamental trees on the Commons was accepted.

1891 Census

On 5 April 1891 James Pateman (45, potato dealer, Cliffe) was living at Tugmutton, Farnborough, Kent, with his wife Jane Reynolds (35, Sittingbourne) and their children, Emmie (8, Farnborough), Phillis (7, Farnborough), Robert (6, Farnborough), Mary (5, Farnborough), Charlotte (3, Farnborough), Phoebe (2, Farnborough) and Jane (1, Farnborough). Betsy had died in 1881 and Hannah had died in 1884.

Also living at Tugmutton were: Jonathan Bird*, Louisa Bird, Charles Lewis, George Reynolds, William Mitchell*, John Reynolds, James Cutbush*, Thomas Weatherly* and George Springett. Those with an * had also been living at Tugmutton in 1881. The son of Charles Lewis, Elias, married Mary Pateman (daughter of William) in 1895. John and George Reynolds were the brothers of Jane Pateman. George Reynolds was married to Mary Pateman.

George, William and Henry Lockyer (who were probably brothers) and their families were living at High Road, Farnborough in 1891. Phyllis Rose Lockyer (daughter of Henry) married Robert Pateman in 1910.

William Pateman was living at Stow Cottages (where Mary Ann Pateman was born in 1886) in Church Road, Farnborough.

As well as these settled, or semi-settled, Gypsies there were also some Travellers recorded on the 1891 Census for Farnborough:

Living in a caravan on White Hill were William Lea (48, Hawker, Kent, Canterbury), his wife Louisa (35, Kent, Greenhithe) and their children Susan (17, Kent, Deal), Oliver (15, Kent, Herne Bay), Betsy (13, Kent, Maidstone), George (11, Kent, Luton), Sarah (9, Kent, Bluebell Hill), Cenemely (7, Kent, Tunbridge Wells), William (3, Kent, Chalk) and Flora (1, Kent, Milton)

Living in a caravan on Farnborough Hill were Owen Corsay (32, Hawker, Kent, Dartford), his wife Olive (25, Kent, Dartford) and William Willnoby (boarder,18, Kent, Pembury).

Living in a caravan and tent in Crofton Road were Levi Boswell (47 let out donkeys and ponies for his living, Essex), his wife Urania (44), and their children Georgina (14, domestic servant, Middlesex), Nora (12, scholar, Surrey) and Levi (scholar, Kent, Chislehurst). See Chapter 5 – The Boswells.

On 11 May 1891 the Conservators reported that 'Lord Derby had planted trees on the Common and his men were now clearing away the gorse on the cricket ground. The lump of earth under Capt. Waring's hedge had been taken and spread over the tube drain.' At their next meeting on 1 July 1891 the clerk reported the death of the Ranger, W. Silas Roberts. The post was filled by W. Abraham Staples at a salary of £12 a year payable quarterly subject to 3 months notice on either side. 'The clerk reported that two of the trees planted by Lord Derby on the Common had been broken and that he had printed and posted handbills offering a reward of £1.'

Alice Pateman (James's older sister, born Wimbledon Common, 1842) died on 22 January 1892, aged 50, at Fulcher's Square, St Mary Cray. Alice was a 'field woman' and she died of broncho pneumonia. The informant was 'Mary Reynolds, sister, present at the death, Tugmutton, Farnborough'. Mary was the wife of George Reynolds. Alice was buried at Star Lane cemetery, which is where Betsy Pateman (James's first child) was buried in 1881. So here is another link between the Gypsy communities of Tugmutton, Farnborough, and Star Lane, St Mary Cray.

On 20 April 1892 the Conservators reported that 'the sergeant in charge of repairing the telegraph wires had complained of a tree on the Common opposite W. Latter's obstructing the wires. That under the instructions of the chairman he had had the tree felled; that Miss Latter had written to complain of this, on the ground that they had always claimed rights over that bit of grass, and that he had answered pointing out that the ground was included in the scheme.' It was agreed to put a railing by the roadside at Farnborough Common due to the dangerous condition of the gravel pit.

'The Ranger was directed to prevent people driving across Green St Green out of the proper track and also to prevent the deposit of manure at Tugmutton and if necessary serve notices'.

On 28 December 1912 Jane Pateman (22, spinster, 5 Willow Walk, father - James Pateman, greengrocer) married James New (21, bachelor, engineer's mate, 4 Yates Cottages, Albert Road, father - William New, labourer) at St Giles.

The southern part of St Mary Cray, nearest to Orpington, bounded by Lower Road, Albert Road, Anglesea Road and Kent Road is a mainly 19th century development known as the New Town. Most of the houses in this area are of stock brick, with their slate roofs surviving in many instances. In Albert Road there is an unusually attractive flint and brick terrace with all its entrance doors to the rear.

The *Royal Albert* public house, on the corner of Albert Road and Lower Road, is a typically robust 19th century design. There were seven steps which connected this pub to the adjacent St Andrew's Cottages in Lower Road. Walter Pateman lived at 2 St Andrews cottages from 1913 until 1916 when he was conscripted into the Army. See *Seven Steps to Glory – Private Pateman Goes to War.*

Jane and James had two children, George and James. There is a photograph of Jane Pateman at the seaside with Daisy, Doris and Bill Pateman.

We do not know when Jane Pateman died or where she is buried.

Celia Pateman (1892-1894)

Celia Pateman was born on 30 May 1892 at Tugmutton. Her father was a general labourer and the informant was 'Jane Pateman, mother, Tugmutton'.

On 7 December 1892 the Conservators reported that a fence had been erected at the gravel pit on Farnborough Common. Also the clerk reported that 'Smith had placed more hop poles against the willow trees by W. Kelly's and as he refused to move them a summons was taken out, on which they were removed at once.' Sir John Lubbock had offered some trees for Green St Green. The Ranger was provided 'with a rough diary to note any encroachments, or any action he took, and lay it before the Board'.

At their next meeting on 4 January 1893 they agreed to write 'to Messrs Gregory of Clapham Junction, builders of the new orphanage near Orpington station, telling them that they had no right to take gravel for the foundations or paths of that building and he received a courteous reply to the effect that they would instruct their foreman to dig no more gravel'. The clerk was instructed to put up notices in the gravel pits to the effect that 'by the Scheme no person has a right to take gravel excepting for the repair of houses or roads in the parish existing previous to the date of the Scheme and then only subject to the direction of the Conservators. Building a new house or making a new path confers no right on the owners to take gravel. Any person taking gravel in contravention of this rule will be proceeded against as the law directs.' The Ranger was instructed 'to put up swing bars at the entrance to the pits, to be locked, with a notice that the key was to be obtained at the house of the Ranger'.

Celia Pateman died of measles and bronchitis on 24 December 1894 at Starts Hill, Farnborough, aged two years. Her father was a general labourer and her mother was present at the death. Celia was buried at St Giles on 8 January 1895. Her siblings Polly (Mary) and John were buried in the same grave on 26 June 1900 and 8 December 1900 respectively.

John Pateman (1893-1900)

John Pateman was born on 5 September 1893 at Locks Bottom. His father was a general hawker and the informant was 'Jane Pateman, mother, Locks Bottom'. John was baptised on 8 October 1893 at St Giles. James Pateman was described as a tradesman, Tugmutton.

On 7 February 1894 the chairman of the Conservators 'expressed his great dissatisfaction at the way the Ranger performed his duties and it was unanimously resolved that the clerk be instructed to give the Ranger notice before next quarter day to terminate his engagement at Midsummer. He was also to find a successor.' A letter was read from the Assistant Surveyor to the County Council asking leave to make a cesspit on the Common at the point where Chelsfield Lane entered Green St Green. This was granted but the request to take gravel from the pit to mend the road was refused. The chairman obtained permission to deposit some rubbish in the hollow at the end of the pit.

At their next meeting on 6 June 1894, the clerk reported that he had given the Ranger notice 'and that he had spoken to Broadway, the attendance officer, and John Bradbury who had just retired from the Police, both of whom were willing to undertake the duties. Broadway, who was in attendance, said that he was willing to do his best if his health would allow and if there was no other candidate, but he did not wish to stand in the way of Bradbury'. The Board agreed to appoint Bradbury. The clerk reported that 'men were getting flints for Kent County Council at Green St Green pit with the object of putting them on the high road between the green and Orpington station. He had written to the clerk of the County Council reminding him that the Conservators had decided that the limited supply of gravel did not warrant them in allowing it to be taken for main roads'. In a reply dated 25 May the County Council challenged this decision and the Board referred it to their Solicitors, who gave the following advice:

'We beg to draw your attention to Clause 20 of the Commons Act 1876 which prohibits any surveyor of highways from searching for, digging, getting or carrying away gravel, sand, stones or other material from any part of a Common which is the subject of a Scheme confirmed by Parliament under the provisions of the Metropolitan Commons Act, without the consent of the Conservators, or in default of such consent, without the order of two or more justices in Petty Sessions. The County Council derive their title under section 11 of the Local Government Act 1888 which gives them such power as a Highway Board possesses. Therefore inasmuch as a Highway Board is restricted by the Commons Act 1876, the County Council is similarly restricted.'

John Pateman died on 4 December 1900, aged 7, at Willow Lane, Farnborough. His father was a greengrocer (master) and the cause of death was meningitis. The informant was Jane Pateman, present at the death. John was buried on 8 December 1900 at St Giles in the same grave as his sister Polly (Mary) buried on 26 June 1900.

Polly Pateman (1894-1900)

Polly Pateman was born on 23 December 1894 at Locks Bottom. Her father was a general hawker and the informant was 'Jane Pateman, mother, Locks Bottom'. The *Bush's Directory of Farnborough* 1904, lists James Pateman as living at Tugmutton.

On 29 March 1895, the clerk to the Conservators reported that he had received a letter from Mr. Dryland the Assistant County Surveyor asking leave to make a catch pit to take the drainage from the road near the *Rose and Crown* and that the chairman had sanctioned it. It was agreed to publish the Board accounts in the parish magazine and that any parishioner could inspect them at the Ranger's house. It was resolved that 'efforts should be made to fill up the pond at Tugmutton without interfering with the spring and that any one having spare earth be invited to deposit it there. The clerk and Mr. Stow had both tried to get some of the earth from the widening of Plough Hill for the pit on Farnborough Common.' The Ranger was asked to attend the meetings and bring his book.

At their next meeting on 6 September 1895, the clerk reported that in the dry weather in the Spring he had employed the Ranger to cut the gorse on the upper part of the Common to prevent its taking fire, paying him £1.4.0 for the work. Since then a fire had taken place which had burnt all the gorse on the lower part. He suggested having all the paper picked up which tempted tramps to light fires and made the Common untidy. It was agreed that posts be put in at top and bottom to stop carriages coming on the bridle path. Mr. Stow said that someone had written to the paper complaining that the Conservators neglected their duty and allowed fires to be lighted. All present denied that they had seen anyone camping on the Commons. 'The chairman reported that a man named Robert Harrow had brought posts and rails and he was informed had given out that he was going to rail in the pond at Green St Green, fill it up and build on it. The Ranger was instructed to inform the clerk if Robert Harrow began to put in the posts, and the clerk was instructed to write to Harrow, telling him that the pond was part of the Common and the Conservators would take legal proceedings against him if he enclosed it.'

It was agreed that the District Council be charged for 'all flints and gravel taken out of Farnborough pits for the repair of by roads and that the money be paid to the account of the Overseers to be applied in diminution of the rate.' The chairman reported that the contractor for the new laundry at the Workhouse had applied for a place to tip the surplus soil. The clerk was instructed to offer him the dangerous place in Farnborough pit. Some discussion took place about the old horse now on the Common, but no decision was arrived at.

At their next meeting on 6 December 1895, 'the clerk reported that he had placed two posts in the bridle path. Also that Robert Harrow had twice put posts round the pond, but that the neighbours had pulled them up again. Also that a quantity of soil from the Workhouse laundry had been tipped into the gravel pit and some had been banked on the edge of the road, making the pit safe. Also that a bank had been placed across the lower end of the bridle path. Also that the District Council had taken a good many loads of flints out of the pit for the by roads, but had not said anything about payment.' The Board agreed to write to the District Council saying that the gate would not be opened again until the District Council agreed to pay for the flints, and to bill them for the flints already taken.

The Board agreed a written application from the National Telephone Co. to be allowed to place four poles on the Common to connect the Workhouse with the office in Bromley. The *Bromley Times* asked if their reporter could attend Board meetings. A lady who was in treaty for a piece of land on the Glentrammon Estate had applied for access to it across the Common. The Board were advised that they had no power to allow a road to be made over any part of the Common, 'nor have they any power to allow the right of way across the Common to Gill's farm to be used for other than the ordinary farm purposes for which it has hitherto been used.' The vicar called attention to the muddy approach to Farnborough Well and asked if a path could be made with gravel. The cover was broken and dirt got washed into the well. It was resolved to call the attention of the Guardians to this as they put up the pump.

On 7 February 1896 it was reported that the Gas Company had removed their pipes from Green St Green and that the Telephone Co. had 'paid one shilling yearly acknowledgement'. The clerk had written to Mr. James Crafter of Green St Green who had built a house at the foot of the Old Hill, and had made two gateways in the side fence opening on to the Common and was making a roadway to them on the Common parallel to the fence. Mr. Crafter was instructed to close the gates and not to use the gateway. Mr. Crafter objected that there was a similar roadway higher up the hill to one of Mr. Fox's fields. The chairman (Mr. Fox!) pointed out that his roadway had existed from time immemorial. 'Certain persons had objected to a fence which Mr. Wilson had put up to protect some ornamental trees which he had planted on his bank. The clerk (Mr. Wilson!) showed by the map that the bank in question was not part of the Common'. The chairman said he had been much annoyed by youths playing football on Sunday and using bad language which he could hear as far as his house. The Ranger was asked to see to the matter.

Several of the trees planted by Lord Derby had died and offers were made to give some Scotch firs and limes. The Board had sent a bill for £23.8.0 to the District Council for 156 loads of gravel which it had taken from Farnborough Common. The Board was advised that 'the gravel with all other minerals under a Common belongs to the owner of the Common and not to the Parish or the Conservators. It is obvious therefore that they have no right to claim payment for them.' But the Conservators could ask the District Council for a contribution towards the conservancy fund. This would be used to restore the Common to a safe condition. The Board therefore agreed 'that without prejudice the District Council be permitted to draw from the pit sufficient gravel for the repair of the roads for this season'.

Polly Pateman (the name given on her death certificate is Mary) died of meningitis on 21 June 1900 at Willow Walk aged 6 years. Her father, a 'greengrocer (master)' was present at the death. Polly (the name given on her burial record is Mary) was buried at St Giles on 26 June 1900. She was buried in the same grave as her sister Celia (buried 8 January 1895) and her brother John (buried 8 December 1900).

4. Willow Walk

- Betsy Pateman (1896-1897)
- Elvy Pateman (1897-1950)
- George Pateman (1899-1921)
- Daisy Pateman (1901-1976)
- Rose Pateman (1903-1993)
- William Pateman (1904-1966)

Blandford: 'Farmers and others who had horses and carts could discharge their rate, or part of it, by carting flints and gravel, and this would be an advantage to them, because the roads were repaired when there was not much work for horses or men in the fields. There were several teams of horses: Stow had four teams, and many others had teams. The Vestry meetings were well attended, and had frequently to be held at *The George Inn,* the Vestry being too small. Wine for the Communion table was obtained from *The George*, and the first voluntary rate was made there.

In the parish accounts there is a charge of nine shillings for liquor that was given to men 'for hunting for the man who murdered a man in the village'; but it does not state if he was captured. There must have been a good quantity of water in Farnborough, for from the accounts there were at least twelve bridges, and the one at Green St Green was a large one, from the quantity of materials that was sent there for repairs. Rewards were given for badgers heads, foxes, pole cats and hedgehogs.'

Kent is affectionately known as The Garden of England. Not just because it has a homely, rolling landscape with small, neat fields bordered by well tended hedgerows, but because historically the county was charged with the task of feeding London - thus it was also the Market Garden of England. Apart from the introduction of steam during the late seventeenth and early eighteenth century to power the threshing machines and enable a limited amount of mechanized ploughing, farming methods had changed little for centuries until the first tractors arrived in the 1930s.

Arable agriculture is labour intensive, ploughing and cultivation relied on horse power, as did sowing, but harvesting, thinning and a certain amount of weeding could only be done by hand. The regular round of seasonal work kept the local workforce busy, but as soon as each crop ripened it needed to be gathered in quickly. Hops had been introduced to Kent during the sixteenth century and although they were not immediately acceptable to many as a flavouring and preservative in beer, by 1724 there were 6,000 acres of hop gardens in East Kent alone.

It is not just at picking time that hop growers require extra labour. Apart from the normal care and cultivation that any crop requires, hops need special attention. Unlike other climbers, they do not naturally find their way up the strings and the new shoots have to be 'trained' or 'twiddled' to encourage them to climb. At the same time, surplus shoots have to be cut out, a considerable task that has to be undertaken within a comparatively short period. Traditionally, hop training was the first job of the year to require an additional work force, in the spring when there was much else to be done on the farm, keeping the locals busy.

The county of Kent was also famous for its cherries that ripened during the hot midsummer months, together with soft fruit including strawberries, blackcurrants and gooseberries. Vegetables also needed harvesting, and although brassicas could be cut over a longer period, picking crops like peas and beans was labour intensive. Plums and damsons were ready in late summer and the hops needed picking in early September.

As each of these crops ripened in succession they had to be quickly harvested in order to be sent to market in peak condition. Although it is well known that East Enders from London came in their droves for the annual hopping, at the end of the last century they represented only a third of the 250,000 strong workforce that arrived in the county to pick the hops.

Apart from the 'home dwellers', most of the rest were itinerants and Travellers from as far afield as Ireland. After hopping, the top fruit was ripening and attention turned to the apple and pear orchards, after which the packing sheds needed to be manned. East Kent and Romney Marsh grew vegetables, particularly potatoes, which were ploughed up in preparation for the back breaking task of being picked up by hand in early winter.

Kent's rural economy depended on its mobile workforce, hanging on at one farm after each crop was harvested before moving on in preparation for the next seasonal task. It was a regular cycle that had existed for generations and today many Travellers still work for farmers whose grandfathers had employed their grandfathers.

Jim Harris: 'When the spring come we'd come up and do the hop training. We used to dress them first, used to have the hoes and knock them out, you know, and cut them off. Then we used to hang on until the hop training. After we'd done the hop training we'd just run up the Derby and then we'd come back and go cherry picking. We used to go from one job to another, do the summer's work right through and then we'd get to the hopping. After that we'd got a job of apple picking and then when they'd finished, about November or something, we used to go potato picking up, we used to pick them up a shilling a bag. Then after that we used to travel round for the winter again, making swag and that. We used to make a few clothes pegs, get a bob here and there, get a bit of hedge cutting from the farmers. We used to do that until the time came round again for the same thing.'

Travellers have always stopped on common land. It was not an unusual sight to see a family unit of two or three horse drawn wagons stopping off for a night or two on the journey between farms, and they were usually tolerated because the locals knew that they would soon be on their way.

Travelling families such as Pateman, Reynolds, Coates and Arnold were attracted to places like Orpington, Farnborough and Crofton because they provided ideal winter stop over places with access to work during the winter months. They also provided opportunities for employment on the local farms. Crofton Pound Farm, for example, was owned by St Thomas's Hospital, who leased it out to tenant farmers. It consisted of 340 acres of arable and woodlands. A 1768 map indicates that Crofton Heath was being used as arable land. A 1791 survey of woods at Crofton shows Chapman's Heath, Darrick Wood, Crofton Hall and Ivy Lodge. A survey of Crofton Pound Farm in 1825 described it as 'situate in the parish of Orpington, and Farnborough, in the County of Kent' and consisted of a house, excellent garden, outbuildings, and a number of fields, commons and woods, including Worley's Field, and Sparrow Common. These were also to be regular stopping families for travellers such as the Arnold and Coates families.

The Tithe Map and Schedule for 1844 lists the land and owners in Crofton, Orpington. At this time it was still possible for travellers to stop over in Great Derrick Wood and Crofton Heath. In 1871 St Thomas's Hospital leased some land (on Crofton Pound Hill, between Crofton Pound Farm and Orpington Station) to Captain Miller who planned to build two roads and seven houses on this land, 'subject to strict details, to the type of houses, and to the materials used in the building of them'. The Hospital sold the farm for development in the early 1930s. A bird's eye view of the farm in 1937 shows the farm yard in a rectangular block, the railways lines, Crofton Pound Hill, Orpington Station and Crofton Lane. The farmyard buildings – including a large barn - backed onto Crofton Road. The farm cottage stood at the top of Crofton Pound Hill, just before Newstead Avenue, and had a very unusual chimney. Crofton Pound Farmhouse was used as a private house after 1939 and was demolished in the late 1950's. In 1957 St Thomas Hospital approved the sale to Kent County Council of 'the area known as Darrick Wood, and land to Worley's Hole, including the Newstead Wood school area, for the sum of £15,460.' Crofton Pound Farm was later developed into the Pound Court Estate.

Betsy Pateman (1896-1897)

Betsy Pateman was born on 26 September 1896 at Locks Bottom. Her father was a general labourer and the informant was 'Jane Pateman, mother, Locks Bottom'.

On 4 December 1896 the Ranger reported to the Board of Conservators 'that Mr. Crafter's gate was locked and the road on the Common not used. He was directed to report if he saw the gate open or road used.' The clerk reported that the fir trees planted in the spring had died and some other trees were broken. The chairman offered trees out of Hollydale to replace them. The dyke round the gravel pit at Green St Green had fallen in and it was decided to put a fence up. The contractor for the Crofton sewer had partly filled in the pond at Tugmutton and filled up the hollows near the Chapel. It was decided to ask him to fill up the ruts he had made across Brasted Green. The Police Station drain had been leveled over and sown with grass seeds. As carts had lately crossed Leach's Green to Capt. Waring's field Mr. Stow pointed out that they had a right of way there.

On 23 April 1897 the clerk reported that the gravel pit at Green St Green had been made secure with posts and an iron rail. The soil placed by the contractor in the hollows near the Chapel had been leveled and the water drained away. Mr. Fawcett the Minister had written requesting leave to put a post at the turn of the path, on which to hang a lamp on Sunday evenings. He was advised that a lamp over the Chapel door would be safer and give a better light. The chairman observed that Tugmutton pond was very offensive from the decaying refuse thrown into it. Also, that the Common on Old Hill was disfigured by old tins and similar rubbish deposited there. It was agreed that a man be set to collect these pieces of paper etc and bury them in the gravel pit. Mr. Plumbridge had offered to move the water channel lower down close to the telegraph post and make level the piece above and sow it with grass seeds.

Betsy Pateman died of 'gastro enteritis, convulsions' on 13 August 1897 at Hockenden, St Mary Cray, aged 10 months. Her father, a general dealer, was present at the death.

Betsy was buried at Star Lane cemetery on 17 August 1897. It is interesting to note that James's very first child, also called Betsy Pateman, had been born at Star Lane, St Mary Cray in 1880.

Gypsy funerals are commonly held in St Mary's Parish Church, St Mary Cray, and it is quite a spectacle to observe a long procession of mourners and masses of floral tributes as they approach Star Lane cemetery. The attractive but redundant cemetery Chapel of 1861 is now in the care of the local authority and was saved from demolition by the St Mary Cray Action Group. Star Lane cemetery contains the graves of many Romany families, including several Patemans.

We do not know why Betsy was in Hockenden in August 1897 or why she was buried in Star Lane Cemetery rather than with the rest of her family at St Giles, Farnborough. According to both *Strong's* and *Bush's Directories of Farnborough*, James Pateman was living at Tugmutton in 1896. And according to *Bush's Directory* James Pateman was still living there in 1898. He was presumably at Hockenden in St Mary Cray in 1897.

Hockenden

Ray Galer describes an ancient path which leads from St Mary Cray to Hockenden: 'By the old church I saw the well worn old path leading right across the Churchyard. It was a much used path and it came across where the station now stands, through the Churchyard and led out through the Bridle path, now called Star Lane, to the hamlet of Hockenden, a way much used by farmers, drovers and merchants on Cray Market Day – and especially on Cray Fair Day – I could hear the shouts of men and the lowing of cattle round the market building in Market Meadow.'

Ray Galer takes his readers on 'A Country Walk' from St Mary Cray to Hockenden. The route he took and the sights he describes would have been very similar to those experienced by James Pateman in 1897:

'We will go up Blacksmith's Lane. Why, as we start I have in my mind the picture of the old blacksmith's forge, and the blacksmith's tree – it was one of the seven wonders of the district. It was said that when Longfellow, the great American poet, stayed for a night at Kevington Manor, he was so charmed with the view of the blacksmith's tree that he wrote his best known poem of The Village Blacksmith, but critics have said that he composed the poem in America. Anyhow, Longfellow did stay for a night at Kevington and he did see the village smithy – also this ugly old vicarage that we have come out of was once the well known bell foundry of the Hodson Brothers, who founded well known bells here in Cray from the year 1650.

Now as we go up the lane, on the right hand side we see the well known strawberry fields of the Orpington district, and the district was as well known for its strawberries as for its Buff Orpington chickens. Now look at those old oak trees – a line of them that have stood the test of calm or storm for generations. Kings have come and kings have gone, battles have been won, mighty storms have arisen, but these old oaks have weathered all sorts of conditions of life, and are still standing and still living – they even faced the Great Storm of 1703, when London and the countryside lost most of their roofs, and trees by the hundred were blown sky high – when even the Market Building in Market Meadow, the centre of the weekly market and the annual fair on the Feast of the Assumption as granted by Edward I was destroyed.

Let us keep to the left hand side of the Manor of Kevington, and let us go down Sweeps Lane – but as we pass Kevington let us see the grounds in front of the house. As one looks on the grass one can see the shadow of the remains of an encampment of Caesar's soldiers – a Roman encampment cut deep into the soil of the Manor of Kevington.

Well, here in Sweeps Lane one really does feel that one is walking down a Kentish country lane. I have been here in the depth of winter when snow has deadened all sounds of life except that of the owl, and I have heard the owl sing out on the coldest, whitest night – it was near mid night. His form, his eyes, against a background of the whitest snow of midnight here in Sweeps Lane – and today as we walk it is so hot, hot as one of those dog days of August. So hot that the 'bread and cheese' growing on the banks are toppling over with the heat, whilst the 'lords and ladies' are bowing one towards another in the drowsiness of this summer afternoon. The wild parsley is a fine crop this year, and the birds of the air will have a good harvest. Well, look to the left now, there's acres of grain growing. Wheat, barley, oats, it seems to stretch all around us, over the hills towards Swanley – grain, corn, whatever it is, it means 'Give us this day our daily bread' and sweetest of all thoughts that whilst there's a cottage beside a field of grain there will always be an England.

Are you enjoying this walk? Well, over the railway bridge and here we are at Sheepcote (sheep fold). Look at the colour of these old houses – can you hear the bleating of the sheep when wool was one of the staple products of England? Sheep, wool, bridle paths, wool pack inns – can you see it all – can you hear it all? Look at that cottage, why it is a converted oast house. Hops – yes, most of this district was full of hops – can you get the twang of the smell of the hops in the oast house – the sulphur from the kilns? Can you see them picking hops – if you are of Kent this will make you romantic.

Well, here we are at Lower Hockenden – one of the charms of the English country side is the names of its villages – Lower Hockenden, nestling snugly in a valley of sheep, of hops, and today of corn. Hockenden, both Upper and Lower, was once a manor, in the Parish of St Mary Cray. In the reign of Edward I it was owned by Sir Robert de Stangrave. He gave to the Prior and Convent of Christ Church in Canterbury, a piece of land in consideration of which they released him from fencing round the wood at Hockendenne. Part of this manor was bequeathed in 1791 to William Wentworth, Earl of Strafford, but has since passed into other hands. During the reign of Edward I, Isabella de Monte held the manor in Gavelkind of the prior of Christ Church, Orpington., by the sum of ten shillings and eleven pence per annum, and by service of ploughing, mowing and carrying the produce of certain lands of the Prior to his granary in Orpington (Orpington Priory).

Well, here at Lower Hockenden is an interesting piece of history. You will notice that by the side of that delightful little old world house of Hockenden Lodge, there is a Four Went way, or Cross Roads – one to Swanley, one to St Mary Cray, one to St Paul's Cray and one to Birchwood. Now in front of Hockenden Lodge there is a lamp – not use now a days - but used until fairly recently. But why a lamp in the midst of lonely country roads, with very little traffic?

Well, this is my fancy – Hockenden Lodge may once have been one of the entrances to the Manor of Hockenden. Because the state of the roads was so bad and the wayfarer was so pestered with highwaymen, rogues and footpads, in the year 1253 Henry III established night watchmen, and in 1830 these watchmen became policemen under Sir Robert Peel's Act. Before 1762 a few wretched oil lamps were placed outside the entrances of great houses and manors, and the watching and the lighting were performed by one and the same man, so the night watchman carried a pole with a cresset on the top of it. James I changed the cresset for a horn lantern.

But in 1416 the state of the roads was so bad and the highway men so busy that the King ordered a lantern to be placed nightly outside each house from the eve of All Hallows (30 September) to Candlemas Day (Feast of Purification, 2 February). Cottagers placed rush candles in their windows. So late in 1744 the Mayor and Aldermen of London petitioned on account of the unsafeness of the roads at night.

Now, as we look at this old lamp standing outside this Hockenden House with its four went way, one feels taken back to the days of watch and ward from evening of All Hallows to the festival of the Feast of Purification – here in this delightful little spot of Lower Hockenden, one can see the candle being lit outside the Manor of Hockendenne and one can still hear the cry of the watchman. Past two of the clock on a clear, frosty morning, 'All's well'. So, I hope that you have enjoyed your walk, and that you have seen and heard of the things that ease the mind and cast out shadows.'

Although James Pateman was described on Betsy's death certificate as a general dealer he may have been in Hockenden in August 1897 to help with the strawberry picking or to take part in the harvest of the wheat, barley, oats, grain and corn. He could then have stayed on for the hop picking in September.

James could have been visiting his brother, Walter, who lived at Vinsons Cottages, Hockenden. This was Walter's address at the time of the 1901 census, so it is possible he was living at Hockenden in 1897. Walter was a 'dealer in green vegetables', so James could have been visiting him for family or business reasons.

James could also have been visiting another branch of the Pateman family (William Pateman, Rose Ann Rich and their children), who lived at Birchwood Terrace, at the end of Hockenden Lane. Whatever his reasons were for being in Hockenden during 1897, James was back at Tugmutton by December for the birth of his next child.

At their meeting on 3 December 1897 the Board of Conservators heard that Tugmutton pond was being filled in. The Ranger reported that 'Mr. Hollingsworth in clearing round his hedge on the south side of the pond had removed the turf from the triangle between the road and the footpath.' The Board was not amused. The District Council wrote to say that they would remove 500 loads of gravel this year, 'of which 350 were already got. The men were clearing out the floor down to the chalk.' The Board received particulars of sale of the Glentrammon Estate with a plan of the estate laid out in building lots. The clerk wrote to the solicitors for the vendors pointing out that 'the front lots could have no access across the Common and over the present approach to the farm house there was no right of way but for farm purposes.'

Elvy Pateman (1897-1950)

Elvy Pateman was born on 26 December 1897 at Farnborough. Her father was a hawker and the informant was 'Jane Pateman, mother, Tugmutton'.

On 4 February 1898 the Board of Conservators were advised that 'the owner of the field on the Glentrammon estate next Capt. Waring's farm had put a gate in the fence adjoining the Common, which was at present locked.' The owner was Mr. Mullins of Moorfield Road, Orpington. The Board instructed their Solicitors to send Mr. Mullins a letter warning him not to use the gate. Messrs Fox asked 'permission to lay a pipe to carry the effluent water of their sewage tanks into the west end of the gravel pit, there to soak away, and offering to pay £20 a year for the privilege. Messrs Fox explained the working of their tanks and guaranteed that the waste would be disinfected, clear and free from smell. It was unanimously resolved that this proposal be accepted.'

Elvy Pateman was baptised on 13 February 1898 at St Giles. James Pateman was described as a labourer, Tugmutton.

On 11 March 1898 the Farnborough Common Conservators were advised by their Solicitors that Mr. Mullins had a right to turn cows onto the Common through his gate. An agreement was signed between Messrs Fox and the Board regarding the waste pipe. The Chairman read a letter from Mr. Child declining to offer himself for re-election on the grounds that the Conservators were 'a mean spirited body, who kept their hands out of other people's pockets'. The Chairman said that a new Girls School was to be built above the Infants School and 'the School Board were anxious by a give and take process to rectify their frontier to the lane'. A rough plan was produced showing a proposed wall and a new footpath alongside the road to Start's Hill. The Board agreed. The Chairman called attention to the continuation of the covered water course under Leach's Green, which was still open by the side of the path from the road to the stile. 'He was informed that the children got their feet wet and sometimes even drank out of it.' A rough estimate was produced of the expense of laying 15 inch pipes and covering with gravel and the Board agreed these works.

On 3 February 1899 it was reported to the Board that the Girls School had been built and the proposed 'rectification of frontier' carried out. The watercourse from Leach's Green to the stile had been laid. Mrs. Butcher asked that her fence running by the side of this watercourse might be straightened by a give and take process, but this was rejected by the Board. The clerk 'produced a notice of the proposed light railway from Orpington to Tatsfield which passing through Messrs Fox's property at the back of the Brewery, would cross Cocksett Hill on the level and take about 20 rods of the strip of Common by the side of the hill'. The Board offered no opposition as this scheme would confer great benefits on the district and there would only be slight interference with an unimportant outlying portion of the Common. The Board agreed to a request from the Cray Gas Co. asking permission to lay gas service onto the Chapel on Broad St Green. The Sanitary Inspector had nearly filled Tugmutton pond with spoil from the Workhouse, but a letter was read from Mr. Griffin complaining that vehicles were driven across the site, stopping up his own surface drain. The clerk was directed to stop this right of way either by a trench or posts. Mr. Fox called attention to the dangerous condition of an old oak opposite *The Larches* at Green St Green which was dead and likely to fall. The clerk undertook to remove it

Elvy Pateman moved to Westcliff on Sea, Essex. On 23 December 1922 Elvie Pateman (24, spinster, Westcliff on Sea, Essex, father - James Pateman, potato merchant) married Edward William Whiffen (27, bachelor, groom, 7 Devonshire Square, father - William Whiffen, coachman) at Bromley Parish Church. The witnesses were William and Gertrude Whiffen. Elvy's name was spelt 'Elvie' on the wedding certificate.

We do not know why Elvy was living at Westcliff on Sea, how she met Edward Whiffen or why they were married at Bromley Parish Church, but it all seems a world away from the Tugmutton Gypsies. Edward (Jack) Whiffen served in the Royal Horse Artillery during the Great War. There is a photograph of him (not in uniform) riding a horse.

Members of the Whiffin family are mentioned in the Farnborough Parish Accounts: Jno Wiffin (1717), George Whiffin (1718), William Whiffin (1718), John Whiffin (1718), Mary Whiffin (1741), Edward Whiffin (1767), Henry Whiffen (1769), George Whiffin (1815). An entry in the Farnborough Commons Conservator's Minute Book for August 1887 notes that the 'last property to be purchased in Farnborough was a piece of landing belonging to Peter Whiffen.' There are three memorials to members of the Whiffin family in St Giles church yard and the graves of Frederick Wiffen (died 30 October 1953, age 80) and his wife Eliza Wiffen (died 26 April 1928, age 53). Dorothy Anderson remembers 'Mr. Whiffin's sweet shop' in Farnborough Village.

On 11 July 1925 the following advertisement appeared in *The Orpington Journal*: 'Your Garden – turf, gravel, manure & crazy paving supplied. Paths & Gardens made up. I will call and estimate on receipt of postcard. G. WHIFFEN, 32 Bridge Road, St Mary Cray. Contract and Removal Work one ton Ford. Moderate charges. Personal supervision to all Work.'

The nature of the work is interesting as it is the kind of work that Gypsies would carry out – the modern day equivalent of landscape gardening, tree felling, and tarmaccing. The location is also significant – Bridge Road was in Ford Croft, St Mary Cray, close to the Pankhurst yard (Phoebe Pateman was married to Frederick Pankhurst) and near to the rag and bone yard owned by Henry Pateman in Poverest Road

There are some photographs of Elvy. One, taken in a studio, shows her as a middle aged woman; another, taken when she was older, shows her picking hops. There are also some group photographs. One shows her about to board a bus for the coast at Farnborough Hill garage with Mrs. Last (landlady at the *Black Horse*, Locks Bottom),

Mrs. Last's sister, Doris Pateman, Frances Pateman and Bill Pateman. Another photo shows her with Boysey Rye and a happy looking crowd as they arrive at the seaside. There are two photos of her in the sea with her sisters Rose and Daisy and others.

Elvie Whiffen died on 16 April 1950, aged 52 years, at Clifton Cottages, Fordcombe Lane, Fordcombe, near Tunbridge Wells, Kent. She was the wife of Edward William Whiffen, private groom. The cause of death was cerebral haemorhage. The informant was E.W. Whiffen, widower of deceased. Elvie was interred in St Peter's Churchyard, Fordcombe. Judging by the gilt edged remembrance card which this information was taken from, Elvy may have gone up in the world. Alternatively, she could also have been returning to her roots – Fordcome is in Kent, west of Tunbridge Wells, and close to the border with East Sussex. The surrounding fields were full of the vegetables, fruit and hops that Gypsies would pick as part of their seasonal employment.

George Pateman (1899-1921)

George Pateman was born on 1 April 1899 at Tugmutton. His father was a general hawker and the informant was 'Jane Pateman, mother, Tugmutton'. The 1899 *Bush's Directory of Farnborough* lists James Pateman as living at Tugmutton.

George died on 23 April 1921 aged 22 years at 5 New Road, Orpington. He was a railway fireman and the cause of death was tuberculosis of the lungs. The informant was F. Pankhurst, brother in law, present at the death, 5 New Road. This was Frederick Pankhurst, husband of Phoebe Pateman. We do not know when and why George moved from Farnborough to Orpington, but we suspect that it was part of the general migration from Farnborough and Locks Bottom to Orpington and the Crays. George's sister, Phoebe, was living at 5 New Road when she married Frederick Pankhurst in 1914. George was buried on 28 April 1921 at St Giles. He was buried in the same grave as his grandfather, Robert (buried 1890).

On 3 November 1899 the clerk of the Board of Conservators reported that a trench had been cut across the site of Tugmutton pond to stop traffic. The Board considered the approach over the Common to Glentrammon Farm being used to carry materials for the houses being built on the estate, but decided not to interfere unless there was an attempt to make the road wider. The Water Co. was written to pointing out that they should have asked leave before breaking the surface. The Bromley Gas Co. was requested to remove the pipes which had been lying on Farnborough Common for a year. Mr. Gawtrey complained of the state of the roadway in front of his house at Locks Bottom. The Board advised Mr. Gawtry to mend the road himself. A traction engine had been left for the night on the cross track in front of Peill's shoot at the Green. It was decided not to interfere with this engine but to warn others off. Mr. Stow said he believed the Orpington to Wickham road was now a main road. If so it was decided to refuse gravel from the pit for it.

On 4 May 1900 the clerk reported that the Water Company had apologized, the Gas Company had taken away their pipes and Mr. Gawtrey had done nothing to the road in front of his house. A willow on the Common near Mr. Session's house had been split by the branches getting top heavy. The Clerk had cut the top off and would top the remaining ones in the autumn. The Board finances were healthy so a rate would not be needed. Mr. Jones wrote complaining that persons made a roadway through the hedge which he claimed at Tugmutton between the road and the strip of Common by the pond. The Board did not believe that he could claim the road or hedge and decided to take no action. Messrs Fox had written that they now only turned the effluent water into the gravel pit occasionally, when they were cleaning out the tanks. They thought that in future £10 would be as much as they ought to pay. Mr. Mullins promised to remove the gate to the side of his projecting corner abutting on the cart track to Capt. Waring's farm. The Chairman said that the gorse on Farnborough Common had grown so high as to be in danger of taking fire. The clerk was instructed to get it cut.

On 7 December 1900 the District Council informed the Board that they were anxious to carry on and widen the road from Lovibond's gate to Pickington's Lane. If the Conservators would offer no objection, the Council would remove the willow trees over the spring, put in the necessary pipes for the spring and drains and straighten and widen the road, carrying it on down the side of Broad St Green into the lane by Springett's pond. It was also proposed to make a curved footpath from the Police Station to Springett's pond and to widen and make up the roadway by this footpath as far as the pump. The Board agreed these proposals. It was directed that the tip by the stone heap at Green St Green was to be leveled and a notice board put up that no rubbish was to be put there.

The 1900 *Bush's Directory of Farnborough* lists James Pateman as living at Tugmutton. A photograph of Locks Bottom police station features PC or Sergeant Ward who was apparently related to the Pateman family in some way, possibly via the Knights. The *Post Office Directory* 1878 notes that William Watson and Arthur Sewell were sergeants at Lock's Bottom police station and there were 12 constables.

The police station also features in another photograph, dated c.1900, which shows a small parade of houses and shops, the *White Lion* pub and a piece of open ground dominated by a large tree. A group of men are staring at the camera from under the tree. A horse drawn cart and an early motor vehicle are parked outside the pub.

Two features give this old part of Locks Bottom a historic interest. One is the site of Godendene, a wonderful country house where Sainsbury's now stands. It was home to the famous March family of sculptors, whose finest work is the magnificent Canadian National War Memorial in Ottawa. Very old residents also recall their statue of Kitchener being taken on a horse drawn low loader through Bromley, on the way to Khartoum.

The other land mark was 'The old grey house at Locks Bottom', or Workhouse (incorporated later into Farnborough Hospital, but now demolished to make way for a new hospital), to which numbers of down and outs could be seen walking along the main Bromley road each evening, to claim beds for the night. Into the 1930's it still had about 600 inmates over Christmas, when the dining hall was lavishly decorated. According to a 1930 account, members of one sporting club visited, to give out presents to each man of tobacco, pipes, snuff and cigarettes. Later, staff and inmates combined in a seasonal entertainment, when it was known as Farnborough Hospital and Institution.

There are three photographs, taken at different times, showing the view of Locks Bottom, from the junction of Crofton Road and Bromley Road, looking towards Tugmutton. The earliest photograph shows some shops on the right, just down from the police station. The left hand side of the road has no houses or shops and there is not a car, lorry or bus in sight.

The second photograph of the same view shows a row of mock tudor shops on the left hand side of the road when they were newly built. The first shop on the corner is a chemist. They still exist, weathered by over seventy winters, and their many gables contribute much of the beauty of Locks Bottom each Christmas, when the whole area is ablaze with fairy lights.

Beyond these shops there are open fields with a large house in the distance. On the other side of the road there are two shops – E. Chave and A. Philips – with Lyons Tea signs and hoardings outside the latter. Beyond these shops there is a weather boarded house (which still exists) and then a bakers, with a distinctive Hovis sign hanging outside, under a gas lamp. There is a motor car parked on the road and a single pedestrian.

The third photograph of the same scene, titled 'the village, Locks Bottom, Kent,' also shows the Hovis sign. E. Chave has been replaced by A.Sansom (confectioners) and A.Phillips has become Barclays Bank. More shops have been built on the other side of the road and the *Black Horse* pub is visible in the distance. The early motor traffic in this undated picture suggest that the period was probably the 1920's or early 1930's, when English hamlets like this were in the process of initial suburbanization.

<u>1901 Census</u>

On 31 March 1901 James Pateman (48, greengrocer, Kent, Cliffe) was living at Tugmutton with Jane (42, Kent, Lidden), Robert (16, greengrocers apprentice, Kent, Farnborough), Mary Ann (15, Farnborough), Charlotte (14, Farnborough), Phoebe (13, Farnborough), Jane (11, Farnborough), Elvy (3, Farnborough) and George (2, Farnborough).

Of the fifteen children which Jane and James had produced between 1880 and 1899: seven were still living at home: Robert, Mary Ann, Charlotte, Phoebe, Jane, Elvy and George; Emmie was not at home but we assume that she was still living in Farnborough because she gave this as her address when she married William Fenton in 1904; Phillis went into domestic service and in the 1901 census she was living at No. 2 Wellclose Villas, Farnborough. She was working for William Plumbridge (fruit grower) who had a wife and three children. Phillis was described as a 'general servant (domestic), Kent, Farnborough'; six were dead : Betsy (1881), Hannah (1884), Celia (1894), Betsy (1897), John (1900), Polly (1900). This reminds us of the very high infant mortality rate in the 19th century when children died of illnesses such as measles, bronchitis, gastro entiritis and meningitis.

The 1901 *Bush's Directory of Farnborough* gives James Pateman's address as 5 Tugmutton. Also living at Tugmutton at the time of the Census were: James Ringer, Eliza Brain, John Springett, John Reynolds, Louisa Bird, James Crane, John Costin, William Mitchell, William Weatherly, George Reynolds and Edward Weatherly.

Only John Reynolds and William Mitchell had been living at Tugmutton with James in 1881. However, Louisa Bird (1891) was related to George and Jonathan Bird (1881); William and Edward Weatherly (1891) were related to Thomas Weatherly (1881); and George Reynolds (1891) had been living in a van in Piggenden's Lane in 1881.

George's move from a van to a cottage at Tugmutton reflected the wider settlement or semi-settlement pattern of Gypsies like James and William Pateman, who had moved from his van in Orpington Lane (1881) to Stow's Cottages in Farnborough Village (1891). By 1901 William Pateman had moved to a far more substantial property in Cobden Road, Farnborough.

So, by 1901 the Tugmutton Gypsy community had consolidated its presence in Farnborough and had become part of the settled and established community: William Pateman at Cobden Road; George Reynolds at Worlegs Hole; John Reynolds, James Pateman and George Reynolds at Tugmutton.

Daisy Pateman (1901-1975)

Daisy Pateman (1901-1976) = Jack Baker (1899-?)
- Anthony John (1938-2004)

Daisy Pateman was born on 25 May 1901 at Wellbrook Road. Her father was a general hawker and the informant was 'Jane Pateman, mother, Wellbrook Road', which is adjacent to Tugmutton Common.

On 26 June 1901 the clerk of the Board of Conservators reported that the willows had been lopped round Springett's pond and the pond fenced. Mr. Good asked permission to shoot garden rubbish in the gravel pit and the Board agreed that only vegetable refuse could be put there. 'The chairman moved the following resolution, saying it was not his wish to cast any reflection on the clerk of whose services he spoke in very handsome terms, but he thought it better to have only one authority in the parish, as at Orpington. As it appears to the Commons Conservators their work should be done by the Parish Council, they desire to transfer their powers to the latter and request the Parish Council to take such steps as may be necessary to carry this proposal into effect.'

On 23 April 1902 the clerk read a letter from Mr. Charles Pearce to say that an elm tree on the Common in front of Gill's farm was decayed and dangerous. He had answered that he saw it was in the line of the new road on the Glentrammon estate but if that road was brought across the Common the Conservators would take proceedings. Having inspected the place with Messrs Fox he had ordered some posts to be placed so as to stop the road. Mr. Griffin (one of the Conservators) complained that Mr. Staples had turned a horse with the mange onto the Common. The Conservators were of the opinion that it was not they but the party aggrieved that ought to take action.

The 1902 *Bush's Directory of Farnborough* confirms that James Pateman was still living at 5 Tugmutton. Other entries in the Directory include: 3 Tugmutton – George

Reynolds; 6 Tugmutton – John Reynolds; 2 Worley's Cottages – John Reynolds, junior; 4 Cobden Road – William Pateman.

On 31 March 1928 Daisy Pateman (25, spinster, daily maid, 5 Willow Walk, father - James Pateman, deceased, potato salesman) married Jack Albert Baker (29, bachelor, builder's labourer, 13 Pitt Road, Farnborough, father - Edward Lawson Baker, deceased, commercial traveler) at Bromley Registry Office. The witnesses were Boysey Rye and Rose Pateman.

It is interesting to note this marriage between a Gypsy traveler and a commercial traveler. This was also the first family wedding to take place in a Registry Office rather than a church. Rose Pateman (a witness at Daisy's wedding) was to be the last Pateman to get wed at St Giles when she married Boysey Rye on 25 December 1928.

Daisy and Jack had one child, Anthony (Tony) John, on 9 December 1938. Tony married Heather Keen and they had three children, Stephen (1965), Julie (1968) and Michael (1972). I met Tony Baker at a family gathering in 2003 and he told me that he lived at Tugmutton until he was 19 years old. His grandmother, Jane Pateman, would not move from 5 Willow Walk because she would have to move to a house with gas and she did not like gas. The rent was 5s 6d per week and went up to 7s6d. The cottage was condemned three times. There was a huge crack in the bedroom wall which Tony could look through and see the stars. Tony slept with a sheaf knife under his bed and was woken one night when he heard noises in the garden. This turned out to be a donkey which had escaped from Boswell's Yard. In the scullery there was a dresser with a machine which measured out flour and silver ball sweets.

Tony remembers hop picking and living on the farm in huts, sleeping on faggots and straw beds. They took their own blankets and the men went down the pub in the evening while the children played in the fields. It was their annual holiday. Tony died in 2004 leaving a wife, three children and two grandchildren.

There is a posed photograph of Daisy as a young woman sitting at a desk with a book open in front of her. And there is a photo of her at the seaside with Doris and Bill Pateman.

Daisy Baker died on 27 October 1976, aged 76, at Bromley Hospital. She was the widow of John Albert Baker, sheet metal worker, of Flat 4, Swingfield Court, 2A Walpole Road, Bromley. The cause of death was bronchopneumonia, chronic bronchitis and emphysema and multiple cerebral infarcts due to atheroma osteoporosis. The informant was Anthony John Baker, son. We do not know where she is buried.

Rose Pateman (1903-1993)

Rose Pateman (1903-1993) = Boysey Rye (1900-1948)
- Dorothy (1929-)
- Geoffrey (1938-)

Rose Pateman was born on 3 January 1903 at Wellbrook Road. Her father was a general labourer and the informant was 'Jane Pateman, mother, Wellbrook Road' The 1903 *Bush's Directory of Farnborough* states that James Pateman was living at 5 Tugmutton, so I'm not sure why Rose's birthplace was given as Wellbrook Road.

On 20 January 1903 the clerk of the Board of Conservators 'related the circumstances connected with Mr. Hubbard's action, who was making a new road to his cottages, starting from the site of the pond opposite the *George* and taking gravel from the Green St Green pit for the purpose.' When challenged Mr. Hubbard claimed that it was within his right as there was no bye law to prevent it and said that if the pit were locked he would break it open. The Board were advised by their Solicitor that Mr. Hubbard would have to prove his right by showing that he or his predecessors in title had for 30 years exercised their right in respect of that road. It was estimated that Mr. Hubbard had taken 84 yards of gravel. The Board agreed to bill Mr. Hubbard for 50 yards of gravel at 2s. a load and ask him to give a written undertaking to take no more gravel, or they would take proceedings. Mr. Alfred Ayres of the *Rose and Crown*, Green St Green, asked leave to put a lamp on the Common at the point where the road from his house joined the Sevenoaks road, as several accidents had happened there. He undertook to keep it lighted. The Board agreed this request.

On 20 April 1903 the clerk reported that the dead oak opposite *The Larches* had been removed and the posts across the end of Gill's road on the Glentrammon estate had been put up. Mr. Hubbard had ignored the request to pay £5 for the gravel he had taken and so the Board asked their Solicitor to take proceedings. Mr. Straker in Wellbrook Road had taken some gravel for the drive to his door, then some time after had picked this gravel up and put it on a new path, and then sent for more gravel to replace it on the old path. When this subterfuge was reported to the clerk, he wrote demanding seven shillings for two loads of gravel. As no answer had been received the Board referred this matter to their Solicitor. Several members called attention to the hedge clippings on the Common and the clerk was requested to have them removed. A proposal was received regarding the widening of the road opposite Lovibond's gate. 'Mr. Lubbock would give a large piece of land for the purpose, if his fence at the other end might be brought up flush with the wall of the girl's playground'. The plan was approved and a letter written to the Rural District Council requesting them to carry it into effect.

At their next meeting on 24 June 1903, 'in the absence of the clerk and the minute book no business was transacted.' On 16 September 1903 the Board discussed how the Ranger should be paid (by cheque at a Board meeting and entered in the minutes) and how the action against Mr. Hubbard was progressing. On 23 September the Board were informed by their Solicitor that Mr. Hubbard's case would come for trial after the Courts resumed on 24 October. It was reported on 17 November that the Board's solicitors had met with Mr. Hubbard's solicitors and agreed a compromise by which Mr. Hubbard would take no more gravel and both parties would pay their own costs up to date. Mr. Hubbard rejected this compromise and said that 'he expected the plaintiff to pay his costs and also that some twenty persons in Farnborough whom he named, should also promise to take no more gravel illegally (he well knowing that none of them had done so). The Board unanimously scouted such an impudent proposal, but were quite willing to entertain the original suggestion'.

The Board instructed Messrs Cronk of Sevenoaks to measure the pit at Green St Green, to see how many years supply was left and to prepare a plan of Gladstone Road.

The 1904 *Bush's Directory of Farnborough* states that James Pateman was living at 5 Tugmutton. On 27 January 1904 the clerk of the Board reported 'that the case Attorney General v. Hubbard was concluded, the Defendant having signed an agreement abandoning all claim to take gravel for new roads. Each party to pay its own costs. He produced a copy of the agreement and was directed to insert it as an advertisement in the *Bromley District Times* and also to put in a paragraph giving a short history of the case, so as to contradict mendacious rumours which were circulated.' The clerk reported a balance of £51 in the bank but the Hubbard case had cost them £88.

At their thirty ninth and final meeting on 30 March 1904 the Board made an application to the Parish Council for £50. 'Mr. Stow said that as Mr. Hughes had by Lord Derby's direction thinned the trees along the top of the Common and repaired the cages round them he thought it would be graceful of the Conservators to thank him. Mr. Shorter said that as he had not sought re-election on the Parish Council he thought he had better resign his seat on this Board now instead of going on till the duties of the Board were taken over by the Parish Council. His resignation was accepted with regret'. And so the life of the Farnborough Commons Conservators came to an abrupt end after sixteen years of incessant meddling in the affairs of the village and the imposition of petty restrictions which ultimately bankrupted the Conservators and forced them to hand over their business to the Parish Council.

On 25 December 1928 Rose Pateman (26, spinster, 5 Willow Walk, father - James Pateman, deceased, salesman) married Boysey Rye (28, bachelor, nursery man, 5 Willow Walk, father - Percy Rye, bailiff) at St Giles. This was to be the last Pateman family wedding at St Giles.

Boysey Geoffrey Rye was born on 7 January 1900 at Barnstable Cottages, Cudham. His father was Percy William Rye, carman, and his mother was Elizabeth Batchelor.

There is a photograph of Boysey Rye, taken in a studio with a rural scene as a backdrop. Boysey looks young and confident with the world at his feet. He wears his hat at a jaunty angle and there is a cigarette in the corner of his mouth. His suit is open to reveal a waistcoat with what look like silver or gold buttons. He holds his hands in front of him and his left foot is forward. He is solid and secure and he looks the camera right in the eye.

There is also a photo of Boysey and Rose in the sea with Elvy Pateman and some other family members. Another photo, also at the seaside, shows Rose and Elvy with Bill Pateman and other relatives. A photo of Rose when she is older shows her with William and Doris Pateman and others. Finally, there is a photo of an elderly Rose enjoying a drink with Jack Baker, William and Doris Pateman.

The Rye's are a well known Orpington family with many Gypsy connections. There is a photograph of a farm worker's home with the caption: 'While the countryside of sixty years ago may seem to modern eyes to have been an idyllic place to live, the accommodation provided for those who actually worked on the land was often cold, damp and comfortless, with no laid on water or other services and usually an outside privy. Some improvements were made, but there was still a housing crisis in 1948 when this photograph was taken and presented to Parliament (along with others) as part of a campaign for better rural housing. Philip Rye and his wife and six children (all under seven) had lived in this tin shack at Crockenhill in Kent for six and a half years.'

The photograph is dominated by the 'tin shack' with smoke coming out of the roof and Philip Rye and his wife standing in the doorway looking awkward and wary. To the left is another corrugated iron building but, more significantly, to the right is the front wheel and steps of a vardo – suggesting that the Rye's were Gypsies and did not all have to live and sleep in the shack. Three older children are standing around a pram containing their younger siblings. The child in the pram looking straight at the camera is Joe Rye.

I met Joe Rye when I was researching the life of my great uncle Walter Pateman, who was killed in the Great War in 1917 (see *Seven Steps to Glory – Private Pateman Goes to War*). Joe knew a lot about Walter Pateman, his wife Priscilla Arnold (who Joe called Aunt Prissy) and their children. Joe has a photograph of Walter Pateman in his uniform and standing by a horse. Like many Gypsies who fought in the Great War, Walter's skill with horses was very useful on the battlefield. Walter was a horse dealer before he was conscripted into the Middlesex Regiment. Joe said that Walter got his head blown off by an enemy shell. Joe also told me that Walter's grandson, Albert, was still alive – and I subsequently made contact with him.

Rose and Boysey had two children, Dorothy (1929) and Geoffrey (1938). I met them both at a family gathering in 2003 and they told me about their mother, who lived on into her 80's. She was the longest surviving child of James and Jane Pateman and she was alive when I started this family history. I should have followed the golden rule of genealogy and spoken to her before she passed away as she could have given me so much personal information about the Tugmutton Gypsies.

Boysey Geoffrey Rye died on 22 September 1948 aged 48 years. He was interred at Bromley Hill Cemetery.

Rose Rye died on 29 March 1993, aged 90, at St Anthony's, 7-11 York Road, Herne Bay. The cause of death was bronchopneumonia. She was the widow of Boysey Geoffrey Rye, nurseryman. The informant was Dorothy Francis Holmes, daughter, 56 Frankswood Avenue, Petts Wood, Orpington, Kent.

William Pateman (1904-1966)

William Pateman (1904-1966) = Doris Maud Abbott (1907-?)
- William David Lawrence (1930-)

William Pateman was born in August 1904 at Tugmutton. His father was a general labourer and the informant was 'Jane Pateman, mother, Tugmutton'. The date of birth is indistinct on the birth certificate.

William was baptized on 20 November 1904 at All Saints, Orpington. James Pateman was described as a labourer, Farnborough. William was the first member of the family to be baptized at All Saints, Orpington, as opposed to St Giles, Farnborough. Orpington had grown in importance and in the years leading up to the Great War, and after, more and more members of the Pateman family left Farnborough and moved to Orpington and the Crays.

On 16 November 1929 William Pateman (25, bachelor, builder's labourer, 5 Willow Walk, father - James Pateman, deceased, general dealer) married Doris Maud Abbott (22, spinster, laundry hand, 5 Willow Walk, father - David Abbott, general stores master) at Bromley Registry Office. The witnesses were Jane and David Abbott junior.

Doris Maud Abbott was born on 19 September 1907 at 12 North Bank Road, Walthamstow. Her father was David Abbott a master confectioner, and her mother was Jane Maud Abbott, formerly Knight.

William and Doris had one child, William David Lawrence Pateman (Bill), who was born 20 May 1930 at 5 Willow Walk. His father was a builders labourer. He was baptized on 6 July 1930 at St Giles.

There are several photographs of William, Doris and Bill Pateman. One photo shows William and Doris on a beach, sitting in deckchairs, with a railway station just behind them. Another photo shows William and Doris in a garden with young Bill, who has a toy horse and cart with a miniature milk churn and milk bottles. Another photo shows William and Doris sitting on a motorbike at Willow Walk. And there is an interesting photo of William, Doris and Bill at Easthill, where they stayed in a converted railway carriage.

There are also some group photographs. One of these shows William and Doris Pateman, plus several members of the Reynolds family, including John, Seaman, Amelia, William, Britannia and Thomas. Another shows William and Bill Pateman with Nonnie Abbott and a number of other people.

William David Lawrence Pateman (21, carpenter, 4 Denmark Cottages, father – William Pateman, bricklayer) married Irene Searle in 1952 and they moved to St Pauls Cray, where they had three children, Alan (1953), Barry (1963) and Gillian (1964). I met Bill Pateman at a family gathering in 2003 and he told me that he was born at 5 Willow Walk and he played in Boswells Yard. As a 3 year old, Bill remembers being left with Amy Whiffen at Colegate Cottages while his mother worked in the laundry. He cut his head open on the mangle and Amy held it under the cold tap and pointed to the laundry chimney and said 'Your mother will be home soon'.

On his way to Farnborough school William would visit his grandmother, Jane Pateman, every morning. He would sit on her lap and she would give him one of the Fox's glacier mints which she always kept in the big pockets of her black dress. She would give William's friends a mint as well and she would give him a mint to take to school. William would also visit Jane at dinner time.

Aunt Daisy lived with Jane, and Daisy's youth kept Jane going. Aunt Rose was called Roya. The family would gather at Jane's on a Sunday afternoon. This was not organized (there were no telephones), but everyone would take some food and make a complete tea between them. William would play under the table. There was no electricity, just an oil lamp with a wick, which was later replaced by an Aladdin lamp with a mantle, which also gave out heat. The lamps burned a circle on the low ceilings. In the kitchen there was a cooker range, with a copper and a black leaded cast iron oven. There was a fire with a side oven and the kettle was always on the go. The old oven eventually burnt out and was replaced with a calor gas cooker.

In 1933 Bill moved to nearby Denmark Cottages in Crofton Road, where he lived at number 4 until 1952. Bill remembers several Romany words including poggered, mullered and pahny. Bill now lives in Milton Keynes with his wife, Irene Searle. They have three children and eight grandchildren.

William Pateman died of stomach cancer on 9 August 1966 at Farnborough Hospital, aged 61 years. His address was 353 Crofton Road and the informant was his son, Bill Pateman, who was living at 13 Meadow View, St Paul's Cray. We do not know when Doris Maud Pateman died or where she is buried.

William Pateman was the last of James and Jane's eighteen children. James continued to live at 5 Tugmutton, as recorded by the *Bush's Directories of Farnborough* for 1905-1908, but in 1909 this address changed to Willow Walk (and was listed as such by *Bush's* until it ceased publication in 1914).

An *Ordnance Survey* map of 1909 shows Tugmutton Common and Willow Walk. It is possible to identify 5 Willow Walk, where James Pateman lived; and 7 Willow Walk, home of Urania and Levi Boswell. Other features on the map include: Broadstreet Green, the Union Workhouse, a smithy and some cottages next to the Black Horse pub (320 Crofton Road); Blackhorse Cottages, Colegate Cottages, Tea Tree Cottages and Denmark Cottages; the Farnborough Schools, Starts Hill Farm, Beulah Chapel (Baptist) and Methodist Chapel (Primitive). A later map of 1933 shows very few changes: the chapels have disappeared and the workhouse has become a hospital.

Bush's Directory of Farnborough, 1910 lists the following residents of Willow Walk, Tugmutton- *From Starts Hill to Crofton Road* ; Boswell, Levi, junior ; Pateman, W ; *Vacant house* ; *Here is Wellbrook Road* ; Reynolds, G ; Reynolds, James ; Pateman, James ; Reynolds, John ; Boswell, Levi, senior ; Bird, Mrs. ; Lockyer, H. ; *Here is Crofton Road.*.

This was still the heart of the Tugmutton Gypsy community, comprising the Boswell, Pateman and Reynolds families. Walter Pateman (William's son) had moved in. Bird was a Tugmutton name from the census returns of 1881, 1891 and 1901. The Lockyers were also a well established Tugmutton family and Robert Pateman had married Phyllis Rose Lockyer on 27 August 1910.

The situation was very similar in *Bush's Directory of Farnborough*, 1911: Willow Walk, Tugmutton – *From Starts Hill to Crofton Road* ; Boswell, Levi, junior; Cooper, H ; *Here is Wellbrook Road* ; Reynolds, G ; Reynolds, James ; Pateman, James;

Reynolds, John ; Boswell, Levi, senior ; Reynolds, G junior ; Lockyer, H ; Pateman, R ; *Here is Crofton Road.*

Walter Pateman and Mrs. Bird had moved out. Robert Pateman, George Reynolds junior and H. Cooper had moved in. Another J. Reynolds was living at 1 Nile Cottages and yet another J. Reynolds was living at 5 Nile Cottages. Given the close ties between the Pateman and Reynolds families, it could be said that these two families formed the nucleus of the Tugmutton Gypsy community – with the gravitas added by the Boswells.

Bush's Directory of Farnborough, 1913 adds further texture and colour to this picture of the Gypsy community. In Church Road we find Stow's Cottages (The Yard) where William Pateman was living before he moved to Cobden Road. G. Bird was living at 4 Stow's Cottages. William Pateman was no longer living at Cobden Road (he had moved to Orpington) but G. Reynolds was living at 8 Cobden Road, George Coates was at 6 Cobden Road and W. Coates was at 8 Cobden Road. See Chapter Six – Fellow Travellers.

At Locks Bottom W. Lewis was at 12 Crofton Road and W. Weatherley was at 1 Locks Bottom Cottages. In Colegate Cottages there were R. Pateman (1) and William Fenton (4). In Tea Tree Cottages there were S. Reynolds (4), C. Rye (3), E. Lewis (1). And in Denmark Cottages there was Chas Lewis (3).

Bush's Directory of Farnborough 1914: 'Farnborough is a large village comprising 1,411 acres, situated about four miles south of Bromley. The population in 1911 was 3210 (including Officers and Inmates of the Bromley Union Workhouse, and Officers and Inmates of St Joseph's Home, which are in this Parish), and the number of houses, 557. The rateable value is £17,734.

At one time, doubtless, Farnborough was more frequented than at present, as, being situate on the main road to Tunbridge Wells and Hastings, numerous coaches passed through daily. At present, in the summer season, large numbers of excursionists by road are in the habit of making it their rendezvous. A considerable area has lately been built upon, and the population is rapidly increasing.

The Church, which is dedicated to St Giles, is an erection of mixed early English and Perpendicular styles. It has Nave, Chancel and a low embattled Tower with two Bells. The main body of the building is of chalk and flint, and the Tower of brick and flint. There is a fine Octagonal Font in the decorated style. The Register dates from 1558, the year of the Act of Queen Elizabeth ordering such to be kept regularly. The Rev, E.J. Welch is the Rector.

The Baptists have a Chapel in Wellbrook Road, and since the development of the Green Street Green district have built an additional one in that portion of the Parish, whilst more recently still the Wesleyans have opened a new building near the centre of the village.

The industries of the Parish are almost entirely agricultural, fruit growing forming a large proportion. The nearest railway station is Orpington, one and a quarter miles. Farnborough is now governed by a Parish Council, elected annually in March.'

This official version of the Farnborough community does not mention the Tugmutton Gypsies although they are scattered liberally throughout its pages. There are the Coates in Cobden Road, the Ryes in Tea Tree Cottages and the Patemans in Willow Walk and Colegate Cottages. The Reynolds are in Willow Walk, Cobden Road, Poplar Cottages and Tea Tree Cottages.

So let us return one last time to Willow Walk and see who was living there in 1914, on the eve of that cataclysmic event – the Great War – which was to change everything for ever. Willow Walk, Tugmutton – *From Starts Hill to Crofton Road* ; Crutch, J ; Cooper, H ; Here is Wellbrook Road ; Reynolds, G ; Reynolds, T ; Pateman, James ; Reynolds, John ; Boswell, Levi ; Crane, W ; Anderson, J ; *Here is Crofton Road.* H. Cooper, G. Reynolds, James Pateman, John Reynolds and Levi Boswell were still living there. Levi Boswell junior, James Reynolds, George Reynolds junior, H. Lockyer and R. Pateman had moved out. J. Crutch, T. Reynolds, W. Crane and J. Anderson had moved in. All of this happened in the space of just three years which indicates how mobile the population was in 1914, although some of those who moved may only have relocated to somewhere else in the village or its environs, perhaps to find a bigger or better house for a growing family.

Members of the Tugmutton Gypsy community featured on the courts pages of the *Kentish Times* in 1914. The following item appeared on 17 April 1914: 'William Reynolds, 6 Tugmutton, Farnborough, was charged with being drunk on licensed premises at the New Inn, Farnborough, on the 11th inst. Acting sergeant 206 P stated that at 10.30 on Friday evening he saw the prisoner staggering about High Street Farnborough. He walked towards the New Inn and entered. Witness followed him in and brought him out. He had not been served. Prisoner, smiling broadly: I am very sorry to say he is telling a story. The Chairman: Have you anything to say to the Court? Prisoner: Nothing at all sir. He was fined 10s and 2s 6d costs.'

On 8 May 1914 it was reported that: 'Daniel Coates, Crofton Farm, Crofton Lane, Orpington, was summoned for allowing a horse to stray at Crofton Pound Hill, Orpington, on April 16th – Police constable 697 said he found the animal near the railway station. A fine was imposed of 2s 6d with 3s 6d costs.' Also on the 8 May 1914: 'Levi Boswell, 7 Willow Walk, Farnborough, was summoned for allowing ten animals to stray at Crofton Road, Orpington. Acting sergeant 200 P deposed to finding on the 6th April six donkeys and two horses, which were owned by defendant. Police constable 418 P on the same day found two of defendants horses at Farnborough. Defendant was fined 10s with 3s 6d costs, the magistrate pointing out the danger of animals being on the roadway unattended.'

Bush's Directory was not published after 1914. The Great War ended its publication and so much else besides. Men from the Tugmutton Gypsy community fought and died in the Great War, including my great Uncle, Walter Pateman, who fell at Bouchavesnes, France, in February 1917. Social relations between men and women, rich and poor, master and servant also changed. All of these forces and factors had their affect on the Tugmutton Gypsies. James Pateman and John Reynolds first arrived at Tugmutton in 1881 – and they were still living there in 1914, thirty three years later. Their children married into local settled families to create a complex pattern of relationships.

5. Farnborough Village

- Mary Pateman (1876-1901)
- Henry Pateman (1880-1961)

Blandford: 'The Vestry Accounts of 1757 record the following tale of poverty and distress: 'On the 2 of May 1757 being at the Sitting of Justices to have my Accts & Seafe signed Elizabeth Coffin of this parish was there and made complaint that John Conford & his Wife were both ill and having 4 Children were in great necessity of more relieve than was allowed by the parish. The poor Woman Received little more than a reprimand for her complaint, though she said Cornford's Wife was in a starving condition for want of proper Relief. I being there and partly knowing the miserable Condition Cornford and his family was in, I could do no less than acquaint the Gentlemen that I believed the Woman's complaint to be very reasonable, which I did by several repetitions and in as respectful a manner as I was capable recommending it strongly as an act of the greatest charity if one of those gentlemen would see the condition they were in. I spoke with all the neighbourly respect as possible of the principle inhabitants of Down, I intended to offend none but was answered several times by one Gentleman, that eight shillings per week was sufficient to keep 16 in family from starving. I was asked by Mr. Hunt if there was an instance of such an expense, I could only answer for the poor parish of Farnborough when we have had neither Minister or Gentleman residing with us to encourage a proper care of the poor that our expense have exceeded eight shillings per week for six in family, when it was happened that a family have been quite reduced the children too small to earn, the man and his wife both ill which was the case of Conford. I would not have noticed this but that I find I am blamed by the parish of Down for taking the part of a poor family which I only looked upon to be the duty of every humane person that knew the deplorable condition they were in.'

Despite this harsh attitude towards Cornford and his family, the poor of Farnborough Parish appear to have been well cared for generally. The Parish owned a large number of small cottages in addition to poor houses. The cottages cost about forty five pounds each to build, and contained two rooms, each ten feet by nine feet, the front room having a brick floor, cupboard and shelves, and the back room oak joists and one inch thick floor boards.

The Vestry accounts give an idea of what the poor received but some of the items are difficult to understand. For instance, 'Clothed a man and woman all over, gave the man a shirt, and the woman a shift', probably these were garments that reached from neck to heel, similar to those worn in Egypt; but it must have been a cold suit when the thermometer was below freezing point. 'Paid for clothing James Gregory and his wife all over with two shirts and two shifts each £3 4s. 2d.' These garments were evidently of some warm material, for they work out at about sixteen shillings each garment. 'Paid for a sack of Charm for Sue'. Crude charcoal was called charms, so the old inhabitants state. Only the women received the sacks of charms, the men received bavins, and other descriptions of wood. The crude charcoal in some years appears to be called chams, so it is difficult from the accounts to tell which is correct.

The Overseers not only helped the poor of the Parish but the poor passing through the Parish. The rates were not heavy, and when a person was too poor to pay the rate he was exempted. The Parish Clerk was the only official till 1827 when an Assistant Overseer was appointed. There appears to have been no difficulty in finding men willing to give their services to the Church or Parish. Well known names in the Parish who have given much time, or both time and financial help, are Lubbock (Sir J., Bart.), Fox, Stow, and Giles, and in older times Cooper, Skeggs, Wynne and Stow. Every man who was capable took his turn when there was a vacancy; but after 1850 Vestry meetings in some cases did not run so smoothly.

Every parish appears to have been compelled to keep their own poor. If a person came into the parish and came on the rates, the Overseers went to the Justice of the Peace in Bromley and obtained a Warrant to send the people back to their legal Parish; but took care of them till they could be handed over, and recovered all costs. The only way a person could settle down in a parish in which he was not a legal inhabitant was to come with a pass, on which was stated that the bearer was acknowledged to belong to a certain parish. This would have posed a difficulty for Gypsies and other travelers who often underwent Settlement Examinations and were sent back to their home parish.

A number of poor boys and girls were apprenticed – and some boys who were not poor. The advantage of being an apprentice was that when the press gangs came to the towns and villages they could not take an apprentice, but could take the others off to the ships – and boys in good positions were often apprenticed to an uncle or other relative. The Parish had to find some militia, and other soldiers; they appear to have had a light kind of compulsory service for the army, but substitutes could be found, as is clear from the following account: 'To the Churchwardens and Overseers of the Poor of the Parish of Farnborough in the said County. By virtue and in pursuance of an Act of Parliament intituled 'an Act to enable His Majesty more effectually to raise and assemble in England, an additional Military Force for the better defence and security of the United Kingdom, and for the more vigorous prosecution of the war.'

We whose names are hereunto subscribed, two of His Majesty's Deputy Lieutenants, acting in and for the said County, do hereby certify, that John Stevens of the said Parish of Farnborough in the said County, having been duly chosen by lot to serve in the Army raised by virtue of the said Act, for the said parish did on the fifteenth day of August 1803 provide one William Bates then lately having left the service of Sir Richard Glode Knight a fit person to serve as his substitute in such army, who was sworn in and enrolled accordingly and duly served therein the time limited by law. We therefore order you the said churchwardens and overseers to pay the said John Stevens the sum of nine guineas which we adjudge to be as near as may be half of the current price paid for a volunteer in the said county of Kent at the time the above substitute was sworn in and enrolled the said John Stevens having sworn that he paid down for the said substitute twenty two guineas and that he hath not at any time since received any part thereof back from the said parish of Farnborough, and that he then was not nor is now bona fide worth the sum of five hundred pounds. Given under our hands, this seventh day of July 1806. Thos Newham (seal) Jos. Faulder (seal).'

At times the Parish suffered terribly from Smallpox and Fever, and did not escape the plague. Smallpox was very bad in 1721, 1725, 1727, 1769, 1781, and 1782, and Fever was the cause of many deaths in 1802. The morals of the Parish were not of a very high standard, if the burials of 1779 may be taken as a guide. There are a few entries for payment for inoculation against Smallpox, also for bleeding; except for a box of pills little or no medicine was given – unless gin and wines were given as medicines. People were found to nurse the sick. 'Gave Widow Dilly rum to bathe her leg.' This remedy appears only to have been once tried, and the result is not recorded.

The Stocks were last repaired in 1819, and were situated between *The George Inn* and the Post Office in Church Lane, which used to be a farm house. The Gibbet was fixed on the brow of the hill on the left hand side of the old coach road which ran between Lord Avebury's and Mr. Fox's estates. The site was just above the old chalk pit near the gate opening into Mr. Fox's field, from the old road going down to Green Street Green. Mr. Fox said that this Gibbet was the last in England made us of. The firs near the site were planted to block out the view from their residence.

No information can be found about a Ducking Stool. Perhaps one was not found necessary and none of the old inhabitants approached by Blandford in 1913 knew anything about it. The women would be most likely to remember if there was such a stool, but they were not approached.

In 1717 a rate of one shilling in the pound amounted to £18 11s. 6d., and in 1749 amounted to £38 6s. In 1782 there were the following Public Houses – *The Queen, The George Inn, Prince of Wales*, and *Black Lion*, and several beer shops, kept principally by widows. In 1806 a burial was recorded of 'Dodson a poor woman who was killed by a wagon passing over her body as she was coming to pick hops aged 63'.

There are several references to Brasted , Basted or Broad Street Green (also known as Bastard Green): 'Thomas Pikely age 26 found dead in a pond at Brasted Green, the verdict of the Coroners Jury Accidental Death (18 October 1803); 'repairing poor houses at Basted Green' (1817). In 1821 some cottages and land situated at Brasted Green were put up for sale: 'In consideration of the parish having only 21 years to come of the estates at Brasted Green concerning which a Vestry was held on the 28 day of September last. The Parishioners have agreed to sell all their rights and Interest to Mr. W.R. Glasier for the sum of one hundred pounds and the said W.R. Glasier agrees to pay the said sum of one hundred pounds to draw Brick sufficient to build 3 cottages and we whose names are hereunder written so far as they can that Mr. Glasier shall inclose the ground in front of his house about 20 feet round to the Lane of Brasted Green and also to enclose the corner at the bend of Penfolds Garden'. In 1870 an 'encroachment on Broad Street Green viz.: stopping and diverting the foot path and enclosing the pond' was reported. At the same meeting it was agreed 'That an application be made to the Education Department for permission to elect a School Board for the Parish of Farnborough'.

'The census taken in this parish in the year 1841 was found to be six hundred and eighty: males 364, females 316'. In 1851 the census was '920 of which were in the Union House 207, eleven only of whom belonged to Farnborough'. In 1861 the census was 750 and in the Workhouse 205. The 1861 Census included Robert Sessions (*New Inn*) and William Stow (estate agent). In 1871 the census was 1086 including the Workhouse. By 1871 the licensed victualler at the *New Inn* was James

Weatherley and Robert Sessions (of Swiss Cottage) had become a 'farmer of 40 acres employing two labourers and a boy'. At a meeting held in the new School Room on 19 February 1874 a Committee was 'appointed to carry out the necessary arrangements for supplying the Village of Farnborough with an adequate supply of water from Farnborough Well or the vicinity thereof.'

In 1878 the residents included Robert Sessions (*White Lion*, Lock's Bottom), Joseph Stow (fruit grower) and James Weatherley (*New Inn*). There was a Post & Telegraph Office (Miss Harriet Baldwin, receiver), Bromley Union Workhouse (Thomas Henry Veall Lukey, master), Police Station (William Watson & Arthur Sewell, sergeants and 12 constables) and Board School (Thomas William Casselden, master).

William Pateman

My great grandfather William Pateman was a Gypsy. His father, Robert Pateman (1821-1890) was born at Hoo St Werbergh on the Hoo peninsular in Kent. William's mother, Mary Ann Enis (1819-?) was born in Chatham. Robert was a chair mender, basket maker and skewer maker who traveled around Kent, Surrey and Middlesex, as evidenced by the birth of his children.

Mary Ann Pateman (1840-1844) was buried at Stockbury, Kent. Alice Pateman (1842-1892) was born on Wimbledon Common, near 'what may be called the grand Metropolitan Gypsyry on the Surrey side of the Thames' (Borrow). Robert returned to the Hoo peninsular for the birth of his next two children: John Pateman (1844-1883) was born in a tent at Cliffe and James Pateman (1846-1926) was born in a tent on Cooling Common. John and James Pateman were baptised at Cliffe in 1846.

Mary Ann Pateman (1851-1929) was born at Westwood 'a very pretty village 3.5 miles south of Gravesend, with a number of gentlemen's seats and private houses'. Elizabeth Pateman (1852-1916), was born at Burham 'in the lathe of Aylesford, West Kent, on the banks of the navigable Medway and foot of the chalk range'. Henry Pateman (1856-?) was born at Snatts Lane Frindsbury.

William Pateman was born in Rochester in 1857, the same year that Charles Dickens purchased Gads Hill House at nearby Higham. Robert Pateman returned to the Hoo Peninsula for the birth of Anne Pateman at St Marys Hoo in 1858. Walter Pateman (1859-1943) was born at Stockbury.

Louisa Pateman and Thomas Pateman were born at Latymer Road, Hammersmith in 1861. Robert was living in one of the disused railway carriages which characterised The Potteries area of Notting Hill, another of the great Metropolitan Gypsyries. Robert returned to Kent for the birth of his last child, Noah Pateman, at Hollowbottom, Bromley in 1866.

Rochester

Chatham, Rochester and Strood have an immensely complex past, but their origins lie with the Rover Medway. On its banks earliest man roamed, and the first farmers settled; 2000 years ago the Belgae established a township. The Romans walled Durobrivae, astride their Watling Street, and built a bridge. The Jutes conquered

Cetham, Strod was recorded by the 9th century and the historian Bede misnamed Hroaescaestre. In 604 a cathedral was founded; by 842 the Danes came plundering but by the time of the Normans it had regained some of its former prosperity.

Bishop Odo, who briefly held Medway, oversaw the building of a castle and glimpsed the beginnings of a new cathedral. Hospitals, churches, and a new bridge were all to follow. The castle, later rebuilt, was besieged and relieved, even gaining a ghost. In Tudor times a dockyard was established. Here, Nelson's flagship *Victory* was built, Brunel's father brought steam, early ironclads were built and submarines developed. For the protection of this dockyard, battlements, forts and redoubts were constructed whilst other enterprises were spawned: private shipbuilding, gun shipments and victualling.

Road, rail, tram and barge also played their part in the Town's history. Fairs, theatres, music halls and cinemas came and went, with the aircraft industry also making headlines building famous planes that undertook perilous journeys. Today's expanded Medway Towns no longer look to industry or the sea, but guard their heritage well.

References to the Medway towns, both by name and implication, appear throughout Dickens's work. Memories of the area where he spent his formative childhood years are evoked in his fiction and magazine articles. In many cases they are presented in a series of impressions, as in this appraisal of Rochester castle and cathedral by Mr. Jingle in *The Pickwick Papers*:

'Ah! Fine place,' said the stranger, 'glorious pile – frowning walls – tottering arches – dark nooks – crumbling staircases – Old cathedral too – earthy smell – pilgrims's feet worn away the old steps – little Saxon doors…'

Dickens's childhood memories were augmented when he took up permanent residence at Gad's Hill Place in 1858 and renewed acquaintance with the area on the long regular walks he took from his new home. In the *Christmas Stories* which he began to write about this time he places himself in one of them. *The Seven Poor Travellers* centres on Watt's Charity, a building in Rochester endowed by the sixteenth century MP, Richard Watts, for the purpose of providing one night's free lodging for six poor travelers who were neither 'Rogues' nor 'Proctors'. The building is still there and open for visits.

Although not mentioned by name, Rochester is clearly the 'market town' used as a specific background in *Great Expectations* (1860), one of the major novels Dickens wrote at Gad's Hill Place. The Guildhall in the High Street is the 'Town Hall' where Pip is formally articled to Joe Gargary; the 'Blue Boar Inn' where this event is celebrated is based on what is now the *Royal Victoria and Bull Hotel* (which also featured in *The Pickwick Papers*); 'Mr Pumblechook's premises' could have been based on several old buildings in the High Street; and Miss Havisham's home, 'Satis House', as so often in Dickens, is an amalgam of two other buildings – the name of one old house grafted onto the appearance of the red brick Tudor 'Restoration House'.

When Dickens embarked on his last book, *The Mystery of Edwin Drood*, which was to remain unfinished at his death, Rochester, under the name of 'Cloisterham', became a significant literary presence. In particular, the cathedral and its precincts are the focal point for most of the characters' lives. So closely associated is Dickens with this part of Rochester that College Gate is often referred to as 'Jasper's Gate'. The present day Eastgate House was the 'Nuns' House'; Canon Row became 'Minor Canon Corner', home to the Revd. Septimus Crisparkle and his mother. At times the cathedral comes across as a dark, oppressive presence, but one of its most vivid evocations occurs in the final pages of the unfinished novel. Dickens had written the description after what was to be his last visit to the city on a warm June afternoon, three days before his death:

'A brilliant morning shines on the old city. Its antiquities and ruins are surpassingly beautiful, with a lusty ivy gleaming in the sun, and the rich trees waving in the balmy air. Changes of glorious light from moving boughs, songs of birds, scents from gardens, woods and fields – or rather, from the one great garden of the whole cultivated island in its yielding time – penetrate into the Cathedral, subdue its earthy odour, and preach the Resurrection and the Life. The cold stone tombs of centuries ago grow warm; and flecks of brightness dart into the sternest marble corners of the building, fluttering there like wings.'

There has been conjecture as to where Dickens obtained the names of his characters. Some are obviously those of relatives, friends and acquaintances with a simple adaptation, others he noted down when seen, as all story writers do, in case they come in useful. He often attended at Rochester cathedral and visited the city. He frequently passed by the graveyard alongside the cathedral. A particular headstone a few feet from the pavement would not have been missed as he walked by. The deceased commemorated are still: John Dorrett, died October 1837, aged 52; Rebecca Dorrett, died September 1839, aged 59 years; Fanny Dorrett died August 1851, aged 79 years. Written and published in 1856 could these be the inspiration for *Little Dorrit*? Across the road from the cathedral's west front is the small burial ground where Dickens hoped to be interred. If he had he would no doubt have been quite as content lying opposite the Dorrett family and among those people he knew and described so skillfully – Benjamin Bassett, Ann Young, William Say, James Brown and other Rochester citizens therein – as among the illustrious in Westminster Abbey. The Abbey is more worthy of him as the burial ground he favoured is now an island bounded by a busy road. But he almost was interred in Rochester cathedral.

The *Chatham News* of June 1870 stated regarding a site for Dickens' interment: 'It was reported that the deceased had expressed a wish to be buried in that part of the St Nicholas' burial ground, Rochester, immediately beneath Rochester Castle Wall. The request was made to the Home Secretary for the burial ground to be opened to receive the body of Mr. Dickens but a refusal was made on the grounds that Mr. Dickens did not live within the parish of St Nicholas'. The newspaper reported that a request had been made to inter Dickens at Cobham church yard, but this was again refused as the church yard was almost full and the parish council wanted the land remaining to be for their own dead, Dickens not being a local resident.

Seeing an opportunity in a situation where no one seemed to want to have the grave of Dickens, the Dean and Chapter of Rochester cathedral employed 'a strong party of workmen to execute the work' and dig a grave in St Mary's Chapel, Rochester cathedral, at the east end of the nave and a vault formed 'for the reception of the remains of the illustrious dead'. But while they were still preparing this vault it was decided to inter him in Westminster Abbey and, says the *Chatham News*, 'the grave was prepared in great secrecy. Early on Tuesday morning the body was removed in a hearse from Gad's Hill Place to Higham Station for conveyance to London by special train which also carried mourners. This train left Higham at 8 o'clock and very few people knew about it.

From Charing Cross terminus the coffin was removed from the train to a plain hearse and taken to Westminster Abbey. The funeral took place at 9.30, only close relatives being admitted to the simple private burial in Poet's Corner. The grave is situated at the foot of the coffin of Handel and at the head of the coffin of Sheridan. The grave was left open all day and thousands of people filed past it.' Meanwhile, back at Rochester cathedral on the same morning the vault was filled up with the earth taken from digging the grave and the paving restored so there was little indication of where Dickens' grave could have been, 'the bell of the cathedral tolling for the funeral of the dead Dickens [in London] while the workmen were refilling the vault [at Rochester]'.

In the High Street, behind the red brick Tudor Eastgate House is a small public garden, pleasant with a fountain and goldfish ponds. On one side is the Swiss chalet from Gad's Hill given to Dickens by his actor friend, Charles Fechter, in which he often worked on his novels. It was acquired by Rochester City Council in 1961, fully restored and re-erected here. Nearby is another item from Dickens' home at Gad's Hill, the horse powered pump with its large iron wheel, installed there by Dickens in 1857 to raise water from a well for the household. It was brought from Gad's Hill and placed on its present site for preservation in 1973. Adjoining it is something else brought here to protect it, a section of medieval road. It was part of the approach road to the 1387 Rochester Bridge being excavated at Strood in 1897. It is similar to cobblestones and one of the ruts made in it by the transport of the time can be seen.

Leaning over the Esplanade's balustrade as the wide Medway flows past now and much cleaner, it is not difficult to realize why the Mayor and Corporation have had age-old rights over the 'floating fish', an archaic term for the river's marine inhabitants which even included oysters and other shell fish. In centuries past these are known from records to have been profusely abundant. As far back as Edward IV a charter was granted to the Mayor and 'citizens' entitling them to 'all fishes to be caught within the liberty and precincts of the city and belonging to us and our heirs.' This included the royal fish, the sturgeon. In July 1630 a sturgeon was caught by one John Porritt and taken to the Mayor and 'eaten by him and his brethren'. In the nineteenth century two more were caught. One was presented to the Archbishop of Canterbury and its fate is unknown. In the 1870's the other, weighing about 100 lbs, 6 ft 9 inches long, was caught by a Strood fisherman with hook and line in the Medway here. It took him and his son over an hour to land it. On doing so he presented it to Rochester's Mayor and Corporation, but they put it in a box with ice, a very long box too, and a corporation official delivered it personally to Windsor Castle, Queen Victoria apparently having been graciously pleased to accept it.

William spent his child hood traveling around Kent, Surrey and Middlesex with his family, picking fruit, vegetables and hops and making baskets, skewers and pegs. These journeys took him to St Mary Hoo (1858), Stockbury (1859), Hammersmith (1861) and Bromley (1866)

1871 Census

On 2 April 1871 William Pateman (19, Rochester, Pedlar) was living with his family in an old stable on a brick field at Becks Lane, Beckenham, Kent. Sometime after 1871 William left his family and 'married' Mercy Reynolds. Mercy was the sister of Jane Reynolds, who was 'married' to James Pateman. For more information about Mercy and her family, see Chapter 6 – Fellow Travellers.

William and Mercy had eight children between 1876 and 1896: Mary (1876), Henry (1880), Noah (1883), Walter (1886), Alice (1889), Phoebe (1892), William (1894), Amy (1896).

After William moved to Farnborough in 1881 he lived there for many years at various addresses: Orpington Lane (1881, in a van), Locksbottom (1883, housecart), Farnborough Common (1886), Farnborough (1889, housecart), Stow Cottages (1890), Church Road (1891), 4 Cobden Road (1902). Some time after 1902 William moved to Orpington. He was not living at Cobden Road in 1913 according to *Bush's Directory*. In 1921 he was living in Chislehurst Road, Orpington

William Pateman was described as: pedlar (1871), beehive maker (1881), hawker (1883), agricultural labourer (1891), general labourer (1892), labourer (1895), and farm labourer (1901)

From this we can surmise that William carried out a number of occupations which can be categorized as follows: Hawker, Pedlar, beehive maker - this was when William was living the life of a Gypsy, traveling around Kent and selling Gypsy crafts such as pegs, wooden flowers and skewers; agricultural labourer, labourer, general labourer, farm labourer - this was when William was leading a more settled life, in the winter months at least, at Farnborough and offering his services to local farmers.

William Pateman died on 24 October 1921 aged 65 years at Chislehurst Road, Orpington. He was a retired labourer and the cause of death was pleurisy and bronchitis as certified by A. Tennyson Smith, MD. The informant was 'A. Lee, daughter, 4 Broadway, St Mary Cray.' This was Alice Pateman, who was married to Jesse Lee. William Pateman was buried at All Saints Churchyard on 29 October 1921. Mercy Pateman died on 3 January 1940 and was buried in the same grave as William on 9 January 1940.

Mary Pateman (1876-1901)

Mary Pateman (1876-1901) =Elias Lewis (1876-1953)
- Charles (1898-?)

Mary Pateman was born in 1876 at Crockenhill, Kent. Even Kentish born people are confused as to which is which between this place and Crockham Hill. Crockenhill is south west of Swanley, on the B258; Crockham Hill is south west of Westerham on the B2026. The former was the most important area in Kent for growing peppermint. George Miller at Wested Farm, Crockenhill, planted three fields with the herb. Miller was known as 'The Peppermint King', also having land under peppermint cultivation at Warren Road, Chelsfield. When Albert Miller took over from his father, 420 acres of peppermint were growing, supplying British demand and even exporting it to Europe. The young plants of peppermint, *Mentha x piperta*, were obtained from rooted dark green leaved plants and planted in fields in the spring. They were kept hoed between the rows and hand weeded to prevent other plants growing among them.

In the late summer when about 20 inches high they came into bloom with spikes of pinkish-mauve flowers and it was then that they were harvested. The parts of commercial use are the leaves and flowers. The stems were usually cut by hand and left in rows. The women did not care much for the hand cutting as they seemed regularly to get sniffling colds at the same time, they claimed through the peppermint, but this is dubious as peppermint contains menthol, a powerful antiseptic.

The cut rows were called windrows and were lightly lifted up periodically and turned like hay to let air thoroughly dry the stems of flowers and leaves. The stems were then collected into piles and put into open-ended hessian bags and tied. These were loaded on to horse drawn carts and hauled to the farm, then taken to the Mitcham distillery company, W.J. Bush. Incidentally, Albert Miller was also the last farmer to grow Mitcham lavender at Mitcham for distilling there.

On arriving at Mitcham the peppermint was put into a still which would contain an average of the crop from one to two acres. It was trodden down by the man filling the still, who then sealed the still and passed steam through the peppermint. The resulting liquid was condensed and then drawn off to yield an oil of varying quality. William Pateman's father, Robert, was living in a tent on Mitcham Common in 1881.

Albert Miller founded Albert Miller (Swanley) Ltd with his son Cyril. On his father's death Cyril Miller took over and cultivation of peppermint continued, but it was no longer a valuable sideline to the farmer's income from fruits, vegetables and corn. Even when it fell to only 14 acres, this was claimed to be the largest peppermint crop in England. The last peppermint crop was grown and marketed from Wested Farm and so ended the cultivation of peppermint on a large scale in Kent. Wested Farm's eighteenth century farmhouse, the oast houses and large timber framed barn survive in use though today cultivation has expanded into different crops. Could the cultivation of peppermint and lavender return? No doubt it all depends on economics.

Elias Lewis

On 7 September 1895 Mary Pateman (19, spinster, Farnborough, father - William Pateman, labourer) married Elias Lewis (20, bachelor, labourer, Tugmutton, Farnborough, father - Charles Lewis, general dealer) at St Giles parish church, Farnborough. The witnesses were John and Annie Durrant.

Elias Lewis was born on 12 May 1876 at Locksbottom, Farnborough. His father was Charles Lewis, farm labourer, and his mother was Sarah Lewis, formerly Reynolds.

Mary and Elias had one child, Charles William Lewis, born on 1 January 1898 at Farnborough. His father was Elias Lewis, general labourer, and his mother was Mary Pateman.

Jim Davey: 'My wife Pam's paternal grandfather was Elias Lewis. Pam is the oldest living family member and was unaware of her Gypsy ancestry and her grandfather's first marriage until recently. It was either a closely kept family secret or just something that no one talked about. Elias died at Pope Road, Bromley on 6 June1953 and both of Pam's parents are deceased so there is no one living from whom she can obtain information. I met Elias in 1952/3 just before he died but we kept in contact with his widow up to the time of her death, as my wife was quite close to her grandmother. It seems that Elias was at least a third generation Gypsy but probably the first to leave that lifestyle.'

First generation: William Lewis (1819, Downe, Kent) married Mary ? (1821, Farnborough, Kent) and they had five children: Sarah Ann (1847, Farnborough, Kent), John (1849), Charles (1851, Farnborough), George (1857, Farnborough) and Lewis (1859, Farnborough).

Second generation: Charles Lewis (1851) married Sarah Reynolds (1852, Wrotham) in 1875 and they had eight children: George (1875, Farnborough), Elias (1876, Bromley), William (1880, Hookham, Kent), Mercy (1884, Farnborough), Charlotte (1888, Farnborough), Mary (1890, Farnborough), Charles (1892, Farnborough) and Thomas (1894, Farnborough). In 1881 Charles Lewis (labourer / general dealer) and his family were living at Bastard Green, Farnborough. In 1891 Charles Lewis (greengrocer) and his family were living at Tugmutton Green, Farnborough.

Third generation: Elias Lewis (1876) married Mary Pateman (1876) in 1895 and they had one child, Charles (1897, Farnborough). In 1900 Mary Lewis was present at the death of her brother, William Thomas, aged 7, at 23 Alexander Terrace, Swanley Junction, Sutton at Hone. In the 1901 Census, Elias Lewis (son in law, builder's labourer) and Charles Lewis (grandson) were living with Mary and her family at Cobden Road, Farnborough. Charles Lewis (general dealer / fruit broker) and his family were living at Locksbottom.

On 28 September 1901 Mary Lewis died aged 23 years at 4 Cobden Road, Farnborough. She was the wife of Elias Lewis, a bricklayer's labourer. The cause of death was ineffectual labour, five days. This sounds like she died during a protracted child birth. The informant was Elias Lewis, widower of the deceased, present at the death, 4 Cobden Road, Farnborough. We do not know where she was buried, but it was probably St Giles church yard, Farnborough.

On 4 July 1903, Elias Lewis (widower, Motor Fitter, London Transport, 2 Crofton Road, Farnborough) married Ellen Lidlow (born 14 January 1885, Faversham), at St Giles Farnborough, and they had seven children: Elias James Francis (30 April 1904, Stows Cottages, Farnborough), Alice, Lily, Victor, Frederick, Oliver and Ivy. As far as I know there was no contact with Elias's first son Charles.

Elias Lewis died on 6 June 1953 at 55 Pope Road, Bromley, aged 77 years. He was a motor fitter (London Transport Board Garage), retired. The cause of death was inoperable carcinoma of rectum. The informant was E.L.Lewis, widow of the deceased, present at the death, 55 Pope Road, Bromley.

Jim Davis: 'Elias James Francis Lewis was also known as Sailor, which could be Elias spelt backwards. With regard to Elias's other six children we lost touch with them long ago but they all lived in the Bromley area and Frederick and Victor both lived in Pope Road near their mother. Lily worked at Woolwich Arsenal at some time during the Second World War and died of tuberculosis towards the end of the war, aged about sixteen.'

Sailor Lewis (1904-1973) married Doris Jerome (1909-2001) on 14 January 1933 and they had five children: Pamela (1933), Joyce (1935), Sylvia (1937), Ivan (1939) and Barbara (1941-1982). Sailor's wedding report states that he served in the Norfolk Regiment for 13 years, from 1919-1932. Jim Davey sent me two photographs of Sailor Lewis in military uniform. The message on the reverse of one of these, dated 1919-24, said 'With love from your ever loving son, these are two of my mates'. Sailor died on 3 July 1973 at Ashford, Kent.

Jim Davey also sent me two photographs of Ellen Lewis (Lidlow): one, dated 1953, shows Ellen standing with Jim's wife, Pam, in front of General Wolfe's statue at Westerham, Kent; the other, undated, shows Ellen standing in a garden (almost certainly taken at Pope Road, Bromley) with a dog in her arms. Ellen Lewis died on 6 June 1989 at Lewisham.

The Lewis family was living in Farnborough in 1847 and this makes them some of the original Tugmutton Gypsies.

Henry Pateman (1880-1961)

Henry Pateman (1880-1961) = Lottie Edith Tilley (1885-1961)
- Noah William (1905-1967)

Henry Pateman, was born at Crockenhill in 1880. Henry later moved to Orpington. On 9 November 1902 Henry Pateman (22, bachelor, labourer, Orpington, father - William Pateman, labourer) married Lottie Edith Tilley (18, spinster, Orpington, father - William Tilley, fitter) at All Saints Church, Orpington. The witnesses were Henry's siblings, Noah and Alice.

Lottie Edith Tilley was born on 2 September 1885 at 25 Somers Road, Southsea, Portsea Island. Her father was William Tilley, Engine Fitter, Hill Dockyard. Her mother was Kate Elizabeth Tilley, formerly Smithers. William Tilley lived at Carlisle Street, Southsea.

In 1901 Henry Pateman was working as a bricklayer's labourer in Portsmouth. He was lodging with his brother, Noah, and Thomas Reynolds (son of George Reynolds and Mary Ann Pateman, Henry's aunt).

On 1 June 1902 Noah Pateman married Annie Honeysett, who was also born on Portsea Island. It seems that Henry and Noah went to Portsmouth looking for work and found wives as well.

Henry and Lottie had one child, Noah William, who was born on 21 April 1905 at Crofton Road, Orpington. Noah William married Ada Bristow in 1927 and one of the witnesses was Lottie Edith.

Henry Pateman moved from Crofton Road, Orpington, to St Mary Cray where he worked as a labourer at Dippers Slip. From 1932-37 Henry was a 'marine store dealer' at Fordcroft, Poverest. From 1938-40 'Henry & Son' were 'marine store dealers' at Dipper Slip, Fordcroft. From 1934-38 Ada Pateman was a 'wardrobe dealer' at 38 Wellington Road. Noah William was listed at this address from 1939-40. The family later moved to 3 Felstead Road, Orpington.

Henry Pateman had various occupations: labourer (1902), bricklayer's labourer (1905), marine store dealer (1932), scrap metal dealer and hop kiln maker.

Henry Pateman died on 5 February 1961 aged 81 at Cray Valley Hospital, St Pauls Cray. He was a scrap metal merchant (retired) of 3 Felstead Road, Orpington. The cause of death was 'uraemia, pyelonephritis, chronic nephrolithiasis, influenza and senile myocarditis'. The informant was W. Pateman, son, 3 Felstead Road, Orpington. This was Noah William Pateman, who they may have called William? The following obituary appeared in the *Kentish Times* on 10 February 1961: 'The death occurred at Cray valley Hospital on Sunday, aged 81, of Mr. Henry Pateman of West View, Craven Road, Chelsfield. Mr. Pateman was well known in the St Mary Cray area, and carried on a scrap metal business at Poverest Road. A resident all his life, he used to make hop kilns for the hop drying industry which once flourished in Orpington. He is survived by a widow and a son.' It is interesting to note that his address was given as West View, Craven Road, Chelsfield, but his death certificate gave it as 3 Felstead Road, Orpington. Henry was buried on 10 February 1961 at All Saints. His burial record also gave his address as 3 Felstead Road.

Lottie Edith Pateman died on 11 June 1961 age 77 at 3 Felstead Road, Orpington. She was the widow of Henry Pateman, metal dealer (retired). The cause of death was 'pernicious anaemia, pneumonia, left ventricular failure'. The informant was W. Pateman, son, 3 Felstead Road. This was Noah William Pateman. Lottie was buried on 16 June 1961 at All Saints, in the same grave as her husband.

Noah William Pateman died on 26 October 1967 aged 62 at 3 Felstead Road. Ada Pateman died on 19 June 1971 aged 70 at 3 Felstead Road. Noah and Ada were buried in the same grave (DJ9) as his parents, in the New Churchyard at All Saints, Orpington. The gravestone is still visible today in Newell Meadow Churchyard.

Oast Houses

'I need only notice the oast houses in use in the county of Kent. Are there any two of these alike? Is not some arrangement in each different from that adopted in others? Has not every farmer some favourite plan of his own? To describe even a portion of these would be an endless task'. (Viscount Torrington, 1845)

Lord Torrington was right. Each oasthouse is different from all the others in some way, not just in Kent but wherever they were built. The sheer numbers of them built is testimony to the importance of hops in the agrarian history of the south and east of

England. The buildings themselves really are crucial to a proper understanding of the history of the industry. Beer is traditionally the drink of the Englishman but this tradition takes no real account of the revolution in beer brewing which took place, in England at least, over the fourteenth and fifteenth centuries. It was then that hopped beer as opposed to unhopped ale (until then the 'traditional' brew), became accepted.

Beer brewing had increased on the continent from the 13th century onwards and it is clear that it was even then appreciated in England; in 1289 a Norwich ale seller imported some for sale and was subsequently charged with 'selling Flanders beer privily'. More widespread introduction aroused quite a lot of initial hostility, but gradually beer increased in popularity. In 1400 it was being imported into Winchelsea but within a few years hops themselves were being imported for brewing beer in this country. Flemings and Dutchmen were the first to brew hopped beer here. When in 1436 attacks were made on foreign beer brewers in London, this resulted in the passing of the Act of Parliament by Henry VI which allowed them to remain and to continue their trade. By the end of the 15th century most of the prejudices against the use of this 'additive' had been overcome and beer was brewed by native brewers in almost every town in the kingdom.

Hops are grown from cuttings or 'sets' which in the past could be bought locally from many of the large growers. They take two to three years to mature and the plants then will continue to produce their cones for a further ten to fifteen years when planted in poorer soils, and for up to fifty years in better soils. Hops produce a perfumed yellow resin or pollen, which both imparts the bitter flavour to the beer and also acts as a preservative. The beer can then be kept in good condition for much longer than had been possible with unhopped ale and the preservative quality gives the advantage of allowing the beer to be transported, exported even – as the Flemings had proved – without immediate deterioration.

Hops are a labour intensive crop in every stage of their production. First they need to be planted 6 to 7 feet apart in a specially prepared ground usually called a hop garden or a hop yard. Poles, replaced more recently by a complicated system of wires and strings, are needed for their growth and they demand rich manuring and constant attention to cultivation as well as a series of measures to counteract the pests and diseases to which they are all too prone. The labour does not end once the hops are picked: to be of most value to the brewer they need to be dried and it was for this process that oasthouses were developed. After the drying it became standard practice to tread them into pockets or bags in order to exclude the air and to preserve as large a quantity as possible of the resin.

In England, notably in Kent, Sussex, Surrey, Hertfordshire, Worcestershire and Hampshire, up to four centuries of experience went towards the perfecting of the process of drying and pressing as practiced by the growers until recently. Although grown in other countries as well, hops there had largely disappeared from the farms by the end of the 19th century. That century saw both the peak years of the industry and the beginning of its decline and during those peak years most of the oasthouses now familiar in the landscape belong; by the mid 19th century an oasthouse had to be provided for any grower who seriously hoped to make a good profit from his hops.

It is possible that Henry Pateman helped to build the St Mary Cray oasthouse, as described by Ray Galer: 'The spot on which I was now calling was the spot of the first hop garden in the Garden of Kent that our fathers saw as they came out from London into the countryside. In my mind I could see the hops trailing up the poles, I could see hosts of hop pickers filling their bins, as quickly as only true Kentish women can. I could still see and hear the children playing in and out of the 'hills' or hop lines, when little fingers refused to pick more. I could see the measurer going round – now using a heavy and now a light hand. Yes ! five bushels to the shilling. Yes! The money man registering the total number on many a card of man, woman and child. Near one house I saw a piece of hop still growing, still striving to bring forth a little harvest – still clinging to a leisurely past. And as I looked behind me, over in the distance I could still see part of the old oast house. That oast house gave me once again the scent of hops drying in the kiln on a warm September night. The scent of hop and charcoal hanging heavy in the darkness of evening – of nights, which were all day for the kiln minders and the hop dryers. Yes! and anxious nights too, for a little too much coal and the flavour was spoilt, and a little too much drying and the pocket was ruined – and did ever a roast potato taste as nice as when it was well cooked in the ashes of the oast house fires.'

Farmers have probably known the principles of drying from prehistoric times; corn drying kilns have certainly been in use since Roman times and malt kilns are known from medieval days. The simple principle of convection was applied: all that was necessary was a source of heat on or in the ground, some form of perforated floor above, on which was spread the substance to be dried, and sufficient expertise to know when the right level of desiccation had been achieved. The first experiments in drying hops must have been on such kilns; the expertise grew with the industry.

Essentially the familiar oasthouse had five main functions: to receive the green hops after they had been picked off the bine; to dry them in the kiln; to provide space for their controlled cooling after removal from the kiln; to provide facilities for pressing them into long bags called pockets; and to provide storage space for the pockets until they were sent to market. In order to fulfil those functions the buildings were divided into two areas: the kiln or kilns, where the hops would be dried; and the stowage, where the hops would first be received, then after drying, cooled, pressed or bagged, and stored. By the 19th century there were usually two floors to both stowage and kilns.

The Kilns

The kilns of the oasthouses familiar today are either square or round and built either at one end of the stowage or alongside it, with intercommunicating doors between stowage and kiln on both floors. The ground floor housed the source of heat and this could be provided by an enclosed grate, by a honeycombed brick furnace or by fires lit in open grates. Where an enclosed stove was used, a system of pipes carried the heat up to concentrate it close to the drying floor. The honeycombed brick furnace stood in the centre or just inside the door of the kiln, and above it often hung a spark plate which also helped to spread the heat across the full width of the drying floor. Open grates were normally screened by a wall which either funneled outwards to join the external wall of the kiln just below the drying floor or formed a tunnel across the centre.

Using charcoal and anthracite as fuel, drying could take anything up to 14 to 16 hours. Once the fires were lit, the heat was gradually intensified to about 60C to drive off the moisture before being allowed to fall to about 49C again. It was crucial to keep the fires lit and the temperature controlled throughout the process. Undue loss of heat meant damage to that load of hops. If the fires actually went out the load was totally spoiled. Where any form of open firing was used it was important to have a good intake of air at the right level in order to keep the fires constant. Small openings were constructed in the lowest courses of the walls of the kilns and these openings had, usually on the inside face of the wall, wooden shutters which could be raised or lowered according to the need to increase or lessen the draft. Where an enclosed stove or furnace was in use, draught was sometimes ducted under the floor. In these kilns a small window was often built into the external wall so that the drier could see what he was doing. With brickwork furnaces or open fires the drier normally relied upon the firelight to see by.

In order to allow the heat from the fires to pass through the hops the joists of the first floor supported slats of either timber or metal, although in some kilns perforated tiles were used instead. Where a tiled floor was used, there was no danger of the hops falling through onto the fires because the perforations were too small; where the drying floor was slatted, a coarsely woven cloth of horsehair was laid over the slats and either looped over hooks in the kiln wall or tacked to a timber plate recessed into the wall just above the floor. This cloth then kept the hops from falling down between the slats and reduced waste and the danger of fire.

Onto this 'hair', as it was called, the pokes of green hops were emptied, usually to a depth of 16 inches or so. The load of hops emptied into the kiln would vary according to whether the season was wet or dry and, therefore, to the levels of moisture in the hops themselves. When the hops were loaded, they were leveled with a widely toothed rake to ensure even drying. The length of the drying depended upon the depth of the load. A good draught was essential to pull the hot air up through the hops and then out at the top of the kiln. Cowls which swung round against the wind and created a vacuum helped pull up the hot air, thereby increasing the speed at which the hops would dry. They are believed to have been introduced during the middle years of the 18th century.

The Stowage

The layout of the ground floor of the stowage was dictated by the position of the kilns. Adjacent to them was usually a partitioned area which might serve all or any of three main purposes: to screen the area in order to allow a controlled intake of air into the kilns whose doors normally incorporated some form of shuttered opening; to allow the driers some comfort – they normally did not leave the building while the drying was in process (beds or armchairs were often brought in); to house a convenient supply of fuel.

The rest of the ground floor might then be used to store the pockets until they were dispatched and in some oasthouses special raised and slatted racks were installed in order to allow free passage of air around them. They were normally stored upside down so that, in years when they were stored for a long period, the damage possible to the hops at the bottom from the sheer weight of the contents could easily be remedied by re-opening the sewn end and replacing the damaged hops.

In traditional oasthouses green hops arriving from the garden were received directly into the first floor of the building. The loosely woven pokes, used to transport them, prevented them from sweating and growing hot, which caused deterioration. Care was taken to get each load of hops into the kiln as quickly as possible after picking. Once large acreages were grown and large amounts of hops were arriving at the oasthouses for drying, 'greenstages' with widely slatted floors were introduced, again to prevent sweating. When dry, the hops were removed from the kiln, heaped or spread over the floor of the stowage and left to cool. In most buildings familiar today the cooling area equaled or was just slightly greater than the area of the kilns. Its floor was closely boarded with its walls either fully or partially matchboarded. Where the walls were left unboarded, they were whitewashed. These were measures of 'hop hygiene' and served to prevent hop residues from collecting in the cracks and crannies, thereby becoming a source of contamination during the pressing.

When first removed from the kiln, the hops were extremely dry and brittle and if pressed in that condition would break or shatter. During the cooling process they re-absorbed some moisture from the air and became less fragile. Cooling times varied enormously and depended partly on the size of the load, partly on the temperature and humidity levels prevailing, and partly on the beliefs and practices of the drier himself. The hops might be left to lie for up to a day or more and recourse might be made to scientific instruments to measure temperature and humidity. More frequently, however, when the practiced hand of the drier could take a hop, crush it and detect just the right amount of resistance in the leaves of the cone and when his equally experienced nose could perceive just the right pungency from the pollen, the hops were ready for pressing.

The first floor of the stowage had a trap opening into which a circular frame could be fitted and from this the pocket was suspended. Up to about 1850 a man got down into the pocket, the hops were shoveled in and he carefully trod them down beneath him until the hops, tightly compressed, filed the whole pocket. About 1850 a mechanical press was patented and widely adopted on the farms: it took 10 to 15 minutes to fill the pocket whereas a man's feet had taken 60. Once full, the pocket was sewn up, stenciled with the name of the farmer and the name and county of the farm, and was then stored on the ground floor until the samples were taken. This was a process normally carried out by an itinerant hop sampler who skillfully opened the side of the pocket and withdrew a block of hops which were then trimmed into a neat rectangular packet. These were sent to the Hop Market and when the samples had been judged and bargained for, a process organised by the hop factors, the pockets from the samples which had been taken were sent up to market and sold.

The Hop Exchange

Ray Galer: 'And I am still looking down the river, towards the Kentish marshes. Why, even behind me and very near to me is the Hop Exchange, and if anything spells of Kent that does. The Hop Exchange – the very livelihood of many a man, and woman and child all the year round down in Kent, and what a romance of the season. The Tally Man, the Lolly Man, the five bushels a shilling, and Kent has, for many generations, been the holiday-de-luxe for many a Londoner from the district of the Hop Exchange, the Borough. There is many an old man and old lady who still dream the dream that I am dreaming, of the yearly holiday, the yearly pilgrimage down into the hop gardens. Starting here from London Bridge Station at 10pm, get there when you do, fare 3s., and no reserved compartment, for we are all one party, with one object, a fair measure and 'Get your hops ready'.

The oast house described above did not take shape until the 19th century. With the innovations brought by the 20th century it remained in general use until the 1960s and 70s. So oasthouses which Henry Pateman built as a young man were still being used at the time of his death in 1961. Over the centuries, better heating and handling of hops improved their quality but that quality could never be guaranteed; there were too many variables whose control was beyond the power of the growers. The weather was obviously one. Very wet or very dry seasons greatly affected how and when the hop bines matured and produced their cones. Extremes of weather, wet or dry, also affected the incidence of hop diseases and insect attack. Heavy rainfall during September could lengthen the drying process and reduce the amount of hops which could be dried at any one time; it also adversely affected the condition of those still left unpicked.

The oasthouse itself was another variable. Careful construction and design played their part in the fine control of the heat and in the efficient handling of the hops into and out of the kiln. This control and efficiency were also affected by the position of the oasthouse within the farmstead. Given that undue loss of heat at a crucial stage could severely reduce the money made from the dried crop, the oasthouse needed to be carefully sited to take advantage of even the gentlest breeze from any of the four quarters.

The knowledge and ability of the driers themselves varied. In many cases the skills of the craft were handed down from father to son and their expertise was recognized in the rates of pay which oast work could command. Just occasionally, adherence to traditional methods led to obstinate prejudice in the face of new ideas. Once accepted, however, successive innovations and experiments brought hop drying to the pitch of perfection attainable today when controlled cultivation and the use of highly sophisticated machinery can almost guarantee a dried crop of uniform quality. Such techniques and installation depend on capital; its availability or lack of it remains the most crucial variable of all.

Whenever possible, a suitable draughty position next to the farm pond was adopted for oasthouses because of the ever present danger of fire – quite a number did burn down. Where possible, it was also better to have them conveniently close to a road in order to get the hops to market. When the last bags or pockets had finally gone, and that was sometimes not until April of the following year, the building would remain in use for storing implements and husbandry tackle on the ground floor, for grains or seeds on the first floor. On small farms some even served as stables or cattle sheds.

Decline in the Hop Trade

'You are dealing with what was one of the most flourishing, and is one of the most important industries of the country, and an industry which we can singularly little afford to lose, because so many of our agricultural interests are passing through this period of depression'. (Lord Salisbury, 1887)

Lord Salisbury, addressing the Commissioners who were to enquire into the reasons for the decline in the Hop Trade, was already looking back on 15 to 17 years of difficulty in the corn markets. Serious loss of revenue here had affected other branches of agriculture. Shortage of money for the purchase of seeds and manure resulted in arable land reverting to grass as farmers in corn growing areas desperately turned to dairy and beef cattle and to poultry rearing in order to try and keep going. To some extent, the hop growers had been able to hold out for rather longer because they were less dependent on corn; serious decline was deferred until the end of the 1880s.

The larger growers had for many years run the dual economy of hops and stock, feeding their hops with the manure produced and buying in less artificial manure than they would otherwise have needed. Both for them and for the smaller growers any increase in stock farming in the years of depression meant more home produced and less bought manure for their hops – diversification was also an economy. They were not to escape for ever. Eventually the major cause of the depression, namely free trade, cold storage and faster transportation were to affect their trade as well. As with the corn duty, the removal of the excise duty on hops in 1862 had resulted in a steady rise in imports. By the end of the century imports had been swelled both by a staggering rise in output of cheap hops in America and by a growing preference for lighter beers like those brewed in Germany. For the lighter beers many of the British hops were unsuitable. For ordinary stock beers American hops were quite as suitable and much cheaper and brewers regularly used one third American hops to two thirds English. Fewer English hops were therefore needed.

New expertise in cold storage further affected the former structure of the market by making possible the long term storage of hops. This enabled the large brewers to lay in huge stocks at very low prices in years of glut, and to keep out of the market altogether in years of scarcity. Any brewers who did need to buy could make up any shortage by turning to cheap, refrigerated imports brought across the oceans in the new improved steam ships. This new ability to transport and store hops in peak condition deprived the growers in England of the customary rise in prices in years when the hop crop was short. To have hops for sale when other people's crops had failed had up till then been the foundation of all fortunes made from hops.

The new trend towards greater importation aggravated the problem which over the 19th century had become the most serious for the hop growers, that of over supply. The days were gone when farmers needed to be urged to plant up with hops. Therefore a series of bad seasons in the 1890s only made an already bad situation worse. The worst hit were the small producers and the grubbing of hop gardens began. By 1908 it was claimed that 40,000 acres had gone. In October 1908 a major demonstration in London on the part of hop growers and hop pickers demanded that the government should re-impose the excise duty.

The government with more pressing problems to attend to turned a deaf ear to their demands. Hop growers were further upset in 1914 when the beer duty was raised, which resulted in a decrease in the amount of beer brewed. Again they petitioned for a duty on imported hops as the market was again found to be over supplied. In 1916 imports were prohibited but the government also decided to restrict the amount of beer brewed, and following new regulations beer was brewed at half the pre-War level. Further restrictions to one quarter of the pre-War level followed in 1917 and emergency measures were drawn up to allow the Government to handle the sale of the 1917 crop. The Hop Control was set up and did not finally lapse until 1925. During those years the growers sold their hops to the Hop Controller and received from him a pre-determined sum (decided annually) which allowed them a small profit. When there was a shortage, fixed amounts of foreign hops were imported. The scheme did not operate without difficulty and it provoked a lot of criticism from growers.

The Control was eventually replaced by another body, English Hop Growers Limited. This was to rely on the voluntary co-operation of the growers and it eventually failed because not all the growers would agree to market their hops through its organization. The prospect of chaos in an over supplied market loomed again, the more so because the amount of beer being brewed was falling again by government decree. Control over the market was re-imposed with the setting up of the Hops Marketing Board in 1932. The Board imposed quotas on registered growers and guaranteed a market for the hops grown within the quota. A period of calm returned to the hop world interrupted only by the arable demands of the Second World War.

Technical progress continued in oast house design in the late 19th and early 20th centuries. In Kent new oast houses built on the larger hop farms were designed with a third storey. This was used for the reception and temporary storage of the green hops. The middle floor served for cooling and the ground floor for storage of the filled pockets. Experiments with the use of fans to increase the air speed through the kilns began by using the drive power of the stationery steam engine. The ability to push air through the hops greatly reduced the drying time and allowed the hops to be loaded to greater depths. By the end of the 19th century the attention of the Irish manufacturing firm Davidson & Co. of Belfast, had been drawn towards hop drying. They were well known for their tea drying plants, marketed under the trade name Sirocco, and experiments began to use similar machines for hop drying. Installation of these machines began on hop farms in the early years of the 20th century but given the economic climate of the times the machines were probably only taken up fairly slowly.

After 1919 when electricity became available in rural areas and when the hop market had settled down again after the disruptions of the Great War, many growers invested in these kilns. From the savings they offered, some claimed to have regained the interest on the outlay, sometimes even the capital itself. The furnaces could be fitted to existing buildings and many were. Oast houses did not have to be built so tall and cowls became redundant, as the hop drier was no longer dependent on natural draught. Louvred caps or long louvred ridges took their place. Diesel was extensively used on British farms by the 1930s and superseded all other types of furnace after the Second World War. Fans and diesel firing made the heating of the kiln much easier to control and brought great advances in the quality of the final product. With the stability offered to the industry by the quota system further improvements were still being undertaken in the 1950s and 60s.

How long any oasthouses will survive is a matter of speculation. Latest developments in hop processing suggest that all buildings will soon become redundant, and as a new technique of dissolving hops in vast baths of liquid carbon dioxide is adopted the resulting product will be easily transported and preserved over years as are the hop pellets already in production. The national crop itself is nothing like as large as it once was. The years of comparative prosperity and technological progress under the quota system were brought to an end through a combination of various factors. The ebb and flow of the market, already drastically affected by refrigeration and importation, was further affected by the perfecting of processes for producing hop essences. The oasthouses on which so much capital was expended, in which so much pride was taken, are left redundant and deserve urgent attention. Many of them are the only surviving evidence of the once confident expectation of profit that many growers felt. The other well known aspect is that of the hop picking, the hop holiday that scores of people, young and old, enjoyed in spite of the crowded and often insanitary conditions in which they lived. Gypsies played an important role in the hop picking and were badly affected when this source of employment was gradually reduced and eventually disappeared.

1881 Census

On 3 April 1881 William Pateman (22, beehive maker, Dartford) was living with his wife, Mercy Reynolds (25, Crockenhill) and their children Mary (5, Crockenhill) and Henry (1, Crockenhill) in a 'van on side of Orpington Lane' at Farnborough.

The ancient parish of Farnborough included the western side of Green Street Green high street, and Locks Bottom. The returns to the census of 1881 show a population of about 1,200 with just over 230 families. Today the area contains a population of over 20,000 with about 6,000 households. One hundred years ago the area consisted for the most part of the homes of hard-working and poorly paid labourers who were employed in agriculture or any other form of labour that was available. About 70 of the 300 working men were engaged in some form of agricultural work, which included farming, fruit growing and market gardening. Much of the life of the villages was closely connected with the land around them. The journey from Orpington Station to Green Street Green was described as passing through acres and acres of strawberry fields.

Nearly 100 men described themselves simply as labourers. But in addition there were some of the higher classes of society who found the village a pleasant place in which to live. Henry J. Latter was a bank manager, there was a stock holder; there were those who lived on the income from houses and land; commercial travelers and various clerks. Also there were the tradesmen who supplied the goods and services the villagers required, including five bakers, three grocers, two drapers and two general shops, a post office, a tailor and a bootmaker. Among the number of trades practiced were two fellmongers (fur and skin merchants) a vermin destroyer, three wheelwrights, a cabinet maker, a beehive maker, four punnet makers and five blacksmiths.

The workhouse at Locks Bottom in 1881 had a population of 254 -153 males and 101 females. These figures include the staff, a master and a matron, two porters, a labour master, a baker, two nurses and a carpenter. There were 26 boys under 15 years of age and 16 girls. Most of the youngsters were described in the census as scholars. At Christmas the paupers in the workhouse had a dinner of roast beef followed by plum pudding and each adult had a pint of beer. It was then a workhouse and not a hospital, but when a labourer at Holwood Farm Keston fell off a load of hay, he was taken there. The gate porter refused to admit him without the authority of the master who, when found, got on his tricycle and went to Bromley to get the workhouse doctor. He said it would have taken longer if he had used the Union horse and cart. The man died and at the inquest it was agreed that he should have been admitted to the workhouse for attention without the unfortunate delay.

6. Stow Cottages

- Noah Pateman (1883-1949)
- Walter Pateman (1886-1917)
- Alice Pateman (1889-?)
- Phoebe Pateman (1892-?)

Farnborough situated between Bromley and Orpington is now often thought by outsiders to be a suburb of Bromley. Although a lot has disappeared over the ages, a lot of the Old Village still exists if one looks closely. The name Farnborough is actually an adaptation of the village's original name of Feanbioginga, meaning 'village among the ferns'. Although Farnborough is not mentioned in *The Domesday Book*, records do exist from 861AD. The oldest known things in Farnborough are the Post-Neolithic Dene Holes which suddenly started reappearing after heavy rains in the 1950's. Two opened up in The Firs Wood, one of which had tunnels leading for miles from it; others appeared in the woods at High Elms, as well as other places. Almost all have now been filled in.

Before the advent of the horseless carriage, Farnborough was a well known stopping off point for the stage coaches taking the well to do traveler from Hastings to London. *The New Inn* (circa 1860) has now been renamed the *Change of Horses*, for it was here that travelers stayed the night and the horses were stabled, fed and watered. Two other old inns still exist in the High Street. *The Woodman* was built in 1698 and just a short distance further on adjacent to the High Street and Church Lane stands *The George at Farnborough*, a 16th century inn which was originally called *The George and Dragon.*

Farnborough was also well known in days gone by for its Horse Fairs. Gypsies from all over Kent would bring their horses to buy and sell. They would run their horses up and down the High Street so that the would-be buyer could see their performance. Apparently this was a very popular spectacle for the villagers to watch. In those days the village had a very picturesque pond in the High Street. This was filled in and the site is now the garden of a bungalow. The village pump, no longer in evidence, was situated opposite Pleasant View, however, another antique pump has been placed on the site of the old pond, as a reminder of the original. Opposite the new pump is an old milestone declaring London 14 miles, Sevenoaks 10.

Between Viners Farm and the Bakery used to stand a ramshackle old wooden shed containing the Farnborough Fire Engine. It was considered to be very old. The Village Hall, standing in the High Street, was built in 1897, and next to it stands the Old Chapel, now called the Gospel Hall. The Working Man's Club is very old and still opens daily at the top of Pleasant View.

Another survivor of days gone by is The Parish Church of St Giles The Abbott (rebuilt 1639). This still proudly sits on the outskirts of the village, overlooking the beautiful country side towards Downe as it has done for centuries. It once had two towers, but one was destroyed by a violent storm in 1724, and the second was struck by lightning in 1838. The tower was rebuilt in 1838 and was given the now familiar Low Pyramidal Crowning Cap. At one time the church had two bells cast by John

Hodson in 1667. After they were recast by Messrs Gilbert and Johnson of Croydon in 1905, one later had to be taken down because it cracked. This now stands inside the church.

In the cemetery behind the church stands a marble monument to members of the March family. This consists of a large oblong tomb with a life sized marble statue of a reclining angel on the top. The statue was sculpted in the March's own workshop in the village and the sitter for the statue was a beautiful young Farnborough woman called Lillian Still. Lillian, however, had a chilblain on her right foot, so they used the foot of her younger sister Rose instead.

Urania Boswell (Gypsy Lee) 'Queen' of the Kent Gypsies, died in 1933. 15,000 spectators and mourners watched as her coffin was carried through the village in a ceremonial hearse pulled by six black horses. It must have been very picturesque. Urania is buried in the church yard with her husband Levi Boswell, the Gypsy chief who died in 1924. An elaborate stone was erected to them both but was vandalized some years ago and restored, very badly, by Bromley council workmen. It can still be seen today beside the main footpath through the church yard.

At one time most of the countryside surrounding the village was owned by two important families, the Lubbocks and Foxs of the brewery. The most important house was High Elms the seat of Baron Avebury (surname Lubbock). In those days the Lubbocks owned the important Hill Top Race Course on their land in Farnborough. The old house was sold and taken over by Kings College hospital as a nurses training centre. It was destroyed by fire in 1967 and the remains pulled down. However, some of the out buildings survived: the ancient ice well is now open to the public; the shell grotto has been vandalized; and the gardens are now a public park. The house had a celebrated Beech Walk (Beechy Walk), which stood for centuries until the hurricane in 1987 destroyed all but a few of the wonderful trees. At some time the family bred edible snails for culinary purposes and descendants of these can still be found in the gardens.

The Lubbocks once owned all the land towards St Giles church and built a monument to the memory of Harold Fox Pitt Lubbock who died in action in 1918. His father John Lubbock, 3rd Baron Avebury, was buried on the site in 1971. The memorial was very elaborate and had: part of an aeroplane on it; some stone model aeroplanes; and a free standing Celtic cross. Due to vandalism, most of the monument was dismantled and is now in a museum. The cross, however, was moved into the church yard and now stands near the garden of remembrance. The grave stones still remain in the little wood near the church. The name of Ursula Moyra Williams (presumably a relative) was added to the monument in 1992. The last member of the family to live on the High Elms estate was Eric Lubbock (one time MP for Orpington). Eric Lubbock became Baron (Lord) Avebury, who lived for many years in Clock House which is in Shire Lane on the edge of the High Elms estate.

In the 1940/50s the shops at the top end of the village were very popular. One was owned by the Waller sisters and another by the Wrays. There was also: Hills newsagents; Mathews the butchers; and on the opposite side of the road a bakery. There were once two laundries in the village – the Limes situated in the High Street opposite Pleasant View and the Cedars near the hospital. In the old days most of the women from the village, those who were not in service at one of the big houses, worked in one laundry or the other.

Air raid shelters from World War Two are still under the village green and could be reopened if necessary, and their outlines can be seen during times of drought. As Farnborough is so close to Biggin Hill aerodrome it came in for its share of bombing during the war and some bomb craters, the most noticeable one being in the field near Firs Wood, still exist.

During the 1950s, before the advent of a car for every family, Farnborough Village was a place of pilgrimage for Londoners wanting a day out in the fresh air away from all the pollution. On summer days families would crowd on the 47 or 51 buses and descend to Farnborough Village in their hundreds. To cater for the crowds there were the Orange Tea Rooms, the Cosy Nook Café and pubs. At around five o'clock in the evening there would be long queues of people, as many as 400 strong, and reaching a good way down Church Lane, heading for home and waiting for the buses. Extra buses were laid on and a great time was had by all.

Farnborough School (formerly the Farnborough Board School) was cut off from the village some years ago when the busy by pass to Bromley was built. This was a problem for the children of the old village for many years until a new school was built behind the village.

Noah Pateman (1883-1949)

Noah Pateman (1883-1949) =Annie Honeysett (1880-1961)
- Nellie Alice (1902-1976)
- Walter Arthur (1904)
- May Annie (1905-1955)
- Ivy Amy (1907-?)
- Noah (1909)
- Harry William (1912-1979)
- Alfred (1914-1915)
- Arthur Frederick (1916-1966)
- Noah (1919-1972)
- Frank George (1920-1977)

On 13 May 1883 Noah Pateman was born in a house cart at Locks Bottom, a hamlet three quarters of a mile from Farnborough. His father was a hawker. The villagers were not then affected by industrialisation except for the Oak Brewery at Green Street Green. They were not affected by the coming of the railway as the nearest station was at Orpington. Nor were they then affected by the spread of urban Bromley.

In 1901 Noah was working as a bricklayer's labourer in Portsmouth with his brother, Henry, and Thomas Reynolds (son of George Reynolds and Mary Ann Pateman, Noah's aunt). It was here that Noah met Annie Honeysett. Henry Pateman also met a local girl from Portsea Island, Lottie Edith Tilley, and married her in November 1902.

On 1 June 1902 Noah Pateman (19, bachelor, labourer, St Mary Cray, father - William Pateman, labourer) married Annie Honeysett (20, spinster, St Mary Cray, father - Edgar Honeysett, seaman) at the parish church of St Pauls Cray. The witnesses were Noah's brother, Walter, and Nellie Honeysett.

Annie Honeysett was born on 26 October 1880 at 6 Nelson Square, Landport, near Southampton. Her father, Edgar Honeysett, was a Seaman, R.N., on *HM Ship Alexandria*. Her mother was Sarah Ann Upsdell (born 1854). Edgar Honeysett was born on 9 July 1851 at the Union Workhouse, Hollingbourne. His mother was Louisa Honeysett.

In 1871 Edgar Honeysett (23, single, Maidstone, Kent) was serving as an ordinary seaman on board *H.M. Crocodile* at the time of the census on Sunday 2 April.

Edgar (21, bachelor, seaman, father - John Honeysett, labourer) married Sarah Ann Upsdell (18, spinster, father - George Upsdell, labourer) in 1872 at Portsea. Their son, Arthur Edgar Honeysett, was born at Portsea, Hampshire, on 22 May 1878.

In 1881 Annie Honeysett (5 months) was living at Nelson Square with her mother, Sarah Ann Honeysett (27), her brother Arthur Honeysett (2) and her grandfather, George Upsdell (63). Annie's father died sometime between 1886 and 1891.

In 1891 Annie Honeysett (10) was living at George Street, Portsea with her mother (37, widow, shop keeper) and her siblings Arthur (12), Alfred (7) and Ellen (5).

Noah and Annie had several children: Nellie (1902, Chislehurst), Walter Arthur (1904, Portsmouth), May Annie (1905, Portsmouth), Ivy Amy (1907, Portsmouth), Noah (1909, Portsmouth), Harry William (1912, Orpington), Alfred (1914, Orpington), Arthur Frederick (1916, Orpington), Noah (1919, Orpington), and Frank George (1920, Orpington).

Noah had his first child in Orpington in 1902 and his next four children were born in Portsmouth between 1904-1909. It is not clear if he stayed and lived down in Portsmouth during this period, or if he traveled between Orpington and Portsmouth, or wherever the work took him. He had two sons named Noah, one who was born and died in 1909 and another born in 1919, known locally as 'young Noah'.

Noah Pateman was described as a bricklayer's labourer (1901), labourer (1902), general labourer (1907), builder's labourer (1912), water pipe layer (1919), pipe layer (1925) and road labourer (1925). He shifted from working on the land to working on the roads. He specialized in laying water pipes and in 1934 he became a foreman for the Metropolitan Water Board. According to Len Hodson, it was Noah Pateman who could get you a job on the roads if you met him in the pub and bought him enough drinks. But he could give you the sack just as easily as well.

Noah Pateman died on 24 November 1949 at 19 Poverest Road, St Mary Cray, aged 66. His occupation was road worker labourer (retired) and he died of carcinoma of the larynx and rheumatoid arthritis. No doubt this was caused by too much smoking and too much exposure to the elements. The informant was M. Lee, daughter, present at the death, 5 Fordcroft Road, St Mary Cray. This was May Annie Pateman, who married Herbert Lee. Noah Pateman was buried on 28 November 1949 in the new churchyard at All Saints, Orpington.

Annie Pateman died on 10 October 1961 at Farnborough Hospital, aged 81. Her address was 19 Poverset Road and she was the widow of Noah Pateman, pipe layer builder. She died of senile decay and the informant was her son Arthur Frederick Pateman, of 32 Petten Grove, Orpington. Annie Pateman was buried on 14 October 1961 in the same grave (V.25) as her husband. There are two Honeysetts buried at St Giles Farnborough, who could have been related to Annie: William Henry Honeysett (died 29 September 1931, aged 68) and Daisy Honeysett (died 11 August 1978, aged 95 years).

Village Life

There were nine public houses in the parish of Farnborough: the *Royal Oak* and *Rose and Crown* at Green Street Green; *The Coach and Horses*, *Woodman*, *New Inn* (now the *Change of Horses*) and the *George* at Farnborough village; and *The British Queen*, *Black Horse* and *Whyte Lyon* at Locks Bottom. (The *Queen's Head* in Green Street Green High Street is in Chelsfield Parish). The landlords often had other trades. In the *1885 Directory* John Goodchild of the *Woodman* is described as a beer retailer and fruit grower. Owen Kenward of The *British Queen* was a beer retailer and butcher, while Robert Sessions who when the 1881 census was taken, was head of the household at *The Whyte Lyon*, described himself as a farmer and made no reference to his duties as landlord of the inn. By 1885 the landlord of *The Whyte Lyon* was W. Wright.

The village inns were male centres. Men went there for companionship, warmth and the exchange of news and views, with no children under their feet or wives to nag them. Games such as skittles, dominoes, cribbage and pitch and toss were provided. It was also a place of commerce where local farmers, fruit growers, market gardeners, carriers and tradesmen transacted business over their pipes and pints. Most of the local horses were so accustomed to stopping at the public houses that they did so of their own accord, partly perhaps because of the horse troughs standing by the entrances to the premises. The water trough outside *The George* was put there in 1885, for the use of the horses pulling the horse buses.

The age of the *New Inn* is not known exactly, but it is probably early 19th century although there have been a number of modifications to the structure during the years. Its origin was probably a way side ale house for pilgrims and travellers. Brewing was carried out on the premises as is evident by the well still to be seen in the cellars, although it has now been filled in. The name *New Inn* usually indicates that an old inn had been there before. The traditional sign board has a religious design, and was often described as the house of Our Lady. Farnborough's *New Inn* was a stage stop for the stage coach from the Old Kent Road to Sevenoaks and Tunbridge. The passengers would alight at the *White Lion* Public House at Locks Bottom where they found comfortable accommodation for the night. The coach and horses would then proceed to the *New Inn*, Farnborough, where the horses were unharnessed and turned loose into the fields opposite the *New Inn* which were known as the New Inn Fields. In winter they were stabled at the back of the *New Inn*. Bed and board were provided at the *New Inn* for the coachman and his assistant. The following morning the horses would be harnessed and back tracked to Locks Bottom where they would take on the passengers once more who would then proceed to Sevenoaks. Livery and bait was also sold at the *New Inn*.

Some odd looking bottles made by Mr Cod have been found at the back of the *New Inn*. The outstanding feature of these bottles was that instead of a cork or stopper a glass marble was inserted into the neck to stop the liquor from spilling out, when tipped on its side. These bottles were generally made for the sale of lemonade and were called Cods bottles. As the lemonade was sold in public houses and the regular patrons of these places went to have their pint of wallop it was said by them that the contents of Mr. Cods bottles was very poor wallop indeed, hence the saying 'a load of cods wallop'.

Before the Great War market gardeners, who were mainly strawberry growers, would gather in the *New Inn* to decide what price they would ask for their produce, before setting off for Covent Garden and other London markets. Later on a regular Sunday feature outside the inn was horse trading, which was conducted mainly by the Gypsies of the district, who after much bargaining and inspecting of teeth and fetlocks, flanks and hind quarters would test the horses out by racing them along the High Street, round the Green and back to the *New Inn*. This activity came to an end with the outbreak of World War Two. At the rear of the *New Inn* is a bowling alley.

Walter Pateman (1886-1917)

Walter Pateman (1886-1917) = Priscilla Arnold (1889-1971)
- Walter (1909-1913)
- Albert (1910-1962)
- Lena (1912-1923)
- William (1913-1930)
- Edmund (1915-1935)

On 9 May 1886 Walter Pateman was born on the common, Farnborough, Kent. His father was a pedlar. At the time of Walter's birth machinery was being used on some of the farms and in the market gardens but it was not yet general use because of the availability of cheap labour from the villages. Harvest was a busy time. Although mechanical reaper-binders were used on some farms, on others the corn was cut by hand scythe. This was hard and slow work and a gang of five led by a good scytheman needed a full day to cut and sheave two acres. The tendency was to employ a regular labour force on the farm, using casual labour when necessary. James R. Tile of Tubbenden farm had 150 acres and was also a hay dealer. At the time of the 1881 census, he employed eight men, four boys and four women. Robert Milne of Den Barn, Green Street Green, had 77 acres and employed four men and two boys, while John L. Lovibond of Starts Hill, farmed 106 acres and employed four men and a boy. The dozen or so fruit orchards and market gardens in the area would also have a small regular workforce, but much of the work of planting, picking, preparing and packing the produce would be done by casual labour, which included women and children.

By comparison with most industrial workers, the agricultural and general labourers were poorly paid. The agricultural labourer usually got extra money at harvest time and, like many of the general labourers, grew produce in his garden or on his allotment. He probably kept poultry, bees, rabbits and a pig and sold any surplus. This helped to improve his standard of living. Ill-health for the labourer, particularly the elderly, was common and consisted of almost permanent rheumatism, lumbago, arthritis and the results of accidents. For many, poverty was caused not only by ill health, but by low income due to irregular work.

In the 1901 census Walter was described as a farm labourer. On 24 February 1909 Walter Pateman (23, bachelor, general labourer, Crofton Road, Orpington, father - William Pateman, farm labourer) married Priscilla Arnold (23, spinster, field hand, Crofton Old Farm, Orpington, father - Edmund Arnold, farm labourer) at Bromley Register Office. The witnesses were Walter's sisters, Alice and Phoebe. For more information about Priscilla Arnold, see Chapter 8 - Fellow Travellers.

Walter and Priscilla had five children: Walter (1909, Crofton Road), Albert (1910, Willow Walk, Tugmutton), Lena (1912, Mount Pleasant, Orpington), William (1913, St Andrew's Cottages, Lower Road, Orpington), Edmund (1915, St Andrews Cottages). Walter was a labourer when his children were all baptized at St Andrews Church, Orpington on 12 April 1916. Walter was also described as a farm labourer (1909) and general labourer (1910).

Conscription was introduced on 24 May 1916 and Walter joined the Middlesex Regiment, which had been decimated at the Battle of the Somme on 1 July 1916. After a short period of training Walter arrived in France in October 1916. He was in the front line at Hulloch and Le Transloy and on 23 October he took part in the attack on Zenith Trench. After another spell in the front line at Les Boeufs, he spent six weeks resting and training at St Maulvis. He was then back in the front line at Maurepas and Rancourt.

Walter Pateman (G.50399, Private, Middlesex Regiment) was killed in action at Bouchavesnes on 27 February 1917. His body was never found. His name is remembered on the Thiepval Memorial to the Missing of the Somme and also on Orpington War Memorial, and the War Shrines at All Saints, St Andrews and St Pauls, Crofton. For more information about Walter Pateman see *Seven Steps to Glory: Private Pateman Goes to War*.

Alice Pateman (1889-?)

Alice Pateman was born in a house cart at Farnborough on 6 July 1889. Her father was a pedlar. She was baptised at St Giles on 13 July. Alice Pateman later moved to St Mary Cray. On 7 August 1911 Alice Pateman (23, spinster, 6 Epsom Cottages, Fordcroft, St Mary Cray, father - William Pateman, farm labourer) married Jesse Lee (23, bachelor, motor smith, 4 Wellington Road, St Mary Cray, father - John Jacob Lee, caretaker) at Bromley Register Office. The witnesses were J. Lee and A. Carter. Alice Pateman was the informant at the death of her father on 24 October 1921. She was living at 4 Broadway, St Mary Cray. We do not know if Alice Pateman had any children, when she died or where she is buried.

According to the *1890 Strong Directory of Farnborough*, William Pateman moved to Stow Cottages in Farnborough Village, which had a population of 1,283. These cottages were named after the local Stow family. Joseph Stow, for example, was a fruit grower. The Stows were active on the Farnborough Commons Conservation Board. It is significant that this Board was established in July 1888 and that one of its first acts – on 9 April 1889 – was to 'bank up the common at the places where vans were drawn on'. This happened just 3 months before Alice Pateman was born. Alice was the last of William's children to be born in a house cart. It is possible that the enclosure of Tugmutton Common forced William out of his house cart and into Stow Cottages; in the same way that James Pateman had been turned off Tugmutton Common and forced into Willow Cottages.

Moving into a cottage was a significant development for William who was living in a barn in 1871 and in a van on the side of the road in 1881. He had spent his life traveling around Kent, Surrey and Middlesex. Now he was breaking with tradition and moving into a cottage. His nomadic lifestyle, however, was not ended. During the summer months he continued to travel around the countryside picking vegetables, hops and fruit. In the winter he returned to his cottage in Farnborough and lived by repairing pots and pans, sharpening knives, making pegs and hawking them around the houses.

1891 Census

In 1891 the Farnborough census population was 1283. The 1891 Census was taken on 5 April 1891. Each house holder was required to complete a census schedule giving the address of the household, the names, ages, sex, occupation and place of birth of each individual residing in his or her accomodation. Householders were also asked to state their relationship to each resident, their marital status and the nature of any disabilities from which they might have suffered. In 1891 householders were asked how many rooms (if less than five) their family occupied and additional occupational data was collected.

In 1891 William Pateman was living in one house, three rooms at 3, Church Road, Farnborough. This small cottage consisted of one room downstairs, with a small kitchen, and one room upstairs. In this small area William lived with Mercy and their five children: Mary (15), Henry (13), Noah (8), Walter (5) and Alice (1).

Some cottages would have two rooms downstairs and two upstairs. In these, the front door opened straight into the front room which, despite the pressures of a large family, was used only for weddings, christenings and funerals and perhaps on Sundays. In most of the cottages lamps and candles were used for lighting although Farnborough and Locks Bottom in the 1880s were being supplied with gas by the St. Mary Cray Gas Company. Some of the cottages had a cast-iron kitchen range with an oven on one side and perhaps a water boiler on the other side. The table in the living room was usually covered with oilcloth. On the mantelshelf stood candlesticks, a decorated tea caddy, and photographs. In the kitchen would be a mangle and a slop stone sink. The low rents which labourers could afford did not encourage the building of better quality houses for them.

Church Road retained the rural character of the past and the path to the lychgate connected church and village. There were 20 addresses in Church Road and some of these buildings were historical, including: No.3 (nineteenth century - where William lived), No.5 (with overhanging weatherboard), Nos. 15 and 18 (eighteenth century) and No 20 (seventeenth century).

The Post Office was at 16 Church Road and the postmistress in 1891 was Harriett Giles. Letters, which had to be collected, arrived from Beckenham via Hayes twice during the morning. Post was dispatched from the post office twice during the afternoon and once on Sundays. There was a wall box at Locks Bottom which was also cleared twice in the afternoon and once on Sundays. Green Street Green residents dealt with the Orpington Post Office.

Farnborough Board School

Mary Pateman (15) and Henry (13) were described as scholars in the 1891 census, which suggests that they may have gone to Farnborough Board School, which opened in 1873. On the face of it this seems unlikely for two reasons: their ages and because it was unusual for Gypsy children to go to school at this time. School leaving age was 14, although some children stayed on an extra year and others, who applied for and were granted leave, left before their 14th birthday. As we shall see, William Pateman was starting to move up in the world and sending his children to school may have been part of his new social scene. The 1876 Education Act made full-time attendance at school compulsory and now that William lived in a house rather than a house cart it was easier for the School Attendance Officer to come knocking on his door to enquire why his children were not at school. The census shows that many of the children of William's neighbours were also scholars in 1891 and probably attended the Farnborough Schools.

I would have liked to have checked the school registers for 1891 to see if any Pateman children did in fact attend Farnborough School. But on enquiry I was told that these registers have gone missing. When the school closed the records should have gone to Bromley Council's Education Department. But they are not there and I was advised to try the Local History Library. They are not there either, and I was told to try the Kent County Council Record Office in Maidstone. This is because Farnborough was in Kent until 1965, and this included most of the years that the school was open. I drew a blank at Maidstone as well.

In 1870 a law was passed through Parliament making it compulsory for every child in the land to have some sort of formal education. Prior to this learning was obtained in a number of ways. If you belonged to a wealthy family you were either sent to a private school or had a tutor to teach you at home. Children of working class parents whether agricultural or industrial were expected to help maintain the family as soon as they were able. This was done by working on the land with their father, working in a factory for wages, as assistants in shops or working in coal mines.

So, in 1870 when the government said that all children must go to school a number of parents were not happy about it. There was considerable doubt about the value of education for working class children above the lowest minimum standard as it was claimed that it made the youngsters discontented. Some parents were annoyed and felt slighted by the teachers' efforts at improving the hygiene, manners and speech of their children. In Farnborough it didn't make such a great difference because this was farming country and the children could always do their jobs before or after school, at weekends and during holidays. For those children who had to complete their farm and garden chores before going to school this meant a very early start and often resulted in them falling asleep in class.

During the early to mid 19th century there were two small schools in Farnborough called Dame Schools. One was held in a cottage where the Police Station at Locks Bottom once stood and the other in a cottage in Church Road, where the Public Toilets now stand. They were called Dame Schools because the ladies who ran them were usually elderly and unqualified in teaching. Each pupil paid a few pence a week for the privilege of being taught but the real finance came from Sir John Lubbock and Mr. John Fox. Another of these Dame Schools was held at North End Farm which was also sponsored by Sir John Lubbock.

In 1872 the Local Authorities decided to build a school in Farnborough and in 1873 the first School Board of Managers was formed. This Board consisted of Sir John Lubbock, Mr. John Fox, Mr. Isaac Laslett (Clerk), Mr. Stow and Mr. William Charles Broadway (Attendance Officer). The first school building was erected in 1872 and consisted of a School House and 3 School Rooms. Mr. Edwin Wills was the Master and Mrs. Augustin Jullie Wills was the Mistress. They jointly received £10 pa and when the register was called for the first time it had 140 names on it. There are very few records of the early years of the school life in existence today so we must form a picture of those pioneer days as best we can. The buildings consisted of a School House and three school rooms roughly 20' x 20' x 15' high. Quite naturally the School Managers were determined to make Farnborough's first school a great success and there were many visits made to the school by the Managers and their ladies.

Furniture in the first school was rather primitive and in short supply, as were books and slates on which the pupils did their lessons. Great care had to be taken of these as replacements were very slow in coming through. Each year an examination was set by a Minister of the Church to test the pupils on their knowledge of the scriptures and to ensure that they could recite the commandments, creed and other parts of the Bible. There were also tests for songs and some of the early songs that were taught in Farnborough School were entitled The Cock, The Robin, In Merriest Creature, Sunbeam, The Squirrel, Oh Merry is the Bright Schoolboy, Greetings Song, There is Beauty Everywhere, Lovely June, Laughing Morn, What Say the Birds, Singing Bird and Busy Bee.

On 31 January 1873 a mortgage of £2000 was raised for the building of the original School House and school rooms. The first school records date from 23 April 1877 when Mrs. Mary Ann Casseldon took up her duties as Mistress of the Infant's Department of Farnborough Board School. This appointment enabled Mr. and Mrs. Wills to devote their entire energies to the senior pupils. Mrs. Casseldon soon had herself organized with strict time tables and improved standards of learning. Mr. and Mrs. Fox were regular visitors, Mrs. Fox supplying calico for the needlework class and wool for knitting. Mrs. Fox was a member of Messrs Fox and Sons, Oak Brewer, Farnborough New Fermenting House.

In November 1877 two dozen books and slates were received from supplies and it wasn't long before the class room was filled with the sound of happy infants making the slates screech as they copied their letters and numbers. The Rev. R. Groves was a regular visitor also to the school as was the Rev. G. Ingstone, Curate of St Giles but it was the Rev. H.G. Atington who set the annual scripture examination in 1878 and in 1880 thirty prizes were distributed to children who qualified for the Government examination. This out of a total of about 45 infants says much for the standards set by the Headmistress. On 10 May 1878 there were 26 infants drafted into the Mixed School, this being the Junior School of both boys and girls for which an additional mortgage of £650 was entered into on 23 January 1878.

According to the 1881 census, there were two schoolmasters, three schoolmistresses and two pupil teachers, for well over 250 scholars. There were two schools, one at Farnborough and the other at Green Street Green. Rules had to be obeyed by children and teachers alike and the Inspector of Schools threatened to cut the grant if needlework was not taught strictly in accordance with the Third Standard. Boys were excused needlework, although they had to learn to knit and were sometimes kept in after school to finish their knitting, but alternative subjects were introduced during the sewing hours. Her Majesty's Inspector, in his report of 1881 said the Infant's School was "creditably efficient" but in 1882 threatened to withhold the whole of the next year grant if more spacious accommodation was not found. Mrs. Casseldon was helped during this period by Miss M.A. Session, who was a paid monitoress.

Life for the children of Farnborough was not all school and although entertainment was not as spontaneous as today, the youngsters made the most of fun time when it came their way. There were the annual Sunday School outings, a school treat given by Sir John Lubbock; Baptist Hall treats, a popular treat of their own for the Union House Children; and of course the Forester's Fete. In the winter there was an occasional evening watching dissolving views and the records show that the school was closed early to allow children to attend these Magic Lantern shows. But before the children were allowed to dash off and join friends in the darkened hall there were jobs to be done at home. From an early age children had to help with home chores and one of these was the making of punnets for fruit picking. As Farnborough was an agricultural area, it was essential to have these baskets ready when the cherries, strawberries, plums and gooseberries ripened. Families tended to be larger in the 19th century which contributed to some of the children's illnesses reaching epidemic proportions.

It was not uncommon for the schools to be closed for two or three weeks during winter on account of smallpox, mumps, measles, chicken pox, the itch, to mention but a few ailments prevalent at the end of the 19th century. In 1885 the village school was closed for a fortnight on account of the prevalence of smallpox in Farnborough. The conditions inside the school rooms during the hard winters did not help the fight against illness – one day in 1886 the Infant School children had to stand on their forms for two hours because the Teacher considered the floor, which was cleaned the evening before, too damp for the children to put their feet on. They were given the afternoon off in the hope that on the morrow the room would be fit for use.

On 10 April 1886 the following were elected to serve on the School Board: Isaac Balard of Beulah Villa, Thomas Hamilton Fox of Beechwood, Walter St John Fox of Beechwood, Joseph Watson Stow of the Village and James Weatherley of the Village. Five months later the school was closed for an afternoon in order that the children could attend the funeral of Mr. Thomas T. Fox, late Chairman of the Board. Later in

October of the same year Mrs. Mary Ann Casseldon resigned and Miss Georgina Fanny Stocks started her 35 year term as Headmistress of 50 children in the Infant's Department. She was assisted by Monitoress Blanche Elizabeth Tile.

1887 was the year that Queen Victoria celebrated her Silver Jubilee and the schools were closed as there was a general holiday on the 21 June. Despite constant warnings by the Board to keep attendances down to an average of 50 a week and a threat of withholding the grant, the total on the books in the Infant's School was 65. They were being taught in cramped conditions by the Headmistress and one Monitoress. Painstaking and diligent as she was in her duties she found it too much and on 21 August 1888 Miss Tile found employment elsewhere. Before the year was out the Headmistress had noted in her Log Book that one boy had been unable to attend school for 8 weeks because he hadn't any boots and that Percy Sawyer was admitted to the school.

In the early years of the Board Schools each pupil was expected to bring 'school pence' weekly, as a fee for being taught. There were times when some children didn't arrive with their school pence and if this happened too frequently they were sent home again to collect it. But kind hearted Miss Stocks overlooked the fee if a child's father was without work through ill health.

In 1888 there was a very bad report on the Board School and later on that year Mr. Wills found it necessary to resign his appointment as Headmaster and a new Headship was advertised at £120 per annum. 56 applications were made for the position which was eventually filled by Mr. J. Ashworth and Mrs. M. Ashworth (they were both First Class Certificated) and they had as their Assistant Teacher an ex-pupil teacher Mr. E.C. Death.

By 1889 the Government Inspector reported that the school grant would be allowed only on the undertaking that the enlargement of the school be proceeded with forthwith. On the 31 March 1890 Miss Stocks and her two Monitoresses commenced school in the new building. An additional mortgage of £1,220 was taken out for the new school which was a great step forward for the Village. Two days later a supply of school furniture arrived, including 6 scholar's desks, one teacher's desk, one table, two chairs, two easels and two blackboards and by 13 October there were 75 infant scholars on the books of whom 71 had been in attendance some time during the week.

Mr. Harbour, Her Majesty's Inspector, gave instructions that no child over the age of 7 years was to be retained in the Infant School and so we find the Headmistress sorting out to see who she could send up to the Mixed School, but after careful examination of her records she found that there were only two who were over the age of 7. When these two were sent to the Mixed School they were returned by Mr. Ashworth who considered them insufficiently advanced to work with his Standard 1 and wished them to still remain with the infants. The Board agreed with his findings, which only goes to show that rules are meant to be broken very soon after they are made, in some cases. However, in March of 1890 twenty one children were sent to the Mixed School, all of whom were well up in their First Class work, five others who should have gone up were kept back until they had reached a better standard. So with 27 boys and 24 girls on the books, the fixed grant of 9/- per pupil, a merit grant of 4/-, a needlework grant of 1/-, and a singing grant of 6d. Miss Stocks received a total grant for the year of £36.19.6.

Despite the new school, new equipment and fewer children, Miss Bradbery and Miss Brown resigned their position as Monitoresses, but in November 1891, Miss Jane Hassell of Green Street Green School was transferred to Farnborough Infant School as a teacher under Article 68. Miss Jane is not to be confused with Miss Gertrude Hassell who was already a teacher in the Farnborough Mixed School. With, once more, a full staff the total on the books again reached high proportions, this time to the grand total of 90 children. Whether or not it was in the way of a reward we are not sure but there is a note in the School Log that on 2 October a harmonium was received for use in the school. This no doubt came in very useful for the singing and drill which was inspected by Mrs. Shannon. Through 1890/91/92 we find Monitoresses came and went with great rapidity. Gradually the number of children increased and at the end of 1892 there were 94 on the books. This was probably due in part to boys and girls from the Workhouse or "Bromley Union" as it was sometimes called being admitted to the schools.

The School Board consisted of Isaac Ballard, the Baptist Church Minister, H. G. Cheel, a baker in Church Road; J. W. Fox, the brewer and farmer of Green Street Green; John Hassell, the fellmonger, woolstapler and rug dresser, and J.W. Stow, a fruit grower. The Clerk to the board was Isaac Laslett, the local builder and undertaker. The Farnborough Schools are now listed buildings and have been made into flats in recent years.

Phoebe Pateman (1892-?)

Phoebe Pateman, was born on 1 January 1892 at Stow Cottages, Farnborough. Her father was a general labourer. Phoebe was baptised on 14 February 1892 at St Giles church. Phoebe Pateman later moved to Orpington. On 25 December 1911 Phoebe Pateman (21, spinster, Mount Pleasant, Orpington, father - William Pateman, labourer) married Charles Edward Smith (21, bachelor, miller, Mount Pleasant, Orpington, father -Edward Smith, labourer) at All Saints Church, Orpington. The witnesses were Henry and Lottie Pateman, Phoebe's brother and sister in law. We do not know if Phoebe Pateman had any children, when she died or where she is buried.

The agricultural industry was having a hard time in 1892. There had been bad weather for a number of years which had resulted in poor harvests and the loss of livestock through diseases. Prices had been forced down by the flood of cheap corn from America and the import of frozen meat. Dairying, fruit growing and the growing of other perishable foodstuffs increased in this area to supply the demands from London for butter, cheese, fresh milk, fruit and vegetables. Strawberries, currants and raspberries were grown over a wide area and rushed to the London market at dawn. It seems to have been a matter of pride - and also probably of price - to get the fruit to the market as early as possible. There were more than 300 acres of strawberries in the area.

The village shops were beginning to stock the mass products from the factories. In 1841 the villages had four boot and shoe makers. Forty years later there was only one. This is surprising because the labourer relied upon good, heavy, well-made boots to protect his feet and keep them dry. Whereas there had previously been two tailors in the village, there was only one in 1885.

Many people had more than one trade. Mr. Ballard in the High Street was a smith, coachbuilder and farrier. Mrs. Giles was a grocer, draper and fruit grower. John Hassell was a fellmonger, woolstapler and rug dresser. Isaac Laslett made bricks and tiles and was also a builder and undertaker. Mrs. Mills described herself as a brazier, tinman, grocer and draper. William Mitchell was a woodman and plasterer. The villages had four dressmakers, a milliner and a needlewoman. Nearly 100 of the local people were engaged in some form of domestic service. It was the major form of employment for women, most of whom preferred this type of work to labouring in the fields because it was better for their complexions and far less wear and tear on their clothes.

The population of Farnborough was not increasing anything like as rapidly as that of the country as a whole. The expanding population was not spreading into the rural areas, as for most people, particularly the labouring classes, life in towns was much preferred. Country people were seeking the wider range of employment, better housing and general facilities which were becoming available in the towns. Housewives did not like living in small cottages in country areas where mud from the unpaved roads was brought in on the boots of her family, where water had to be carried from the pump or spring and the privy was at the end of the garden.

1892 was the first year in which there are records for the Farnborough Mixed School - the number on the roll was 155, plus the 94 infants, which was a sizeable increase in the first 20 years of the School. On 22 November 1892 Mr. Weatherly and Mr. Stow had to visit the school in the afternoon to see why the stoke hole was flooded. The wet weather did not deter Mrs. Evans of Tubbenden from visiting the school one afternoon and the Rev. W. Nunn held the annual scripture examination. The Revs. F.K. Kelly and I. Ballard also visited during these examinations.

1893 was the beginning of a new era for Farnborough School. In October Walter John Fox presented the First Class Boys with a football which was very much appreciated. This enabled them to demonstrate their talents on the Village Green which served as playground and sports ground for the schools. In those days there was no recreation ground in Farnborough but as the Farnborough by pass had not been built the grass patch at the lower end of Starts Hill extended right through to the High Street.

Two sad events brought 1893 to a close at the School, one being the funeral of little Daisy Owen, to which the majority of the school children marched in procession, on 9 November, and on 5 December Mr. Death informed the Headmaster that he would be leaving as he had gained an appointment under the Bromley School Board. 1894 started with very heavy snow storms and it was because of this and also through sickness that several children were absent on 4 January from the drawing examination. It was mainly the children who came from Crofton who were unable to attend through bad weather and the Inspectors took this into consideration when allowing for the grant.

In February 1894 the Infants School registers reached a total of 100 and in March 26 children were transferred to the Mixed School which was finding difficulty in securing an assistant master. Mrs. Ashworth was finding the numbers too many to cope with and so sought the help of her daughter to assist her, whilst Mr. Ashworth placed Standard 2 under his son. This over crowding also necessitated the staggering of recreation times as the playground was too small for all the children to be there together. In April 1894, Mr. William Henry Holmes commenced duties as an assistant teacher to Mr. Ashworth which still left them a little below the minimum required and so in May it was decided by the Inspectors that only children residing within the Parish boundary should be admitted to Farnborough School. In consequence 15 children from the Mixed School and 8 from the Infants were sent home. On 20 August 1894 a proud Mr. Ashworth noted that he had received a notification that the pupil teacher Albert E. Ashworth had gained a first class in model drawing and a first class in free hand at South Kensington Science and Art Department.

Punishment in the early days of the school included children having to stay in to complete the lessons, forfeiting leisure play time because of disobedience and in severe cases of misconduct, especially in the Junior School, the cane was given. Should a boy in Mr. Ashworth's class push him too far he would say 'Go out and cut me a cane, I'm going to cane you now'. These boys, being brought up in the country knew how to cut a cane for if it was cut very thing it stung very much but soon went, and if it was cut thicker it didn't sting so much but the pain lasted longer. So the boys had to decide between a quick sting or a longer lasting but not so sharp pain. After a caning Mr. Ashworth broke the cane across his knee, so that a new cane was used every time it was necessary and this was sometimes more than once a day.

Games have changed very little over the years, though it has become necessary to revise some of them due to the increase in traffic on the roads. One of the favorite games with the boys in the late 19th century was for six or so boys to stand in the middle of the road and each other boy in turn had to try to hop across with the six in the middle doing their best on one foot, to make him put both his feet down to the ground. George Springett was the champion road crosser around about the turn of the century. One game that has gone completely out of fashion is the hoop. This was generally made of iron and with Farnborough School being on a very steep hill it was great fun to take your hoop to the top of Starts Hill and bowl it down at great speed when a boy, placed at the bottom, would try to put his arm through the hoop as it rushed by in order to stop it. Marbles were also very popular.

One ex pupil of the Girl's School remembers the double desks with tip up seats which were so convenient for practical jokes and caused many a giggle in the class room. The heating was by open fires and lighting was by gas lamps mounted on circular brackets. The teacher or Governess as she was known sat behind the large desk on a raised platform at the front of the class. The beginning of school was marked by the tolling of a bell and the morning began with a hymn from Sankey's (a girl from the class played the harmonium) then followed a prayer. Drill was performed in the play ground and was done to music from records. Both needlework and knitting were done, though cooking was of the simplest form mainly mixing batter and peeling potatoes. Lunch was brought to school and eaten in the playground although if wet it was consumed in the sheds at the back of the school. When the Inspectors were expected the Governess was all nerves. The usual alert was sent up with a boy from her husband's school at the bottom of the hill and then a girl was posted on the steps to watch for the Inspector's carriage to arrive. The fun started when he took over the lesson, the Governess stood behind the Inspector and became very agitated when the children did not come up with the answers to his questions. All eyes were glued to watching her try to mime the answer from behind the Inspector's back but they failed often to understand her efforts, and they were told off by her when the Inspector left.

Morning and afternoon playtime was about 15 minutes long and just to loosen up the children would climb over the main wall and drop down outside, run round the farm side and have a run in the grass fields and back into the shed again. In winter great excitement was experienced when the heavens darkened and a thunder storm approached. It was then that all the lights were put out and at the first flash of lightning all the rings on the Governesses fingers were taken off and put in her desk, also her large bell, and the children's knitting needles stopped work.

Farnborough Village: continuity and change

Once a year in the ancient parish church of St Giles the Abbott, in the village of Farnborough Kent, a sermon is preached on the uncertainty of life. It is a theme which might be applied to the village itself. Had someone not had the foresight to build Farnborough bypass about 50 years ago, one shudders to think what would have happened to little Fearnbiorginga, 'the village among the ferns upon the hill'. It might now be dead as a community, for it straddles what used to be the main road between London and Hastings. And we all know what heavy traffic can do to towns and villages it passes through. Not only has Farnborough survived. It still has its village life and character – even though it is these days part of Bromley borough, in Greater London. It has managed to retain its sense of identity. And it also has a very friendly nature.

Commuter residents have merged well with the village residents, some of whom have lived in Farnborough all their lives. One such character was Nobby Haines, who lived in Palmerston Road, one of a group of old streets known as the Prime Minister Roads, including Gladstone, Chatham, Peel and Pitt. He was born about 200 yards away, at a cottage near *The George*. A fireman on the old Southern Railway, until he met with an accident, he helped stoke the boilers at Orpington and Farnborough hospitals until his retirement. But he is best known as a great sportsman, having played centre forward for Crystal Palace. His cups and medals filled a showcase and he was still winning awards on his allotment at the age of 79.

Long before it switched from Kent to London for administrative purposes Farnborough has always been a favourite spot for Londoners seeking its beautiful surrounding countryside and its marvellous air. On 13 April 1914 Thomas Tillings launched their first Shoreditch – Farnborough omnibus service (11 old pence all the way) with the slogan 'country breezes for city workers.' The buses turned for the return journey outside *The George*, with long queues forming at Bank Holidays. And there is another local link, for the Bank Holidays Act, 1871, was passed through the efforts of Sir John Lubbock, later Lord Avebury, of High Elms, a short distance across the valley from Farnborough.

The Lubbocks and Aveburys are linked with the village, and some members of the family are buried at Farnborough. In fact the churchyard at St Giles seems to be the last resting place of a number of notable people. The 'queen's grave', as it is called, is that of Urania Boswell, 'queen' of the Kentish Gypsies. Her funeral was attended by 15,000 people. Another grave is that of the March family, famous sculptors who lived near Locksbottom and whose work includes the Vimy Ridge memorial and the huge Canadian national memorial in Ottawa.

The records of the village go back to the year 862 and it is reckoned to be one of the oldest Kent villages. Farnborough Hall, mentioned in the reign of Henry III (1216-1272) was the former home of the local lord of the manor. The present house, which lies almost out of sight at the end of a drive off Tubbenden Lane, is Queen Anne, and still has some old beams and low ceilings. The village is a conservation area, and one of its watchdogs is the Farnborough Village Society. It represents many of the households in the village and is the largest village association. Its aims are to protect and improve the amenities and environment, and the interests of the residents. Many residents still regard Farnborough as a Kentish village and they didn't want to become part of the London Borough of Bromley.

Back at Locks Bottom, in the area which used to be called Brasted Green, things have changed rather more than in the village itself. There are many new homes, including the Farnborough Park and Keston Park estates, with beautiful properties built in a landscaped setting. And in Crofton Road, which leads to Orpington, the original row of mock Tudor fronted shops known as Park Parade has been augmented by Princess Parade, on the other side, which has really brought the shopping up to date with a vengeance. Not all residents are happy with the appearance of the new shopping centre, for they still regard the area as a village. But it has helped to keep Locks Bottom alive. Local shopkeepers and business men are trying to preserve the local community and village atmosphere, despite the march of progress. An association was formed to promote a Christmas lighting scheme for the shops. It was so successful that the illuminations have even been featured on television. People came a long way to see the lights.

Ye Olde Whyte Lyon, just round the corner in the main road at Locks Bottom, a former coaching inn, dates back to 1626 and has its ostler's bell and letters from royalty. Another link with the past is the nearby police station, still sited in a little cottage type building where it has been since at least 1851, the date of the first record. That is a mere 22 years after the Metropolitan Police Force, or 'Peelers' were formed by Sir Robert Peel. Before that it was a butcher's shop. So while it looks to the future, Farnborough clings to the past. And perhaps the best illustration of that is the sermon on the uncertainty of life. It dates back over four centuries and commemorates an event which – to give it its due – does not appear to be very significant in itself, the drowning in a pond of rushes of a villager of the 16th century, on his way home one night.

Not only is the Rush Sermon, as it is called, still preached under the terms of the Dalton bequest, but the preacher gets ten shillings for so doing. Out of kindness of heart, and recognition of the rising cost of living, the preacher, in fact, gets an additional payment in these days of inflation. The church itself has had an uncertain life, being damaged by storms throughout the centuries. A bottle found during one of the periodic rebuildings contained a note about the work carried out after a great tempest in 1639. In 1292 Edward I granted permission for an annual fair in the village and St Giles Fair is still held to the present day, though these days it is run by the Round Table.

There are photographs of: old weatherboard cottages in Farnborough High Street, near Farnborough Common; Mr Nobby Haines, 79, of Palmerston Road, Farnborough; *Ye Olde Whyte Lyon*, on the main road at Locksbottom; there are four views of Church Road, 'the hub of Farnborough' including some picturesque old buildings in Church Road, near St Giles Church; Farnborough Police Station, Locks Bottom, is one of the oldest police stations in the London area; St Giles, Farnborough Parish Church, is perched on a hillside overlooking some glorious countryside; Mock Tudor shopping arcade; the famous grave of Urania Boswell, the Kentish 'Gypsy' queen; the *New Fantail Restaurant*, Locksbottom; some of the high street shops in 1926; *The George and Dragon*, before rebuilding; High Street with *George and Dragon* and the bus terminus; The Square, Farnborough; Post Office, Farnborough; The 'Cosy Nook' tea gardens, Farnborough Road. A sign by the road indicates facilities for parties of cyclists.

In many ways Farnborough Village has not changed much. *Ye Olde Whyte Lyon* is still open for business, but *The George* is now closed and awaiting redevelopment. Stow Cottages and Cobden Road are still standing, but the *New Fantail Restaurant* has changed its name to *Chapter One*. The Christmas lights at Locksbottom are now nothing but a fond memory and the shopping arcade has lost much of its business to a massive new Sainsburys supermarket. The Workhouse – which was converted into Farnborough Hospital – has been demolished and replaced by the Princess Alexandra Hospital. Brasted Green, Tugmutton Common and Willow Walk still look much as they did when William and James Pateman first arrived in Locksbottom and Farnborough in 1881.

There are also some old photographs of :Farnborough Village and Schools; *The New Inn* (1865); Farnborough Boys School, 'The First Cricket Bat' (1895); Queen Victoria Jubilee Celebrations (June 1897); The Foresters (1905); May Queen (1907); The Violin Class (1908); *George and Dragon* (1910); the first bus to leave the *George and Dragon* (April 1913) ; Farnborough Girls School (1919); Farnborough Boys Football Team (1930/31); funeral of Gypsy Lee (1933); Farnborough Girls Netball Team (1933/34); Farnborough Old Boys Guild – production of 'Sinbad The Sailor' (1935); Handicrafts (1939/40); Recorder Class (1948); Country Dancing (1950); Flagpole raising ceremony (1973).

More photographs of Farnborough Village can be found in old picture postcards. There are some places that manage to remain timeless despite the gallop of modernisation. Farnborough is still essentially a country village though only perhaps a twenty minutes drive from Bromley. To walk under St Giles' lychgate and come upon that great expanse of dazzlingly sunlit green meadowland, as far as the eye can see, is to come upon another world that feels a thousand miles away instead of barely four. Merely to take the footpath thence towards High Elms is to automatically unwind from the stress of shops, street and noise; exactly as our grand parents and great grand parents found when they came out here by horse or char-a-banc to cast off the cares of their own periods of history: the Depression, two great wars, or too many mouths to feed on too little pay. And the most satisfying thing of all is to realise that we are seeing virtually unchanged the Farnborough that they knew.

A Canute of a Village, Farnborough saw the swamping tide of suburbanisation flood out from the Orpington direction in the 1920s and 1930s as if it would never cease until all the greenery was gone. But it came to the verges of Green Street Green and Locks Bottom and then stopped; and there it remains to this day. The handful of shops serving the local community preserve their old nature of country emporia having unlimited stocks of unlikely useful necessities. Only about eight years before the first picture postcards began leaving the local post office for the outside world, a famous late-Victorian professor drove out under four footed horse power from either Orpington or Bromley to visit Darwin at Down House. The description he gave of his ride through Farnborough towards his destination could well have been written today instead of over a century ago, so little has this terrain altered:

'I drove one sunny morning in October, through the graceful, hilly landscape of Kent, with its stretches of purple heath, yellow broom, and evergreen oaks, arrayed in its fairest autumnal dress.' The most noticeable features of a similar journey today are exactly the same: the purple late summer heather of the Commons and the brilliant gold of the gorse growing wherever it can resist cultivation, not to mention the similar flower of the broom that gave the parent town of Bromley its original name. It is said that in virtually every month of the year, some twig of gorse will be found bearing its yellow flowers, even outside the main blossoming season, if one walks far enough in these parts.

Walking was one of the most fashionable forms of exercise in Edwardian times, one of the reasons for the public popularity of Farnborough, with the nearby community of Green Street Green, which was also a cyclist's mecca. Where there were droves of hikers, cyclists and snapshotters, there was potential trade in refreshments, accounting for the great number of cafes and tea gardens all over this area which, in their turn, attracted yet more people to discover it for relaxation. Many came for the gentler pastime variously described as spooning or canoodling, when a young couple could spend an entire afternoon holding hands over an outdoor table, by spending a few coppers on successive cups of tea, or home made cakes.

For our forefathers simple pleasures in homely surroundings were their answer to long hours in often poorly paid jobs. They lingered over their scones and butter no farther from home than Farnborough Village, and penned the penny postcards that now fetch several pounds – or considerably more – at collectors' fairs. Most surviving antique cards of Bromley town centre are valued as records of scenes long vanished; often of entire streets that are gone. Those showing Farnborough are in a happier category; showing costumes, vehicles and shop goods of the past, but within the framework of a street or lane that is still recognisable. In this respect, they make us appreciate our local villages more than ever, by reminding us that development has failed to obliterate their underlying character.

Farnborough past is vividly summed up in a postcard of a long vanished group of pretty cottages with a picturesque lamp outside. Built mainly from wood, they were on the corner of Pleasant View and the High Street. Other postcards include: Farnborough Board Schools; St Giles church; Farnborough Common; Godendene; Church Street; the lane running past St Giles; the old Post Office and Lych Gate; the shops (including the family grocer and cheesemonger, the shoe shop, the sweet shop and the stationers shop); The High Street, once part of the main road from London to

Hastings; boys wearing sailor suits and girls wearing black stockings and black buttoned boots that were universal during the 1880s and 90s; the *New Inn* (previously the *Change of Horses*); the Cosy Nook Tea Gardens (visitors would mark their postcard with a cross and the explanation 'We are sitting at this table'); Bird's Tea Garden; Tubbenden Lane; troops at Farnborough Garage (1915); walking wounded relax outside the Red Cross Hospital during the Great War; the High Elms Estate (which hosted an annual treat for Workhouse inmates and a Christmas dinner for the estate workers); Beechy Walk (destroyed by the 1987 hurricane); Clock House Farm; Farnborough Hill; a wonderful group of horse drawn vehicles at the *George and Dragon*; boneshaker open topped buses on the classic 47 route which ran every 15 minutes and terminated at the *George*.

Farnborough's primary attraction was as a gateway from outer London into the best Kentish countryside for ramblers. Not least of its interests, for such folk as came out by horse bus for a few hours in the fields, was its pretty orchards of blossom in spring, and the scent of its ripening fruit in summer; over 300 acres were given to strawberries alone in 1900. Gypsy horse fairs were once held in the village; horses were trotted along the main road to demonstrate their paces to prospective buyers.

7. Cobden Road

- William Pateman (1894-1900)
- Amy Pateman (1896-?)

Dorothy Anderson's family have lived and worked in Farnborough for many generations. The earliest date which can be found is George and Susannah Baldwyn 1584, who are buried in St Giles Church yard. The Baldwin Bible is in a glass case in St Giles – the case was provided by John Lubbock. The Bible was hand written by Edward Baldwin. In 1722 Edward Baldwin was clerk of Farnborough Parish. His wife and daughter were both named Anne. In 1750 Edward Baldwin was a verger. All the Baldwins, man and boy, were choristers up to 1915, when they volunteered for General Haig's army during the Great War. Charles Henry Baldwin was killed in France in 1916 and is buried in Rouen.

In 1736 the population of Farnborough, four and a half miles south east of Bromley, was 553. The families were all inter married - the Weatherley's, Alchornes, Sessions, Stows, Picketts, Olivers and Goodchilds. The Baldwins ran the general stores, the Thatchers, the post office and the *George and Dragon*. The Goodchilds lived at the *Woodman,* the *New Inn* (*Change of Horses*) and the *British Queen*. Dr Fowler, who lived next to the Limes laundry, was a physician and surgeon during the late 1800s.

Farnborough police station opened in 1839 when the village population was 1003. Legend has it that Sir Robert Peel, Chief of the Police, had a friend living at Farnborough Lodge. The main road from London to Hastings (A21) passed near by with plenty of highway men lurking from time to time and he was rather worried for his friend's safety. He requested the police station to be built, to safeguard all travellers. In 1940 a plaque was put on the wall of the police station to commemorate the formation of the 52nd Battalion of the Home Guard. It was removed to Bromley Museum in Orpington when the police station building was sold.

The *Whyte Lyon* was a coaching inn – the horses were watered at the pond opposite. If it was necessary to stay over night they were fed and stabled at the attached stable, which much later was turned into Pratt's Garage. The pub is haunted by a lady smelling of lilacs who passes through the bars. Next to the *Whyte Lyon* was the March family residence. The six brothers and one sister were all sculptors. Only Sydney March married and he had one daughter, who was an artist. The March family worked on Great War memorials in Canada, South Africa and many other countries. The March family home, Godendene, was demolished to make way for the new Sainsbury supermarket. The middle sized English country house was epitomised by the lovely rambling Godendene, with its comfortable bays, sheltered verandah, and then fashionable covering of creepers and other ornamental climbers.

The hill going up towards Farnborough is 'Union Hill' so called as it passed by the Union and Workhouse, which was later Farnborough Hospital. The second turning on the left past the hospital is Hildavale Road where John Alderton, a market gardener, formed the Farnborough Aviation Works in 1909. The first plane built there in 1910 is in the RAF Museum at Hendon. The village pump was beside Brook Cottage on the left going towards the village. There is a triangular green and at the rear stood the pump. It remained there until a few years ago when the Council dismantled it for cleaning and it disappeared. It has subsequently been replaced.

Poplar Cottages between Brook House and the Cedar's laundry were four very old wooden cottages in a terrace, built in the early 19th century. They lost their conservation value when they were updated and modernised. Opposite on the grass verge is a mile stone – 14 miles to London. As you approach the beginning of the Village after passing the Cedar's laundry you would see several weeping willow trees, behind which Farnborough Board School was built in 1873. The Fox brothers and the Weatherlys raised a mortgage to pay for the original building. The boy's playground was around the willow trees.

Starts Hill at the top was the lovely Elizabethan mansion built 1558-61. It has been refurbished and is delightfully kept by the London Borough Bromley Area Health Authority. In the grounds today are several bungalow type buildings for social services. It was a general arable farm in days gone by owned by the Basset family. John Lovibond married their daughter Mada, hence we have Lovibonds Avenue, Mada Road and Bassetts Way.

Darrickwood House belonged to Crofton Manor – it was a home for Army Cadets, they were marched to Farnborough School every day and back again for lunch. On Sunday afternoon they attended a church parade at St Giles. On the approach to the village main road there was a huge post in the centre of the rough road, requesting traffic to go 'Slow Through Village' for the dust. The first shops were wooden. If you entered the door and turned into the right room you were in the barbers shop, if you went left you were in a sweet shop. The original chemist shop was in the same parade run by Mr Snow.

After passing Nile Cottages you now come to Matthews Butchers, originally on this site was the *Coach and Horses* pub with a pond for watering horses abutting the road. It was commonly referred to as 'Old Mother Penfold's Pub' by locals. After Mr Matthews retired the business was purchased by Mr and Mrs Smith. Their grandson ran a very successful business there. Opposite was Chapman's Farm and Session's Farms – today known as Viner's Farm. The two maisonettes in the front of Viners were originally called the New Bakery – this was because when the A21 cut through at the school green Mr Fuller's bakery was demolished and the up to date shop opened there.

On the corner of Pleasant View there is a very nice bungalow. Behind it, almost, were three wooden cottages very old but kept in good condition for the early 30's. Along Pleasant View are two very old cottages built around 1700. Further up is the red tiled Victorian home of the Alchorne family, several other small dwellings and the ex service men's club, and the public footpath through to Tye Lane. At the left hand side as you approach Pleasant View, is an old double fronted house, which was originally Mr Follett's grocers shop.

Opposite was the Limes laundry which was owned by the Ballard family – Mary Ballard married Arthur Goodchild. They were going to emigrate on the Titanic to set up home in Vancouver, but fortunately as it turned out the liner was over crowded and they were referred back to the next voyage. The Titanic sank in 1912 after hitting an iceberg. Almost next door dwelt Dr Fowler, physician and surgeon, who married Mr Goodchild the proprietor of *The Woodman*. They had several sons and daughters.

Charles Goodchild and his wife May kept the *New Inn*. Opposite (which is now referred to as the recreation ground) was the New Inn Field and when the horse drawn carriages arrived from London for the day they were provided with a cooked breakfast, carried across the road and served to the customers from long trestle tables. As many as 180 breakfasts were sold in any hot summer's day. Next to the field was Mr Rainey's garage.

Opposite *The Woodman* was the Parish Room (or village hall) which was built by George St Pierres Harris. His trade mark was the monument on the roof of any building he designed. Next door was the Wesylan chapel, a small corregated iron building, referred to as the Tin Chapel. They had many sewing and knitting classes for the younger folk during the winter evenings. Next to there were the Green Gardens, or allotments, which were tilled by the villagers. Next door, divided by a right of way, was the Cosy Nook Tea Rooms kept by the Wells family. It was a great haunt for cyclists who flocked in their droves to Farnborough – the New Cross Wheelers, the Catford Wheelers and many more. Visitors from the 47 bus terminus at Church Road used to go there for tea – strawberries and fresh cream 6d.

Close by was the village pond, which has been replaced by a housing estate. The roads include The Green Gardens and Ladycroft Way, named after the field behind the swings and roundabout, used now by the sports club. There was a very marshy pond near the hedge, but that was filled in. On the long straight piece of the field was the local football pitch, all the boys who were interested played there each Saturday. The Two Elms, a large house built in the 1600s opposite Church Road was the Stow family residence. Grandfather Stow was the fire master and when word came of a house on fire a rocket would be sent up. The old fire engine was always kept full of water but the horse was in the paddock which was at the corner of Gladstone Road. Old grandfather Stow had to rush around, chasing the horse to put it in the shafts of the fire engine – by the time he had achieved that the old boy was almost as red as the engine.

Gladstone, Peel, Pitt and Cobden Roads were known as the Building Field, because they were the really modern villas of the day. On the left as you enter Gladstone Road was a huge iron constructed building, which was to be the tram terminus – the trams ran as far as Catford, then extended to Downham but the powers in Bromley of the day refused to allow tram lines to be laid to Farnborough. The site was used by Haines Jones garage and Sutty Pumps factory.

The first shop in the parade of shops in the High Street was a florist, it then became Farnborough telephone exchange, with one operator and a few lines. The iron mongers was always referred to as the Oil Shop, because the majority of dwellings had no gas or electricity, they used paraffin lamps for light and the cooking was done on an old black open range fire. There was always a big black pot hanging over the fire – nothing was wasted, all the plate scrapings went into the pot and were eventually turned into soup. The Oil Shop also exchanged accumulators, which were needed to run the radio. Around the early 30s it cost 6d for an exchange and so the radio was only used for the news or special items of particular interest.

There was a boot repair shop, Mr Whiffin's sweet shop, the dairy, paper shop, gentleman's outfitters and haberdashers, which was Mr Crafter's then Mr and Mrs Moodie; Mr Wallis the butcher and the Temperance Hotel, commonly known as Old Mother Savage's Cook Shop. The front room over the shop was kept as a dentist, he came from Orpington on Thursday afternoons to attend to folk. The rest of the road to Tubbenden Lane was orchard belonging to The Shrubberies, a big house on the corner which was demolished with a view to build some flats, a doctors surgery and clinic. The planning application was rejected. The terminus for the 47 bus was Church Road, and there was a horse trough in the centre abutting the High Street.

As you entered Church Road on the left there was a house and big old grocers shop and cheese monger. Mr Pyrke sold everything from a tin kettle to a huge tin bath. Big sacks were on the floor, the tops turned over showing sugar, rice, tapioca and lots more, barrels where villagers took their jam jar or pudding basin along and had jam, syrup or treacle ladled into them. Tye Lane turned off Church Road and at the top on the left Mr Dorey ran a wet and dried fish shop. Next in Church Road was Bob Goodchild the greengrocer, and next door was Baldwin's sweet shop. Then Mr Cooling, the saddler and boot repairer, he also worked hard as a postman. The yellow stock cottages next door housed the first post office and was run from the front room by Mary Sessions, Miss Giles and Mr Steadman, three friends who lived at Elm Cottage. There it remained until the new row of shops was built in the High Street when it was transferred to its present position.

The very old cottage that sticks out on the pavement in Church Road was originally two. Old Grannie Durrant (the great grandmother of Tom Durrant V.C. who was killed at Arnham and Durrant Way is named after) lived in the first one. Her grand daughter used to be sent to the baker every Tuesday for two penny worth of yeast. This old lady used to pull a bit off, roll it round in her old hard worked hands, it looked black by then, and she swallowed it. Her staple diet was a lamb chop, greens and potatoes fresh every day. She was very alert and agile but when she was 95 her daughter who lived close by moved to Bromley so she went to live with them. The other cottage was the Staples family. Miss Staples was employed as a nurse maid. Next there were three cottages, abutting the pavement and where the toilets now are were two flint cottages with long front gardens. Then came the gateway into the orchard, looked after by Fred Goodchild.

The large telephone exchange lay back from Elm Cottage and was built in the 30s. Then there is Mary Harman's home, abutting the path and very old but in excellent condition. The wooden cottage in the yard at the back of it was purchased freehold some years ago for £75. It is now worth a mint. Mr Wickins the baker was excellent, and was well known for his gingerbread – huge slices from an old black tray for an old penny. The bake house at the back was all on the bricks as they term it and every Christmas he would cook turkeys, rabbits, chickens etc for people in the village.

The old *George and Dragon* abutted Church Road and every summer week end when folk were queuing for their buses there would be buskers entertaining the crowd. Sometimes some of the local families, where there were lots of sons, would have a disagreement and start fighting and then the police man on point duty at the blue police box on the corner of Gladstone Road would intervene and it was quickly stopped.

William Thomas Pateman (1894-1900)

William Thomas Pateman was born on 1 November 1894 at Farnborough. Although no address is given on the birth certificate, William Pateman is recorded as living at Stow Cottages in the *1894 Bush Directory of Farnborough*. William Pateman was a general labourer. The mother's name was given as 'Alice Pateman, formerly Reynolds'. I am not sure how Alice could have been mistaken for Mercy! William Thomas was baptized at St Giles on 13 January 1895.

William Thomas died on 22 November 1900, aged 7, at 23 Alexander Terrace, Swanley Junction, Sutton at Hone, Kent. The cause of death was typhoid fever and pneumonia. His father was a farm labourer. The informant was Mary Lewis, sister, present at the death. This was Mary Pateman who married Elias Lewis in 1895. It is possible that William Thomas died at Mary's house at Swanley Junction. This may have been bigger and less crowded than William's house at Cobden Road. Typhoid was a highly infectious disease and Mary would have been concerned for the health of her own son, Charles Lewis, born in 1897. We know he survived because in the 1901 Census, Elias Lewis (son in law, builder's labourer) and Charles Lewis (grandson) were living with Mary Pateman and her family at Cobden Road, Farnborough.

For most of the village children life began in a small, overcrowded, badly ventilated cottage. For a shilling (5p) or so the untrained, but experienced, village midwife would be present to help with the birth. Older children were expected to look after their younger brothers and sisters, but most children from labouring families were sent to work as early as possible so that they could contribute to the family income. During the cold weather many of these young workers, inadequately fed and clothed, living and sleeping in overcrowded conditions, fell easy prey to illness and disease.

Controversial issues at the time William was born were sanitation and the control of infectious diseases. Cholera, typhoid and other infectious diseases were gradually being brought under control, but still existed. The West Kent Main Sewerage Board had been formed and sewers were being laid in the area, but for many of the villagers the wood or brick-built privy was at the end of the garden - sometimes with three seats in a row. In 1877, the Metropolitan Water Board obtained the power to extend the water supply to Farnborough. Mr. Tyacke was the engineer to the West Kent Waterworks in Orpington Road. So a water supply was being provided. But for many homes water was only available from a pump at the wells in the area or from one of the many streams which were shared with the animals regardless of hygiene. A regular task for the older children was to take pails to the pump or stream to get the daily supply of water.

Tuberculosis was ever present and greatly feared. Another killer disease was diptheria which could, and did, wipe out whole families. The wife and children of Augustus Levermore died of diptheria at Crofton in March 1893: Alice Levermore died on 21 March age 37; Alice Mabel died on 8 March age 13; Blanche Augusta died on 10 March age 5; Isabelle died on 18 March age 18 days; and Sybil Beatrice died on 25 March age 1 year 7 months.

1895 started with wintry conditions. At Farnborough School the pipes were so cold and the temperatures in the rooms so low that for several weeks the schools were unfit for the children to attend. Messrs Weatherly and Stow were called in to find out the reason. Questions were asked of all those in authority but it wasn't until Mrs. Curd, a stalwart school cleaner, was approached that it was found she had insufficient wood to light the fires on 28 January. This was a mystery to the Headmaster as she had received the same quantities of coal and wood for the last 4 winters and had never encountered this difficulty before. The school library received 66 new books which brought the total stock to 144 books, at a value of 11 guineas.

Mr. Nettleton Plumbridge (the household where Phyllis Pateman was a maid) of Farnborough Common still remembers his third birthday, on 1 April 1895 when he first attended Farnborough Infant's School, because his mother and the teacher, Jenny Hassell, had great difficulty in getting him over the threshold. But once inside the picture changed for young Plumbridge and soon he was enjoying life with his other young play mates under the watchful eye and kind attention of Miss Georgina Stocks and Miss Jenny Hassell. Miss Stocks, who lived for many years in Orchard Road with her sister after she retired, was not only the Headmistress of the Infant School but was also a founder member of Farnborough Methodist Church and Miss Jenny Hassell was a cousin of Mr. Plumbridge's mother who lived next door to his home. Mr. Plumbridge remembers clearly the day Jenny Hassell married Mr. Brickel of St Mary Cray because he was a page at their wedding.

More visitors arrived at both Infant and Junior Schools during the first quarter of 1895. Mrs. Shannon visited and heard the children sing and recite, Mr. John Goodchild junior arrived with 30 or 40 museum specimens for the use in object lessons and Mrs. Fox of Beechwood gave her usual needlework prizes to the girls in Standards 1-6. In April 1895 the school was treated to specimens in a glass showcase from Messrs Coleman showing the manufacture of mustard, starch and blue and also specimens from Mr. John Reeves, the Turncock, who promised to supply further specimens later on. In May 1895 T.A. Fox Esq., J.P., Chairman of the Board, chaired an entertainment for the children in the afternoon at which a collection was taken which amounted to £2.15.0. This was to be devoted to the purchase of models of animals to illustrate the object lesson and a few days later a further 5/- from Mr. Dyer and several smaller amounts were received making a total of £3.8.1.

In May 1895 the circus came to Farnborough, and school attendance fell dramatically. Both schools were affected and Mr. Ashworth on 22 May considered it advisable not to take any lessons, anticipating the Board's approval. In June 1895 the Rev. E.J. Clarke presented the boys with a complete set of cricketing materials. In August 1895 Mr. Quint entered upon his duties as assistant master in the Mixed School Department and later on that month 30 children went to Crystal Palace for their Annual Treat. Attendance numbers dropped during the late summer and early autumn due to a 13 week fruit and hop picking season to which children from Tugmutton district regularly went. This is probably a reference to the Gypsy children who lived at Tugmutton Common. However, according to the 1891 census, none of James Pateman's children were listed as 'scholars' which indicates that they were probably not attending the Farnborough Schools. In November 1895 Mr. Walter St. John Fox authorized the Headmaster to purchase a new football for the boys.

Amy Pateman (1896-?)

Amy Pateman was born on 17 February 1896 at Farnborough. Although no address is given on the birth certificate, William Pateman is recorded as living at Stow Cottages in the *1896 Bush Directory of Farnborough* and the *1896 Strong Directory of Farnborough*. William Pateman was a general labourer. Amy was baptised on 10 May 1896 at St Giles.

Amy later moved to Chislehurst Road, Orpington. On 26 December 1936 Amy Pateman (39, spinster, 61 Chislehurst Road, Orpington, father - William Pateman, deceased) married Charles Chown (38, bachelor, labourer, 77 Bethel Road, Sevenoaks, father - Charles William Chown, deceased) at All Saints, Orpington. The witnesses were her brothers, Henry and Noah Pateman.

We do not know if Amy Pateman had any children, when she died or where she is buried.

An 1896 Ordnance Survey Map of Farnborough shows Stow Cottages in Church Lane. The map also shows the post office, St Giles church, the grave yard, the smithy, a Mission Room, and two public houses: The *George and Dragon* and *The New Inn*.

The local police force consisted of an inspector, two sergeants and four policemen, based at Locks Bottom. They patrolled the area on horseback and by so doing provided some protection for persons and property. At this period drink was blamed for much of the crime. Ministers, the police and temperance reformers launched assaults against village public houses as being the cause of much trouble.

The Farnborough Schools made another step forward in 1896 when in accordance with the new code football and cricket for the boys and skip rope for the girls were accepted by Her Majesty's Inspectors as physical exercises and qualified for a higher grant. Apart from that it seems to have been rather an uneventful year for both schools until the end of August 1896 when Sir John Lubbock presented the upper class children with 43 entrance tickets to the Zoological Gardens. Mrs. Fox of Beechwood gave 10/- and Mrs. Hamilton Fox of Hollydale a sovereign to the children to spend on this treat on Saturday 12 September 1896.

Whether it was to keep the cost of running the schools down or whether the supply of qualified teachers was insufficient to staff the school adequately, a number of pupil teachers were employed at this time. This meant whilst the children were in attendance the pupil teachers had to teach, but they also had to take lessons on how to teach from the Headmaster. These were generally held early in the morning and in the summer the pupil teachers were hard at work at 6.30am in the morning until 8am, but in winter they started their lessons at 7am until 9am. The autumn of 1896 brought another tragedy to the school, when little Emily Dinan, aged 5, died and was buried with 18 in attendance on 30 October 1896.

A record of staff salaries at Farnborough School dated 1897 reads J.E. Ashworth £6.5.0, M.E. Ashworth £3.15.0, A.L. Ashworth £1.13.4, A.E. Ashworth £1.13.4. In 1903 these had risen to £10.13.5 for Mr. Ashworth and £7.15.3 for Mrs. Ashworth.

22 June 1897 was a day that all school children remembered for many years afterwards. This was the day that Queen Victoria celebrated her diamond jubilee and it was her personal wish that all schools should have a holiday to celebrate this occasion. The celebration took the form of various recreational activities, but Farnborough Board School was treated by Mr. Walter Fox, who was then the Chairman of the School Board, to tea in the large school room, also the presentation to each pupil of a commemoration mug with a picture of the Queen on it. Miss Stocks wrote to the Queen congratulating her upon this happy event and thanking her, on behalf of the school, for her present to the children. She also enclosed a copy of the photograph of that happy occasion – none of the children were wearing school uniforms because these were not introduced until very much later.

On 14 September 1898 the children attended the funeral of the Vicar, who had played such an important part in their schooling. His place was taken by the Rev. G. Lombard who carried on the tradition and visited the schools regularly. In January 1899 Annie Potter died from diphtheria, another of the illnesses which struck so viciously in those days. On 6 March 1899 the girls were transferred to the new Girl's School building, leaving the boys of Standard 4, 5, 6 and 7 being taught by Mr. Ashworth in the main room, Standards 2 and 3 in the large room and Standard 1 in the small classroom under the watchful eye of Mr. Quint and a Monitor. The girls were under the Headmistress Mrs. Ashworth. This was the last of the schools to be built and was sited at the top of Starts Hill where it still remains.

With the opening of the Girl's School all aspects of school life were tightened up. One of the first things to be altered was the prize giving at the end of the year and prizes would only be given to girls who made 95% attendance instead of 90% as hitherto. A fresh copy of the 'Regulations for the Conduct of Public Elementary Schools' was received and pinned to the notice board. T. Hamilton Fox, who was then Chairman of the Board, and H.F. Priter, another member of the Board, were the first to visit the school at 9.15am. They were followed closely by the Clerk of the Board and the Vicar. Additional furniture soon arrived at the new Girls School – cupboards, teacher's desks, chairs, sewing boxes, blackboards, easels and so on. Then came Mr. Weatherley the Vice Chairman who distributed the annual prizes. He was accompanied by the Clerk of the Board and Mrs. Fox of Beechwood who kindly gave as usual 10/- as the needlework prizes and Mrs. Bealby 6/- as second prizes. Before the school closed for Easter in 1899 another new blackboard, desks and chairs arrived and Mrs. Fox of Holydale promised six knitting prizes for next term.

After Easter 1899 Miss Bough, Assistant teacher began work with Standards 1 and 2. But poor Miss Ashworth, who was an assistant teacher at the Girl's School could not resume her duties as she was suffering from nervous exhaustion. On 13 April 1899 Miss Bough informed the Headmistress that she intended leaving the school in June as she considered the work of two Standards too much for her and had accepted an appointment in London. There were now 100 girls on the register in the girl's junior school. Miss Newton, assistant teacher, commenced duties to fill the place of Miss Bough on 5 July 1899.

By the time the bells of Farnborough rang in the new century, even a doubling of the population to 2260 had brought little change to the village. There were still a wheelwright and coach maker and the need for a hay-and-straw dealer, but fewer blacksmiths, one of whom had diversified into bicycle making - within another ten years Farnborough would have its own motor and cycle works. Shops included three florists, and Refreshment Rooms had opened, forerunners of a popular demand. The village Working Man's Club and Reading Room were established in the 1890s, Farnborough Horticultural Society in 1896. The workhouse at Locks Bottom was to be lit by gas in 1901, so doing away with the old paraffin lamps and the necessity for a special Fire Brigade. But it was still a decade away from turning into a hospital although a female infirmary had been built in 1898. Expansion into the Farnborough of today had hardly begun.

The strict discipline imposed by Mrs. Ashworth on not only the scholars but also the assistant teachers seemed to be taking its toll and in January 1900 her daughter Miss Ashworth had time off suffering from hysteria and later on in that same month was compelled to resign her situation owing to ill health. This vacancy was quickly filled by Miss A. Golder, but soon this young lady was to be advised that she had obtained a second class Queen's scholarship and would be admitted as a student into Oxford Training College. It was not only the children that needed discipline – in 1900 one of the pupil's mothers was before the magistrates for assaulting an assistant teacher who had chastised her daughter.

Just seven weeks after the New Year commenced the Farnborough School stoke hole was flooded and so there were no fires in the morning and the children were very cold and damp. Messrs Stow and Weatherley visited to see what they could do in this matter, which may have contributed to the illness of Miss Stocks, which prevented her from attending school. This placed the burden of control and teaching squarely on Miss Hassell. In the Mixed School Mr. Death was also absent through sickness and no doubt a number of the children also had to stay at home. For two days in February 1900 both schools were closed by instructions from the Chairman to enable men to put in the drains through the Girl's yard. Despite these hardships Her Majesty's Inspector gave a favorable report at the end of March, the girls knowing a little more about History and elementary work than the boys, and recommending that a little firmer discipline be maintained, but there was a total grant of £110.10.0 for the Mixed School on that occasion.

On 24 May 1900 all school children were given a day's holiday in honour of the Queen's birthday and also to celebrate the relief of Mafeking. A Fete was given by the gentry of the village. Mr. Plumbridge was traveling to Covent Garden market with his father who had a cart load of strawberries to sell. They had reached Bromley when they heard the news so they stopped and bought several Union Jacks to tie on to the cart. The crowds were so vast and jubilant by the time they reached New Cross that they realized they would not reach Covent Garden that day. They gave away all their strawberries and returned home.

On 10 September 1900 Miss Golder left Farnborough Girl's School and it was not until 1 October that a replacement came along in the person of Miss Mable Spencer. Fourteen days later Miss Newton advised Mrs. Ashworth that she would be leaving as soon as possible to get married and go to America. This again left Mrs. Ashworth short of a teacher, which meant that she had to take Standards 1, 4, 5 and 6 all on her own. When the Junior Mixed School split and the girls went to their new school at the top of Starts Hill the boys took over the bottom school, which was the original school attached to the house, and the mixed infants were housed in the middle school, which was the second school to be built.

By 1901 the Boys School had reached a total of 92 on the books and as the yard was so small the Standards were compelled to take their breaks in two sections during bad weather, but on days when the weather was fair the upper classes were allowed to play on the green in front of the school house. Mr. Plumbridge remembers very well the first violin class that was held in Farnborough School, in fact this was the first musical instrument class to be held. The class was taken by Mr. Stanley Bond and was operated at the Boy's School in the 12-14 year old age group. The cost in those days for a violin was one guinea and the general method of paying was by carol singing at Christmas. A number of scholars clubbed together and went round playing and singing and collected the money, which they then put towards the cost of paying for their instruments. There were also handicrafts carried out at the school, mostly woodwork from about 12 years old.

There were circuses which came to the Village, generally two, one being held in the meadow which was called Diddles Circus. The principal acts were a knife thrower, human butterfly and pony acts; these consisted of two ponies only. The tent held about 30 people at a show and top price for a seat was three old pence. Also at this event a firm called Pettigrew (see Chapter 8 – Fellow Travellers) supplied roundabouts outside the tent area for children to use. The other circus was held in the Orchard Road area and was Fossetts, which belonged to the Fossett Brothers. Mr. Plumbridge remembers that they had an unrideable donkey, as they called it. Archie Lockyer (Robert Pateman married Phyllis Rose Lockyer), a great friend of Mr. Plumbridge in those days had a lot of experience on two of his own donkeys and he got on Fossett's donkey by jumping on backwards, holding on to the donkey's tale and it didn't matter how the donkey kicked it could not get him off. Poor Archie did not get the 10/- for riding it as promised by Fossett Brothers but he did get thrown out of the circus

There was no canteen in the school in the early days and meals of any kind were not provided. Boys and girls went home for their lunch or brought their own sandwiches. Some children came from quite a long way off – the furthest Mr. Plumbridge can remember was Towncourt Farm near Orpington Station, and so those children had to bring sandwiches every day, as they could not walk home and back in time. Another Farnborough activity in the early 20th century was the Farnborough Flower Show. This was quite a major event in the village and was held in Lubbock's Meadow adjacent to the school. Later on it was transferred, by kind permission of Lady Derby, to Holwood Park, where it was held on a Saturday in the summer. The show consisted of all the amateur growers in the area covering fruit and flowers, military bands played, often the Royal Engineers, and the show was given the grand title of Farnborough Horticultural Society Flower Show and was classified as one of the principal events to be held each year in the Village.

1901 Census

In 1901 the census population was 2262. On 31 March 1901 William Pateman (50) was living at Cobden Road, Farnborough, with Mercy (50), Mary (25), Alice (15), Walter (17), Phoebe (13) and Amy (5). Also living with them were Elias Lewis (son in law, 25, builders labourer) and Charles Lewis (grandson, 4). Of the eight children which William and Mercy had produced between 1876 – 1896: five were still living at home: Mary, Alice, Walter, Phoebe and Amy; Henry had moved to Orpington - he married Lottie Edith Tilley in 1902; Noah had moved to St Mary Cray - he married Nellie Honeysett in 1902. William Thomas died in 1900.

In 1901 the children of the Infant School gave two entertainments, the proceeds from which paid for a treat for the children and after the tea special prizes were awarded by T.H. Fox to 23 children of the Infant School. Mr. Elliott took up his post as assistant teacher in the Boys School, a much needed assistant as there were 92 boys in the department. This must have had a very desirable effect on the boys because the Headmaster made a note in his log on 28 May 1901 that there had been no case of corporal punishment to be recorded for a whole month. On 20 June 1901 the schools were closed for a week's holiday in celebration of the coronation of King Edward VII. On 23 August 1901 Mr. F Kelly gave a tea for 22 boys at the school.

According to the *1902 Bush Directory of Farnborough*, William Pateman was living at 4 Cobden Road, Farnborough. An Ordnance Survey Map of Farnborough in 1909 shows very few changes from the OS Map of 1896. The smithy had gone and a lych gate had been added to St Giles Church. The lych gate was a memorial to Rachel Mary Fox who was born 18 May 1826 and died 10 March 1902. The Fox family owned the brewery at Green St Green.

I spoke to Graham Short, who lives at 4 Cobden Road today. He told me that the deeds of the house indicate that Cobden Road formed a boundary between Farnborough Village and neighbouring farms. The 1909 OS Map shows a foot path going between 12 and 14 Cobden Road and leading past Worley's Hole to Tubbenden Farm. Labourers from the village would take this path to and from work.

Cobden Road was at the end of Gladstone Road. Peel Road, Pitt Road and Palmerston Road were built at the same time. They are known locally as the Prime Minister Roads because they were all named after nineteenth century politicians and statesmen. William Pitt was Prime Minister from 1783-1801 and 1804-6. Sir Robert Peel was Prime Minister from 1834-5 and 1841-6. Viscount Palmerston was Prime Minister from 1855-8 and 1859-65. W.E. Gladstone was Prime Minister from 1868-74, 1880-5, 1886 and 1892-4.

Richard Cobden (1804-65) was an English advocate of free trade. The son of a Sussex farmer, he led agitation against the laws restricting import of corn, and they were repealed in 1846. He was impoverished by his public work and was helped by subscription. The houses in Cobden Road are large Victorian villas with several bedrooms and living rooms, and an indoor bathroom and kitchen. They were much bigger than the traditional agricultural labourers' cottage. How, then, had William Pateman managed the transition from the three roomed Stow Cottage to the spacious villa in Cobden Road?

In 1891 William's neighbours in Church Road were 'labourer', 'gardener', 'charwoman', 'carman', 'post mistress' and 'bread baker' but most of them were . 'agricultural labourers'. In 1901 his neighbours in Cobden Road included a 'stage coach groom', 'Commons Keeper' and 'laundress'. William was still a farm labourer but he seems to have moved up in the world in terms of the status of his housing and neighbours. How was this possible?

A clue lies in the fact that William lived close to *The New Inn* (the publican in 1901 was Walter Ferris) and a plaque outside this pub tells us that: 'There was much activity outside *The New Inn* on Sunday lunchtimes. Horses were run up and down the High Street and much buying and selling took place, mainly with Gypsies. Many villagers turned out each week to see the interesting and colourful spectacle.' Perhaps this is how William made his money to enable him to move into Cobden Road?

In 1902 at the age of three years young Leslie Haines left the care of his parents and joined Farnborough Board Infants School. At the age of seven he entered the Boy's School and eventually became Head Boy. This meant that he had to sit near the teacher's desk in order to help. His duties included the marking of composition and arithmetic papers, as well as looking after the class and keeping the pupils in order when the teacher was absent.

Mr. Haines remembers that some pupils came from Farnborough Workhouse and they were known as the Union children, who were usually orphans or children who had been deserted by their parents. They wore distinctive blue jerseys and white collars and were very strictly disciplined. None were allowed to play with other boys until the Master of the Workhouse was satisfied a village family was of a suitable standard. Then a friendship might develop. Each day the Union children were marched to school along the Common. As there were no school dinners the Union children went back to the Workhouse for dinner, but they brought biscuits to eat during playtime.

Up in the Girl's School things weren't going too well for Mrs. Ashworth in 1902. Her new assistant Miss Hodges was away for a considerable time with scarlet fever and Miss Robinson was often away for a few hours with various illnesses. The result of this and the fact that the Board could not provide temporary assistants was that the twelve children recently sent up from Miss Stock's school had to be returned in order to make the Standards in the Girl's School manageable. Despite these difficulties the Inspector's Report on the Girl's School dated 22 April 1902 stated that 'the school is well disciplined and the girl's work as a whole is satisfactory'. This says a lot for the head mistress and her two assistants, Miss Spencer and Miss Hodges, although it was probably the strict discipline of Mrs. Ashworth that kept the standards up. Mrs. Ashworth taught her girls a new song during June 1902 entitled 'God Save our King' which was in preparation for the coronation of King Edward VII.

The next few months were very trying for Mrs. Ashworth with her assistants either leaving or being off sick and many of her pupils were affected by epidemics. In April 1903 her girls performed in the parish rooms during the Easter holidays an operetta entitled 'Bo Peep' and this raised £5.3.4 after paying all expenses. The sum was used for giving a tea to all the girls in Farnborough Girl's School.

On 1 July 1903 the schools were transferred to the Kent County Council Education Committee. The schools were still experiencing staffing difficulties. Mrs. Ashworth applied for and received a teacher on loan from Chislehurst Road School (William Pateman later lived next door to this school) to help fill the gap.

In 1904 one of the pupil's mothers tried to assault one of the assistant teachers but was prevented from doing so by the head mistress until a policeman arrived when the assistant teacher 'went under his protection'. The same woman had assaulted a teacher in 1900. The Board of Governors was made fully aware of such incidents and any action that had been taken.

On 11 January 1904 Mr. George Pond entered upon his duties as assistant master at Farnborough Boy's School and two weeks later Mr. Quint ceased his duties and became attendance officer for the educational authorities. On 28 March 1904 the schools were closed in order that the local parish council could hold their elections in the school rooms. Farnborough was governed by its own parish council, which was elected by the people of the parish.

On 14 October 1904 an assistant teacher accidentally upset the ink on the attendance column of the second class register, and this incident had to be reported in the school log book and reported to Mr. Quint, the Attendance Officer. In December the same assistant teacher gave her notice and left Farnborough School.

On 30 November 1904 the schools had to be closed because the head teachers of the Boys and Girls departments (Mr. and Mrs. Ashworth) had to be away on important business. As a number of the infant children were brought to school by their elder brothers or sisters it was felt best to close all the schools. On another occasion 'the school was closed owing to the prevalence of whooping cough by order of the sanitary authorities'.

The end of 1904 and the beginning of 1905 were very cold months and many a day was passed by the children shivering at their desks wrapped in overcoats to try and keep out the cold. This was due to the lack of fuel supplied for lighting the fires in the various school rooms and also for the boiler to heat the hot water pipes. Some days it was so cold that the Headmaster had to close the Boy's School entirely and send the children home before the morning lessons could really get underway.

On 28 February 1905 Mr. Ashworth ceased his duties as Head Teacher of the Boys School at 12 o'clock. On the same day Mrs. Ashworth also terminated her engagement as Head Teacher of the Girl's School, having been appointed by the Education Authorities for Buckinghamshire as head mistress of one of their schools. Both the Farnborough schools were closed until further notice.

On 13 March 1905 Mr. Charles Rickards took charge of the school on a temporary basis and remained in charge until 10 April when Mr. G.A. Ledgard took up his duties as head master of the school. He only had one uncertificated assistant to help him, although another assistant should have already been appointed, but owing to the scarcity of teachers this had not yet been done.

Also on 13 March 1905 Helena Wise commenced duties as supply Head Teacher at the Girl's School and despite difficulties and not having sufficient material to give the girls needlework lessons she seems to have got well into her stride with other things such as knitting and stitch learning on odd pieces of material. New copy books arrived and arithmetic lessons and writing lessons continued with fervour, but by the middle of April a new head mistress in the person of Margaret Josephine Ledgard took charge of the Girl's School in place of Helena Wise.

On 2 June 1905 help arrived in Miss L.M. Skerry who was appointed assistant in the Girl's School and Miss Hammond was also able to take charge of Standards 3 and 4. School attendance was depleted by such illnesses as scarlet fever, severe colds and throat infections, but despite this and the lack of materials to carry out lessons properly the reports from the school inspectors were favourable and much praise was given to the head mistress and her assistants.

On 5 June 1905 Mr. Thomas Henry Saunders, uncertificated, joined Mr. Ledgard as an assistant master at the Boys School. By the end of the term Mr. Saunders had received notice that he had passed the certificate examination, and this was the beginning of a distinguished career for this future head master. Mr. Haines remembers that Mr. Saunders was well known as a tenor voice in various choirs and this was often heard to good effect during the assembly and prayers at the beginning of the day. After prayers the roll was called first thing in the morning, to which each child would have to answer 'Yes, sir'. Following assembly the routine was the children were marched into their classrooms (boys wore hob nailed boots which made the movement of classes a very noisy affair) and the children sat formally in rows and began the day with arithmetic. This was put up on the board before the day began. Then followed reading, grammar, geography or history. In the afternoon, there was copy book writing and possibly looking after the allotments. There were seven gardens and one for Mr. Ledgard. Each boy who had an allotment to look after also had a junior boy to help him and gardening was a proper lesson, which took place two or three afternoons a week. Vegetables were mainly grown, such as peas, potatoes, carrots etc and a few flowers.

Mr. Haines recalls the early days when the boys of Farnborough School played football on the green at the front of the school house with two willow trees forming one set of goal posts and two telegraph poles the other set. Mr. Haines does not remember the cane being used to excess, only two strokes were given for bullying a younger child, and one stroke for swearing, with another thrown in for good measure, if a boy shuffled his feet or fussed while the caning was in progress. Another use of the cane was for playing truant and this was a deterrent that kept attendances to a high standard. The teachers were very sympathetic towards pupils who had extra jobs to do before or after school. Bobby Sessions often fell asleep during the morning lesson, because he had to be up so early to work at milking and other jobs. The teacher used to say to the boys 'Don't wake him, let the lad sleep'. When Mr. Haines was eight years old there was a very violent storm one night and he saw the tail of Haley's comet. This was also reported in the *Bromley District Times* and in *Lloyd's Weekly News*.

As head boy and a prefect one of Mr. Haine's duties was to wait outside the school for the milkman in order to buy milk and eggs for Mr. Ledgard, who lived in the house alone. It was also his duty to leave the class room at a pre arranged time, collect a bag from the house, and go down to the *Woodman* pub to buy the head master's liquid refreshments. Mr. Haines recalls celebration days such as Empire Day, Sunday School treat, the Forester's Fete and Oak Apple Day. This was not an official celebration but one that pupils celebrated among themselves when they wore firs in their buttonholes.

Empire Day celebrations, held in May, were a great event and children traveled as far as Bromley to take part in specific celebrations. Sir John Lubbock gave a speech and handed each child a Union Jack after the national anthem had been sung and the flag in the school playground saluted. In the afternoon games were played in the fields around the school and much marching and band playing went on.

The Forester's Fete was held in June. Farnborough had two Friendly Societies: the Ancient Order of Foresters and the Loyal Order of Ancient Shepherds, which were connected. They both met at *The New Inn* and J. J. Rumsby was Secretary of one and Scribe of the other. The Foresters met on the second and fourth Tuesday each month and the Shepherds on the fourth Wednesday. The aim of these Societies was to provide financial help to members during sickness and old age and to cover funeral expenses. Members paid an entrance fee and a regular subscription of a few coppers at each meeting. The great incentive was the ever-present spectre of having to enter the workhouse. To many people it was the lowest stage of degradation to enter that institution and eventually receive a pauper's funeral. There was some criticism because these meetings were held at a public house, but it was pointed out that the main business was the collection of subscriptions and that the inn was the only suitable place for the members to meet.

The Farnborough Ancient Order of Foresters was formed on 5 December 1863. The church parade of the Foresters was a very big occasion. The entire 'Court' of Foresters would turn out and meet on the Sunday prior to holding the fete. They met at Green Street Green and were led in procession by the 'Chief Ranger', who was mounted on a white horse, over the hill to Lord Avebury's house, where Sir John Lubbock would then put a gold sovereign into the Forester's bag for collection. The band played and everybody marched back towards the church. The Chief Ranger was dressed in Lincoln Green velvet and wore a large hat with coloured feathers in it. Huge banners, similar to those carried by trade unionists today and needing two men to support them headed the procession with brass bands playing and banners flying. The Ancient Order of Foresters marched up Farnborough Hill dressed in their full regalia with sashes and badges, and accompanied by members of adjoining Courts of the Order, until they arrived at the church. Here a service was held of dedication and prayers were offered for good weather on the following Saturday, so that the fete could be a success.

During the week members of the Court visited houses in the district, making collections for the purchases of items to be used at the fete and on Saturday after many hours of hard work installing all the side shows etc the Fete was underway. Lubbock's Meadow adjoining Farnborough School thronged with happy laughing people of all ages. Athletics were performed, races run, one Court competing against another. The children enjoyed themselves on the roundabouts and other amusements and there was much music from the local bands. Farnborough Court was originally formed from members of the Foxes Brewery and some of their meetings were held in the Farnborough school rooms. The Court met for a final time at the *New Inn* in 1972 and hanging in the saloon bar there is a wall plaque and the 'Forest Axe'.

Within the first quarter of 1906 a new boiler was fixed to the Boy's School, with great hopes that it would dispel all the troubles of heating the class rooms previously experienced. It took several months to get the boiler working effectively, but the comfort was short lived, because in January 1907 the tank which supplied the water to the boiler froze and so no fires could be lit. The Infants School seemed to fare much better in the middle building, although they seemed to have been hit rather more severely with chicken pox and other ailments, which depleted the number on the books considerably during the early part of the 1900s.

On 12 February 1906 the sanitary authorities again closed the school, this time it was owing to an outbreak of 'itch'. Despite all these interruptions 1 March 1906 was a day to make Miss Georgina Stocks very proud. A letter was addressed to the School Managers which read 'Dear Sir, I am directed by the committee to say that they note with great satisfaction the excellent report of H.M. Inspector on your school and they desire me to offer you their congratulations to both Managers and Teachers on the commendable results achieved' and this was signed by Colonel Harrison, Secretary. In March of 1906 a cookery class was formed, which gave an added incentive for the girls of Farnborough to attend their schooling, and records show that attendance improved weekly. By 26 October 1906 there were 126 infants all eager to be taught under the kindly Miss Stocks.

By 1907 the Infant School had become so overcrowded that the Board gave instructions to dismiss all children under the age of 5 and not to admit them until the premises had been sufficiently enlarged. Yet another hazard had cropped up, which hindered the children from attending to their schooling. This time it was the fires smoking and the rooms becoming unusable as a consequence. Several days during April 1907 this happened and the headmistress had to forego the usual scripture lesson. On 1 May 1907 the schools were given a half holiday, as the girls held a May Day Festival.

Van Children

On 28 May 1907 there is a report in the Boys School log that two 'Van' children were admitted. These may have been children from the Gypsy families at Tugmutton. It is interesting to note that there may have been Gypsies in vans on Tugmutton Common as late as 1907. My research suggests that by this date most of the Gypsies – including James Pateman and Urania Boswell – had moved out of their vans and into the cottages in Willow Walk. According to the *1907 Bush Directory of Farnborough* James Pateman was living at 5 Tugmutton which suggests a building rather than a van. None of James Pateman's children are described as 'scholars' in the 1901 census, but five of his children were of school age: Mary Ann (15), Charlotte (14), Phoebe (13), Jane (11) and Elvy (3). It is possible that they attended the Farnborough Schools but were not recorded as scholars in the census. As they were technically house dwellers rather than Van dwellers this might explain why no 'Van' children appeared in the school log before 1907. The 'Van' children of 1907 could have been visitors or relatives of the Gypsies who were living at Tugmutton.

Also in 1907 the walls of the Boys School, which was the original building, had to be underpinned and this interrupted the work in the school rooms as the noise the workmen were making on the walls and the roof was quite considerable. Although this work started in August 1907 it was not finished until January 1908; in fact the Christmas holidays were extended because the work was unfinished.

During this period a number of children were coming from Green St Green to attend the Farnborough Schools, which aggravated the situation as far as accommodation was concerned. So much so that in 1908 a new class room was added to the Girls School. Then in 1909 thirty one girls who lived at Green Street Green left as a new school had opened there.

Farnborough was gradually becoming a large community. This was no doubt due to the influence of the railway coming to Orpington, thereby enabling people to live further out and commute to the city for business. In 1909 there were 144 names on the register of the infant school, 150 in the girl's school and about 150 in the boy's school. The 1909 OS Map also shows the close proximity of Cobden Road to the Farnborough Schools and Tugmutton Common, where James Pateman lived at 5 Willow Walk. A later OS Map of 1933 shows comparatively few changes, with the obvious exception of the Farnborough bypass road, which passed close to the end of Cobden Road and divided Farnborough Village off from Tugmutton.

In 1909 a boy had been employed by local tradesmen for half the day on a number of occasions. Although this was illegal the practice was carried out to some extent and the school authorities tried their hardest to have it stopped. In May 1909 Mr. Pond was hit in the left eye by a cricket ball while supervising the boys at cricket. He suffered a lacerated wound of the cornea and was not able to attend duties for a week or more. On 17 September 1909 a vegetable marrow was cut in the school gardens measuring 2'4" in length.

In 1909 workmen excavated on the side of Gladstone Road, to lay sewers, and deposited all the soil from their digging in the chalk pit at the east end of St Giles church yard. This required a large amount of manual work and gave employment to local people, although a good deal of imported labour was used as well. This all meant additional trade for village shopkeepers and publicans.

1910 was a very cold winter and fires in the Boys School would scarcely burn at all. In the Infants School – the middle school which had been enlarged and improved – there were still more children than could be satisfactorily taught by the existing staff. This was rectified by the introduction of Miss Minnie Pond who commenced duties as an assistant teacher on 10 January 1910. When A.M. Lubbock visited the school in February 1910 he was dismayed to see that the fires in the second room were out and the place was very dirty with soot. On 20 May 1910 King Edward VII was buried and the schools were closed. By now the school managers were taking a greater interest in the school gardens. Mr. Griffin, one of the managers, offered prizes to the value of 10/- for the best kept and best cropped school plots.

There is a postcard of 'Council School Farnborough Kent'. According to the sender's words, penned in 1911: 'These are the Farnborough Board Schools; the front one is the boys and the back one the girls.' Interestingly, the postcard was addressed to Sydney in Australia, but nearly 80 years later was found on an antique dealer's stall in the London area, priced at £2; originally, it probably cost just one old penny.

In 1911 when the census was taken there were 3,210 people living in the parish of Farnborough. This figure included 654 at the Union, and 415 at St Josephs Home. Farnborough is 350 feet above sea level. The village comprised of 1,411 acres, there were 557 dwelling houses and the nearest railway station was at Orpington, one and a quarter miles away. Farnborough was noted for the purity of its air as well as its water for brewing purposes.

On 21 June 1911 the schools were closed to celebrate the coronation of King George V and in November 1911 the boys education was disrupted by gas from the mains filtering through the soil and into the school, which caused several of the boys to be absent due to the effect it had on their stomachs. The gas company gave instructions that all the boilers had to be turned off, and as the school became very cold all the boys were sent home until repairs had been made.

By January 1912 managers stepped in and gave instructions that records of temperatures of the schools be sent to them each week, with a view to making some improvements in the heating arrangements. In February 1912 Mr. Quint paid a visit to the absentees and reported that several parents had kept their children away from school owing to the coldness and it was found that at 9am in the morning the thermometer only registered 37 degrees Fahrenheit. Clearly something needed to be done with the old school.

1912 for the infants seemed fairly smooth running, although in March and April quite a few children had illnesses of one type or another and Florence Still was away with diphtheria. On 24 May 1912 Mr. Lubbock took 12 of the oldest girls to London to pay a visit to the National Gallery and Queen Victoria's Memorial Statue. Not to be outdone, on Empire Day the headmaster took 12 boys to London to see Queen Victoria's Memorial. . In July the Infant School was closed for a fortnight owing to the prevalence of chicken pox.

Overcrowding in the Boys School was becoming a problem once more. The 3rd class had 65 children on the books and the inspector asked that some rearrangement be made. There were 34 boys attending Farnborough School from the children's home, although they seemed to be away as often as they attended, either due to special treats or illnesses, which necessitated the entire home being isolated. At long last a new boiler was installed during the summer holidays of 1912 and a warmer winter was hoped for by both teachers and pupils alike.

In December 1912 the school gave its first carol concert, during which the whole school sang songs and carols and afterwards exchanged presents among their friends. Another bright spot in a cold world was when Keston Fish Ponds froze over and especially during the Christmas holidays when children could spend happy hours skating and sliding and generally being healthy, boisterous children in the open air.

Early in January 1913 H.M. Inspector considered that the number of children in attendance was far in excess of the accommodation available in the three rooms and with only two assistants to organize the school the headmaster could not possibly carry on satisfactorily within the code laid down by the Kent Education Committee. There were 156 boys on the roll. This meant that all grades had to be taught at similar times and little help could be given to those who were falling behind. Mr. Ledgard wrote a letter to the Kent Education Committee laying out the difficulties of the school and pointing out that the same situation arose in 1911. At the end of March 1913 Mr. Ledgard received a reply from Mr. Henry Barnes which stated that the

Managers had instructed Mr. Ledgard not to admit any new boys who resided outside the parish of Farnborough until further notice. In June 1913 the Bromley Guardians withdrew 37 boys attending Farnborough School and sent them to other schools in the neighbourhood. Although there were so many names on the register during the summer months quite a number of children were away for a considerable number of weeks either fruit picking or hop picking. According to the *1913 Bush's Directory of Farnborough*, the rateable value of the parish was £17,756, and William Pateman was no longer living at 4 Cobden Road.

Farnborough 1914

A 1914 'skeleton map of Farnborough and District' shows The Manse, Farnborough Hall, Topcliffe Grange and the *George Inn* in Farnborough Village. The Farnborough Schools are also shown, plus Locks Bottom, Crofton Hall, Crofton Court and Crofton Pound. Also on the map are Crockenhill (where William Pateman was living in 1876-1880) and Orpington (where William was living in 1914).

Bush's Directory of Farnborough 1914: 'At one time doubtless Farnborough was more frequented than at present as being situate on the main road to Tunbridge Wells and Hastings numerous coaches passed through daily. At present in the summer season large numbers of excursionists by road are in the habit of making it their rendezvous. A considerable area has lately been built upon and the population is rapidly increasing.

The Baptists have a Chapel in the Wellbrook Road and since the development of the Green Street Green District have built an additional one in that portion of the Parish, whilst more recently still the Wesleyans have opened a new building near the centre of the village. The industries of the Parish are almost entirely agricultural, fruit growing forming a large proportion. Farnborough is now governed by a Parish Council, elected annually in March'.

Members of the Parish Council in 1914 included Messrs Griffin, Higgs and Stow. The same trio had been Farnborough Commons Conservators until it handed over its powers to the Parish Council in 1904. They were also 'school managers' at the Farnborough Council Schools. And so the same small group of fruit growers still held their grip on power in Farnborough Village at the outbreak of the Great War, which was to change everything forever. Other local notables included the Rev. E.J. Welch (Rector of All Saints) and Miss Giles (Post Mistress).

In 1914 William Pateman was living at Chislehurst Road, Orpington. Four of his children – Alice (1889), Phoebe (1892), William (1895) and Amy (1896) – had been baptized at St Giles, Farnborough. But only one of his children – Mary – was married there, in 1895. And none of his children were buried there. Most of William's family and descendents were baptized, married and buried at All Saints, Orpington. This signifies the shift by William and his family away from Farnborough and towards Orpington at the turn of the century and the years leading up to the Great War.

William Pateman appeared on the courts page of the *Kentish Times* on 10 April 1914: 'For allowing his horse to stray in Chislehurst Road, Orpington, William Pateman, Chislehurst Road, was fined 2s 6d and 3s 6d cost. Police constable 416R said he found the horse, which was subsequently claimed by the defendant.'

Mercy Pateman is listed in the *Bromley Directory* as living at Chislehurst Road, Orpington, from 1924 to 1928. This address changed to 61 Chislehurst Road from 1929 until 1939. The *1939 Bromley Directory* lists seven other Patemans living in the Orpington area: Noah (169 Poverest Road), Noah (38 Wellington Road), Harry William (13 Aynscomb Angle), Frederick (Noli, Chislehurst Road), Simon William (25 Elm Grove), Henry & Son (Dipper Slip, Fordcroft) and Edith (Birchwood, St Mary Cray). Their story will be told in the next volume of this family history, *Corke's Meadow: the life and times of Noah Pateman and his family*.

8. The Boswells

The Boswells were the most well known of the Tugmutton Gypsies. Levi and Urania Boswell were the 'King and Queen' of the Kent Gypsies, and when they died their funerals (which were attended by thousands of people) were reported in the national press.

Levi Boswell (1847-1924)

Levi Boswell (1847-1924) = Urania Lee (1851-1933)
- Sansparella Boswell (1865-1921)
- Ada Boswell (1869-1939)
- Percy Herbert Boswell (1872-1947)
- Georgina Boswell (1877-?)
- Kenzer Boswell (1877-1949)
- Norah Boswell (1879-1934)
- Levi Boswell (1882-1934)

Levi Boswell was born in 1847 at Wanstead, Essex. His father was Daniel Leavy 'Levi' Boswell (baptized 25 December 1832 at Gedney Hill, Lincolnshire). His mother was Justinia Deighton (born 1834, Rainham, Essex). Levi had a full brother, Herbert (1850, Plumstead) and three half siblings (fathered by Zachariah Boswell): Emily (baptized 30 July 1856, Leytonstone), John Neverfess (baptized 22 May 1859, Shoreditch) and Esther (baptized 2 March 1862, Finsbury).

In 1851 Levi Boswell (26, tinker and grinder, Gloucestershire) was living in the 'open air' on Plumstead Common with his wife, Justinia (27, Rainham) and their children Levi (4, Wanstead) and Herbert (10 months, Plumstead). Living with them on the Common were: Samuel Lee (33, chair mender, Middlesex), his wife and five children; Plato Boswell (29, tinman and brazier, Worcestershire), his wife and child; and James Deighton (47, tinker and grinder, Hertfordshire), and his eight children.

Zacharia and Justinia Boswell appeared in the 1861 Census at Hammersmith, London, in a tent. Zacharia (36), Justinia (38) and Levi (14) were all chair bottomers, born, respectively, in Worcestershire, Raynham Essex and Scushershaw (?) Essex. The other children named were Kate (8, Plumshop, Kent); Emily (4, Hammersmith), and John (2, Deptford, Kent). In neighbouring tents were: Levi and Mary Ann Boswell and family; William and Sarah Roberts with children Sampson, Cecilia and George; William and Charlotte Roberts with their younger children Townsley, Mary A., William, Charlotte and Lucy.

Levi married Urania Lee and they had seven children: Sansparella 'Sansby' (1865), Ada (1869), Percy Herbert (1872), Kenzer James (1877), Georgina (1878), Norah (1879) and Levi (1882). Levi and Urania appear on the 1881 Census at Stratford, Middlesex, with an unnamed daughter aged 12, born Shoreditch, Middlesex and a son Herbert aged 10, born Willesden, London.

Levi and family appear on the 1891 census in a caravan and tent at Crofton Road (near Tugmutton), Orpington, Kent. The details are: Levi (44, 'lets out donkeys and ponies', born Wanstead, Essex); Urania (44, Not Known); Georgina (14, domestic servant, born Kensal

New Town, Middlesex); Nora (12, scholar, born Dulwich, Surrey) and Levi (9, scholar, born Chislehurst, Kent)

The Boswells were living at Willow Walk in 1910 and 1911. They lived at 7 Willow Walk, which is still standing today and is now known as Gypsy Cottage. James Pateman lived at 5 Willow Walk and would have known Levi Boswell and his family very well. There are two photographs of the Boswell Camp at Locks Bottom. One photograph shows 'Smiths and Careys making pegs (clothes pins) and drying grass. These families traveled in the bow top wagon and would set up a bender tent for extra space. (Scott Macfie Albums, Lock's Bottom, Orpington, Kent.).' The other photograph is captioned 'On the steps of her vardo home, this Gypsy girl worked on a wooden flower stand to sell to the gaujos. (Photographed in the Boswell Camp at Lock's Bottom, Orpington, Kent, October 1912.).' This little girl was Omi Johnson and the photograph was taken by Fred Shaw on 17 October 1912. Levi Boswell's death was reported in *The Times*, on 8 May 1924:

Death of a Gipsy Chief

'The death has occurred at Farnborough, Kent, of Levi Boswell, the head of the Boswell tribe of Romanies, who have relatives in all parts of the world. His widow, Urania Boswell, known as the Gypsy Queen, is a descendent of the original Gypsy Lee. For 300 years the two great Romany tribes, the Boswells and Lees, have intermarried. Levi Boswell was formerly a widely known horse dealer, but for some years he had been living in retirement in a Farnborough cottage. The funeral at Farnborough this afternoon will be attended by Gypsies from all over the country.' Levi Boswell's funeral was reported in *The District Times*, on 9 May 1924:

The passing of a Gipsy king – Death of Levi Boswell – Yesterday's funeral pageant

'The passing of a great Gypsy King, Levi Boswell (whose spouse is allied to the famous Lee family, and is popularly known as 'the Gypsy Queen') occurred on Thursday of last week, at the age of 77 years. The great Boswell was known to every horse fair and fete in the country. As a horse dealer he was without an equal, and his aid was sought by many in search of a horse if not a kingdom – and they could always rely upon Boswell for a square deal. Then, what of his herds of donkeys – and such donkeys they were. The young people tested their capabilities by the thousands in every quarter of the country at fetes, shows and fairs.

Levi Boswell had acquired the property which he occupied at Willow Walk, Tugmutton Green, Farnborough, and here the family (and donkeys) thrived. Now, alas, there is a widowed Gypsy Queen, and all that remained of the famous Boswell was committed to mother earth at Farnborough churchyard yesterday (Thursday) afternoon. There was an attendance of nearly a thousand people, many of whom came from various parts of the country, and there was a large percentage of the Gypsy tribe amongst them. Shortly after two o'clock the cortege formed up at Willow Walk, Tugmutton Green, and here the funeral car with the six fine black horses attached, the coaches containing the members of the bereaved family, and the many floral tokens of affectionate regard for the late veteran representative of the fraternity in the district were photographed.

The procession from Willow Walk followed the main road by way of Locks Bottom, and as it wended its way towards Farnborough it grew larger and larger, and the special contingent of police drafted into the neighbourhood did excellent service. Bus after bus set down its living freight, until the churchyard was peopled in every part. The funeral car presented quite an imposing spectacle. The coffin, a magnificent casket, was uncovered, but over the horses were thrown purple palls with gold decoration, while on the near horse of the leading pair a postilion was mounted. The canopy of the car was covered with floral emblems. Upon arriving at the church the Vicar (the Rev. E.J. Welch) took the head of the cortege, and the company filed into the church, the widow and the members of the family, including the sons and daughters of the late Mr. Levi Boswell, following immediately behind the coffin. The service was conducted by the Vicar.

After the concluding sentences of the Church of England service, Mr. West (Gypsy camp commissioner) gave out the hymn, 'Safe in the arms of Jesus', which was heartily sung by the congregation, and this was followed by a short address by Mr. West. He said they were only bidding their friend farewell that afternoon until, 'the day breaks and shadows flee away.' He spoke of the frequent occasions that the Boswell family had been bereaved during the past eighteen months, and of the evidence given by the late Mr. Boswell during his illness that his heart had been touched by the Holy Spirit. It had been the speaker's privilege to visit him on several occasions, and after praying with him, Mr. Boswell would lay his hand upon his heart and say, 'I am trusting in the dear Lord Jesus'. If the churches had within them more men of the stamp of their departed friend they would be the better for it. The speaker concluded by commending the widow and her family to the care of Almighty God.

The floral tokens came not only from the bereaved family, but from all parts of the country. They comprised harps with broken strings, horseshoes with whips of gold laid across them and beautiful wreaths, crosses and sheaves of roses. The funeral arrangements were carried out by Messrs. W. Owen and Sons, of Farnborough.

Urania Boswell (1851-1933)

Urania Lee was born in June 1851. Her father was Abraham Lee (born 28 May 1830; baptized 13 June 1830, Charlton, St Luke), a traveling brazier tinker of Charlton. Her mother was Mary Smith (alias Sarah 'Pol' Lee) of Devil's Dyke. Urania had seven siblings: Lizzy (1854, Bethnal Green), Nathaniel (10 July 1856, Bethnal Green), Abraham (1857, Chingford), Sarah (baptized 2 October1859, East Peckham), Randall (baptized 22 April 1861, Buckhurst Hill), Job (born 1863) and Matilda (baptized 26 September 1869, East Peckham.). The *Kentish Independent* reported the following incident involving Urania Boswell on 29 June 1889: 'Selina Boswell (alias Dighton) [her husband, Levi, would have traditionally used his mother's maiden name of Dighton] aged 40, married of no fixed home, was charged with fighting in High Street, Plumstead. PC Sargent said he was called to the prisoner who insisted on fighting a man. He separated the parties but the prisoner followed the man and kept irritating him, and as she had stones in her hands he took her into custody. The prisoner, a masculine Gypsy woman [Urania was no beauty] with jet black ringlets and wearing an immense Spanish hat, said the man in question was the husband of her daughter, only 19 years old with an infant, and he wished to make her run at the donkey's head when giving children rides. She told him his conduct was unmanly and she threatened to knock his brains out. The prisoner had never been charged before and was discharged.'

Urania Boswell died on 24 April 1933 aged 82 years at 7 Willow Walk, Farnborough. She was the 'widow of Levi Boswell, horse dealer'. The cause of death was 'carcinoma of stomach and degenerative myocarditis'. The informant was 'Mary Ann Georgina Costin, daughter, 7 Willow Walk, Farnborough.' This was her daughter, Georgina Boswell. Urania's death was reported by *The Times*, on 25 April 1933: 'Gypsy Lee, Queen of the Kent Gypsies and eldest daughter of the original Gypsy Lee of Brighton, died at her home near Farnborough, Kent, yesterday.' A full report appeared in *The Kentish Times,* on 28 April 1933:

Queen of the Gypsies dies – forecast her own passing – "Death bird" sign for Gypsy Lee

'Outside the tiny bungalow at Farnborough, where for the last 40 years she had spent nearly six months in every year and where now she lies in her coffin, 'Gypsy Lee's' brother told a *Kentish Times* representative of his sister's passing. Even while he was talking some of her relatives arrived and entered the door to gaze for the last time upon her, as she lay, framed in white, with a bunch of flowers on her breast, with the peaceful smile of death on her old, wrinkled face. It was a queen, lying in state, for Mrs. Urania Boswell, widow of the late Mr. Levi Boswell, had been, since her husband's death, the accepted leader of the great clan of Lees and Boswells, almost the last great families of the Romany tribe.

It was like a scene from a Borrow novel, to stand within those walls, hung round with faded photographs of the late queen and her family, with the spotless, polished brass work round the fireplace, and to hear her brother, now the last remaining member of her many brothers and sisters, talking to another of her relatives in the quaint Gypsy tongue, unintelligible to all 'outsiders'. Outside was the group of cottages and bungalows that formed the encampment, an old caravan that still seemed to bear the dust of its many miles of travel, a battered old trap in which she once rode often, a few hens scratching in the dust, her favorite cat still as a statue. It was as though one had been transported back through the years.

And her brother, Mr. Job Lee, 'Joby Lee, well known to all the sporting fraternity throughout the country', as he described himself, a gnarled figure of a man, tough as oak, despite his 70 years, with knotted hands that spoke eloquently of many hard fights in his boxing booth, and mahogany face that told as no words could have done of years spent in the open air, told in simple words of days and nights spent in ceaseless watching at his sister's bedside during the last weeks of her life.

Gypsy Lee, who was 81 years of age, was the daughter of the equally famous Gypsy Lee of Brighton, and like her parent she had a nation wide reputation as a palmist and fortune teller. Among her patrons were people from all classes of society, from the poorest to the greatest in the land. Lords and dukes were not ashamed to listen to her advice, and throughout the district she was a familiar figure in her motor car as she drove about. She owned property in many places, and spent six months of the year at Ramsgate, where she had a home, Margate, and other resorts. The other six months were spent as a rule in her cottage at Willow Walk, Farnborough.

Her husband, Mr. Levi Boswell, the king of his clan, died in 1924 and the magnificence of his funeral at Farnborough is still remembered. The traditional cortege with black horses and outriders, and the following of hundreds of his 'subjects' will be repeated today (Friday) at Mrs. Boswell's funeral. She leaves three sons, Herbert, Kenza, and Levi Boswell, and a daughter, who are also well known, though the daughter is at present lying ill in hospital. One of the sons is a well known figure at Blackheath with his donkeys.

Like all her family, Mrs. Boswell was an expert horsewoman, and she used to drive and break horses for her husband. She met with many accidents from time to time, and some 40 years ago when the wheel of a trap in which she was driving broke she fell and was dragged for a long distance by the runaway horse. Seven years later when driving a mule she was again thrown, and her face was badly cut, but she walked nearly half a mile to Farnborough hospital, bleeding profusely. Scarcely had she recovered from this accident when a branch of a tree under which she was sheltering fell on her.

Three weeks ago she had a fall just outside her door, and when a milkman arrived to deliver there he found her lying unconscious. He roused the family, and she was got into bed, and she never got up again. For the last fortnight her brother was with her, and during the last few days of her life he sat by her side night and day, never sleeping and hardly moving away to change his clothes.

Now let him tell his story of how she foretold her own passing. Try to imagine him, standing before the little thatched cottage in the encampment, in his shirt sleeves, with a bright colored waistcoat half open, his hands thrust deep in his trousers pockets; his head bare to the winds, looking far less than his years, despite the many accidents he has suffered. 'On the morning before she died,' he said, 'a rain thrush came and sat on the tree behind the house. She said to me "My time is getting near now. It is the first time that thrush has been here for three years. My time is getting near and we shall have rain now for a couple of days." Then her death bird came over at night time. It is a bird we never see, and we don't know what it is. But it has a sweet noise. It sang 'sweet, sweet' and it came over three times that night. "Now it is over" she said, "tomorrow morning about six or seven o'clock I shall say adieu to you all." The next morning about a quarter or half past seven, a minute before she died she said, "Good bye to you all. I have finished," and she died.

She never lost her faculties from the time of her illness till her death, nor did she lose her courage, although she knew she was dying. There must be something stoical about the make up of this family, for her brother told our representative that his sister had 'dated him' and he would die 'three years next March'. 'She told me so, and so it will be,' he said, 'and you will remember then what I told you.' And there was not a tremor in his voice, no more emotion than when he told us of his own life, of his triumphs in the boxing ring when he traveled the country with a boxing booth and 'beat all the champions at 9st 6lbs' or of his circus experiences, his falls and broken bones, or of the time when he was injured by a roundabout and lay with broken bones underneath it for an hour.

The funeral takes place at Farnborough Churchyard this afternoon (Friday) and all this week members of the family and friends have been hastening from all parts of the country to be present. It is not every day that a queen dies, and Gypsy Lee will be given a royal funeral. The new queen is Mrs. Selina Lee, wife of Mrs. Job Lee, whose home is in Essex. Arrangements for the funeral have been entrusted to Messrs W. Owen and Sons of Gladstone Road, Farnborough'. A report of Urania's death also appeared in *The Bromley Mercury,* on 28 April 1933:

Queen of Gypsies dies – foretold her own death – arrangements for "Royal" funeral – huge assembly expected at Farnborough this afternoon

'Gypsies from all parts of Kent will attend the funeral at Farnborough today of their Queen, old Gypsy Lee, otherwise Mrs. Urania Boswell, who, by dying early on Monday morning, fulfilled her own prophecy. To relatives who gathered around her bedside a week ago today she said, "On the third day I shall die," and according to her only brother, Job Lee, this was the second occasion that this strange woman had foretold the date of her death. When her husband, Levi Boswell, died in 1924, she is stated to have said, "I shall die in nine years and it will be cold". The ninth anniversary of Levi Boswell's death, at the age of 77, is on Monday. Mrs. Boswell would have been 82 in June.

She was the eldest daughter of the original Gypsy Lee, of Brighton, whose name she assumed to follow her famous mother's profession as palmist. Although she owned a large house at Margate, where she spent the summer, she was most at home with members of her clan in the encampment at Tugmutton, near Locks Bottom. Here, for 35 years, she spent the winter days in a small bungalow that was once a caravan. When I visited the encampment a few hours after her death, I was directed to a little thatched cottage. Here live her two eldest sons, Herbert and Kenza, who have been cripples from birth. They sat on either side of the fire and invited me to sit on a chair just inside the door. Above my head was a gaily colored parrot, on a stand. The bird did not utter a syllable all the time, as though fully sensible of the atmosphere of gloom. On the wall behind me was a large photograph of the procession at the funeral of old Levi Boswell. My attention was directed to this by the brothers with pride.

We had not been speaking a few minutes when there came a timid tap at the door and in walked a woman, weeping. 'It's her oldest friend,' Kenza whispered to me. Aloud he asked her, 'Did Mrs.--- tell you?'. The woman answered, 'No, no one told me. I knew'. 'Well, said Kenza, 'it's no use crying. She's gone, just as she said she would.' Later he told me his mother had been ill for several weeks, and when I asked him what was the cause of death he curtly answered, 'Worry, that's all I can say it was.' According to the medical certificate heart failure caused Mrs. Boswell's death, but recently she had been greatly worried by the grave illness of her daughter, Norah, who is in Farnborough hospital. Altogether there are three sons and three daughters, as well as several grandchildren and great grandchildren.

Despite her age, she had a wealth of the true Romany black hair, and, with a large feather curling round her 'cart wheel' hat, she was a familiar figure in Bromley and district. Before removing to Farnborough she lived for a time in Burnt Ash Lane. For many years she had walked with the aid of a crutch. This was because she dislocated her right hip when she fell backwards across the shafts of a cart. Her husband having been a horse dealer, she was accustomed to horses. Once when she slipped from the saddle while riding she managed to keep one foot in a stirrup although she was dragged for several miles. On another occasion she was thrown by a mule, and although her face was badly cut she walked to Bromley hospital, where she remained three months.

During the past 20 years hundreds of people, who believed she possessed mystic powers to foretell their future by reading their hands, have visited her little bungalow. Many of her 'clients' have been distinguished people who came in cars, and she also frequently visited racecourses and private houses in the West End of London in pursuit of her profession. Vanderbilt, the American millionaire, is said to have once visited her in disguise. She immediately recognized him, the story goes, and warned him not to make his next journey across the sea. He was drowned when the *Titanic* went down. Just before the King's illness she is supposed to have written him that he would be ill, but that he would recover and be able to go shooting again. When her executors visited her bungalow on Monday evening they found in a cupboard a bundle containing 97 £5 notes. She is said to have died worth more than £5000. This is in addition to her jewelry, which includes a £5 gold piece, numerous gold rings, some of the 'buckle' type, weighing between two and three ounces; and gold brooches.

The funeral procession will leave the encampment at 2.30 this afternoon and proceed to Farnborough Churchyard, where old Levi Boswell is buried, via Crofton Road and along the main road. A magnificently plumed hearse will be drawn by six black horses, one of which will be ridden by a postilion in traditional livery of black velvet jockey cap, blue broadcloth coat with four rows of brass buttons, blue crush breeches and riding boots. Herbert and Kenza, the two sons, will ride in separate coaches, each drawn by two black horses. Most of the other members of the clan are expected to make the two mile journey on foot. A service in the church will be conducted by the Rector, the Rev. R.G. Griffith, and at the graveside another service will be conducted by Mr. West, a member of the clan, who is a missioner.

Gypsy Lee's lying in state began on Tuesday, and each day since there has come numerous relatives, friends and Gypsies from other camps to pay their last respects. Her body, dressed in her nightgown and strewn with white narcissi, was placed in one of the best coffins of Messrs. W. Owen and Sons, the Farnborough undertakers, have made. It was of oak, with moulded corners, and on the raised lid was a brass plate inscribed: 'Urania Boswell, Gypsy Lee, died April 24th, 1933, aged 81'. Members of the family, and not the undertaker, will screw down the lid. In the coffin they will probably place her dresses and other articles, in accordance with custom.

Just inside the door of her cabin, four candles have burned since the coffin was placed on trestles where her bed used to be, and all the time relatives have kept watch. On the walls of the cabin, which has always been kept spotlessly clean and which shines with brass and pretty china, are hung photographs of the Gypsy Queen and her family through three successive generations. Many of them are of Gypsies who are said to have died on the day that Gypsy Lee foretold. 'She dated me as well,' Job Lee, her only brother and last of the Lees, is reported to have said on Tuesday. 'Two years next March, she told me, and I know I'll go then for she's always been right.' None of her relatives troubled to wear mourning clothes. 'We believe that when a person is born, then's the time to mourn because of what they must go through. But when they die, that's release for them, and we don't grieve. Give a man a sixpence when he's alive, rather than flowers when he's dead. That's what we believe.'

Urania was buried on 11 May 1933 at St Giles, Farnborough, in the same grave as her husband. Urania's funeral was reported by *The Times*, on 29 April 1933:

Funeral of the Gypsy Queen – Romany Pilgrimage to Farnborough

'About 600 Gypsies from all parts of the country gathered at Farnborough, Kent, yesterday for the funeral of their Queen – Gypsy Lee (Mrs Levi Boswell). The funeral procession started from the encampment where Gypsy Lee lived in a bungalow. A short service was conducted in the encampment by Mr. A. West who for many years has been known as the Gypsies' missionary. The coach was drawn by six jet black horses, adorned by a profusion of black plumes. On the leading horse was mounted a postilion wearing a uniform of dark blue.

Norah, Gypsy Lee's favourite daughter, who has been lying seriously ill at Bromley hospital, begged the authorities to allow her to be present at her mother's funeral, and was permitted to do so. In the coaches behind the hearse were Herbert and Kenza, the 'Queen's' two sons who have been cripples from birth, Levi, her youngest son, Georgina, another daughter, and Job Lee, her brother, the last of the Gypsy Lee family.' A report of Urania's funeral also appeared in *The Kentish Times*, on 5 May 1933:

Gypsy Lee's Burial – amazing scenes at Farnborough – 15,000 people present – black horses and plumed hearse

Amazing scenes were witnessed at Farnborough on Friday when the funeral of Mrs Urania Boswell, known to thousands as 'Gypsy Lee', took place. Throughout the day huge crowds of people had been pouring into the village, on foot, in buses and coaches, in cars, carts, lorries and vans, in fact in every conceivable kind of vehicle. The route of the funeral cortege was thronged for hours before hand, and at half past two, when it was due to start from her old home, the roads were lined with dense masses of people. Many had taken up vantage points in trees and half way up telegraph poles, while on every inch of pavement and on the grass verges spectators were standing three or four deep. At Farnborough Park there was a huge crowd. There was another near the schools, where the road branches off into the village and outside *The George and Dragon* and along Church Road the crowds were denser than ever.

It seemed as though all the world and his wife were determined to get a view of this unusual spectacle, for it is not every day that one can witness the funeral of a Gypsy queen, for so Gypsy Lee was, the accepted queen of the Kent Gypsies and leader of the great clan of Lees and Boswells. Rich and poor mingled in one great concourse. They had come from all parts of the neighbourhood and many from even farther afield, from Bromley, from London, and from the ends of Kent. For hours before hand it was almost impossible to get a seat on a bus to Farnborough, while motor coaches unloaded still more hundreds into the village.

Meanwhile outside the little encampment in Willow Walk, where the queen had made her home for over forty years, there were further amazing scenes. Crowds had collected there, too, and Press and cinema camera men, as well as dozens of amateur photographers, added to the congestion in this narrow country lane. Many of the professional photographers came provided with step ladders, while others levied toll on neighbouring houses to obtain the means of raising themselves above the heads of the crowd to get a better view. Outside the house stood a magnificent hearse, topped by tall waving plumes of sable black, and harnessed by six splendid black horses, with purple trappings. A liveried coachman sat still as a statue in the driving seat, his whip held at the correct angle and by the head of the off fore horse stood an outrider in uniform of soft blue velvet, brilliant with glittering buttons, with a velvet jockey cap on his head, ready to mount when the procession started.

Within there was a vivid scene as friends and relatives of the dead queen gathered to gaze for the last time on her familiar and loved face before the coffin was closed. And visitors, too, came in to satisfy an idle curiosity or to take snapshots of an unforgettable event. In one corner sat three tragic figures, the two crippled sons, Herbert and Kenza Boswell, and the daughter, Mrs Norah Rose, who had left hospital only the day before, against the wish of the authorities, in order to be present at her mother's funeral. Round them clustered the other near relatives and members of the clan, united in their sympathy.

Before the coffin was finally closed Mr Abraham West, London City Missioner to the Gypsies, conducted a short and simple service in the yard of the encampment, just for the family. There was a stir outside as the bearers shouldered their burden and carried it out to the waiting hearse. There was a rustle like the sound of wind in trees as a hundred hats were removed and the crowd stood silent and still, while the coffin was raised into place.

The statue like coachmen moved into life and slowly the cortege moved off towards Grafton Road. At the head walked Mr W. Owen, representing his firm, accompanied by Mr West.

Then came the hearse, its plumes nodding in the breeze, the buttons of the out rider glistening in the spring sunshine. Inside the coffin lay, heaped over with flowers, huge wreaths from mourners all over the country, conspicuous among them a large one in the shape of an empty chair, and among these rich emblems a few simple bunches of flowers.

Behind the hearse came two coaches, each drawn by a pair of jet black horses. In these rode the immediate mourners of the family, including her sons and daughter, who had been assisted to their seats. Behind them again came a procession of over 900 members of the clan, walking two by two, some in sombre mourning garments, others in their ordinary workaday clothes bringing a touch of gay colour to the scene. And behind and around them the watchers took up the march, adding numbers to the procession every minute.

At a solemn pace the train moved gradually along, from Willow Walk into Crofton Road, round by Farnborough Park, into Farnborough Common, where all traffic was held up to let it pass. A bare headed throng stood in silence as it passed, a silence that was only broken by the frequent clicking of cameras.

As they passed Farnborough hospital the crowd was added to by almost the entire staff of the institute, as well as most of the inmates. All work had ceased in the great building, window cleaners' ladders stood tenantless against the walls, the laundry and other parts of the establishment were emptied to catch a glimpse of the procession as it passed. Further along the road, too, the school had emptied itself to watch, and through the village, every shop and doorway and every window framed watching faces. Crowds everywhere, growing denser as the church was neared. Harassed policemen, dozens of them it seems, kept back the throng and kept the roads clear.

In the lovely little village churchyard there were still more people, but inside the old grey stone church there was a welcome stillness and cool peace. At the door the Rector, the Rev. R.G. Griffith, and Mr West, in their white surplices waited to meet the coffin. Presently the opening sentences of the burial service announced its arrival. Borne shoulder high down the nave it was put on to high trestles, while the clan filed quietly into their seats. An occasional muffled sob broke across the hopeful words of the service, but otherwise nothing interrupted the silence save the voices of the clergymen.

After the teeming throngs outside, after all the display of the long procession to the church, the short simple service stood out in striking contrast. The 90th Psalm, a chapter from the Epistle to the Corinthians, read by Mr. West, a few brief prayers, and the funeral was over.

As the party left the church the clouds, which had gradually been overshadowing the sun, broke in the first drops of a sharp thunder shower, but the mourners passed on to the graveside, the grave of her late husband, Levi Boswell, opened now to receive the dead queen. The plain oak coffin, with its brass handles and the simple brass plate bearing the words, 'Urania Boswell – Gypsy Lee – died 24 April 1933 aged 81 years', was laid in place. Round the grave stood the mourners, their swarthy faces lined with tears. The children of the dead queen were almost in a state of collapse as the service proceeded but a soothing word from Mr West, who, after 30 years' work among the Gypsies probably knows them more intimately than any other 'foreigner', calmed their tears. Two verses of 'Abide With Me', sung unaccompanied, brought the service to an end. It was an impressive moment, to stand in that lovely little churchyard, framed on all sides with tall trees, between whose branches one glimpsed long vistas of distant green fields, and to listen to the hymns, sung by a hundred voices.

Mr West then gave a short address to the mourners round the graveside. 'My dear friends', he said, 'I stand here today not only as a representative of the London City Mission, under whose auspices I work as a missionary to the Gypsies but I also represent that vast family of Gypsies scattered all over the country who are to-day mourning the loss of our dear sister, Urania Boswell.'

He learned from the press that it was their custom not to mourn their dead, but he said it would be out of harmony with their warm, affectionate nature, if in any sense they appeared to be cold, callous, or indifferent at the loss of one whom they loved. That same spirit of mourning and affection which Christ showed at the grave of Lazarus animated the hearts of every Gypsy standing there today.

When he looked round that great throng he thought of those who had come from distant parts of the country to see one whom they loved and respected greatly, laid to rest. When he thought that Margate, where she had often lived, was represented there by Deputy-Mayor (Councillor P.B. Osborne), and his wife, he knew how loved and respected she had been in that great Kentish wintering place. There was no doubt that Urania Boswell had always conducted herself in such a queenly fashion to gain the love and respect of all who knew her.

They were not looking down sadly for Urania Boswell in the grave. She had risen and his great word was not only to that throng but to Romany as a whole, that they should live for that great reunion with her in the land where roses ever bloom.' Urania's funeral was also captured on a British Pathe News reel which can be downloaded from www.britishpathe.com. Commenting on the funeral of Urania Boswell, *The Orpington Journal*, asked on 6 May 1933:

Are Gypsies romantic?

'Thanks to the star writers and 'sob sisters' of the London Press there was a crowd of many thousands to witness a Gypsy funeral procession at Farnborough last week. The *Daily Impress* said there were 50,000 present. Readers will arrive at the approximate number by dividing by four, a system which may generally be applied to anything local which appears in its columns.

'Talkie-tone' operators, photographers, reporters were there in dozens and if they, in common with the thousands of others who came from miles around, were disappointed at their 'Romany holiday' it was their own fault. It is a good many years since George Borrow first wrote of the 'Romance' attaching to Gypsies. Today the same idea is industriously pursued by the titled daughter of an ex-lord chancellor. To judge by the remarks passed by those who witnessed the funeral procession there are at least 15,000 persons who in future will want a lot of persuading that Gypsies are romantic.'

The inscription on Urania's gravestone in the churchyard at St Giles, Farnborough states: 'In loving memory of Levi Boswell, The Gypsy Chief who passed away May 4th 1924 aged 77 years. A light is from our household gone, A voice we loved is still, A place is vacant in our home, Which never will be filled.' And when Urania died they added this: 'Also of Urania

Boswell (Gypsy Lee), beloved wife of the above, who died 24 April 1933 aged 81 years. Reunited home at last.'

In many photographs of Urania Boswell she looks every inch a Gypsy Queen, dressed in all her finery and the trademark feathered hat. In one such photograph she is staring royally at the camera with one hand on her hip and the other clutching a large black bag. In another photograph she is standing on the steps of her vardo, wrapped in a black shawl and smoking a clay pipe. There is also a photograph of her standing outside her vardo in 1930. Although aged 79, her hair was still jet black. On 2 February 1934 a news item appeared in *The Orpington and Kentish Times*, concerning:

The estate of the 'Gypsy Queen of Kent'

'In the Probate Court on Wednesday, the President, Sir Boyd Merriman, had before him a motion in the matter of the late Mrs. Urania Boswell, 'Gypsy Queen of Kent', who owned a large house at Margate and lived in a caravan at Farnborough and who died recently.

Mr. Grassbrook moved for the appointment of a chartered accountant, pending suit, the testatrix having died in April 1933, leaving three sons and three daughters. Counsel said she died intestate. There was an alleged will and codicil of April 1933, of which the defendants were the executors. This action had been started by the plaintiff in order to get a pronouncement against the will and codicil, so that the estate could be administered. During the pending of the suit it was desirable to have an independent person to look after matters.

Counsel for the defendants, the executors of the will, opposed an administrator being appointed, as it was only a small estate, viz. £5000. Except for some cottages, there was nothing that required looking after. His lordship thought it a case in which an administrator should be appointed pending suit, and ordered accordingly.'

Journal of the Gypsy Lore Society

The Rev. D.M.M. Bartlett wrote about Gypsy Lee's death in the Journal of the Gypsy Lore Society (Volume XIII, No. 2, 1934): 'On Friday April 28 1933 there took place in the Churchyard of St Giles, Farnborough, Kent, the burial of Urania (Reni) Boswell, wife of Levi Boswell and daughter of Abraham and 'Pol' (Sarah) Lee, of Brighton, aged 81 years.

The Funeral and those present
Great crowds, variously stated as 15,000, 20,000 and even 50,000 thronged the roads and churchyard. Gypsies, estimated at 600, formed the core of the procession: there were actually 52 in the party of mourners. The nearest relatives were Reni's sons, Herbert and Kenza (James) Boswell – both cripples; Levi, another son; and Nora and Georgina, her daughters, Nora having left a hospital bed to attend her mother's funeral. With them was Job Lee, Reni's brother, like her the child of Gypsy Sarah, the Brighton 'Queen', and Abraham Lee, 'the original Gypsy Lee' according to some of the reporters. Let me here explain that I make a rather copious use of inverted commas, implying that statements so designated are asserted as facts by newspapers, usually of small repute, whose names I do not mention: but that I myself by no means necessarily concur. It was a rainy day, and the glory of the 'six draped black horses and postillion in jockey cap' was somewhat spoiled as the 'cortege' made its slow way through crowds variously reported as being silently respectful, or 'according to Gypsy rites, a laughing and happy company.' *The Times* says, no doubt more truly, that 'the crowds were

drawn by the mystery, the aloofness and the fascination of this inscrutable race, which moves among us without contact, about whose very origins there is uncertainty and questioning.'
At the graveside the last rites were conducted by the Rev. R.G. Griffiths, Rector of Farnborough; and Mr A. West, 'the Gypsies' parson', made an oration prior to the starting of the procession, but not in Romani, as wrongly reported. He is quoted as saying: 'I can speak Romany, but I never do. It is a habit I try to break them of!' – an attitude of which other Romane rashaia will profoundly and indignantly disapprove. Urania was buried in the grave of her husband.

They were stated to have been married at 'the Red Church', Bethnal Green Road, in 1869. But a search kindly made by the present Vicar revealed no record. Several of the papers have vivid descriptions of the grief of some of the mourners at the final scene - the *Morning Post* quotes Job Lee, the surviving brother as saying: 'We mourn when people are born, but when they die there is release for them and we do not grieve'.

Disposal of the Caravan and Effects
The traditional burning of the vardo did not happen in this case. Nevertheless, something of the ancient attitude toward the dead was maintained in the decision that the living wagon, 'well equipped with gold and silver ornaments', should have its door shut immediately the funeral was over, and there stand exactly as she ordered it, till it should drop to pieces with age, decay and exposure to the elements. 'All her gems and priceless souvenirs will rot away and only when a visitor comes will the door be opened.' Some scepticism may be excused to the likelihood of this provision. The Rector of Farnborough writes: 'Folk were allowed to see the body in the coffin up to the time of the screwing down of it; I think a charge was made.'

The Will and Disposal of Property
The actual internment being over, it is stated – and also, I may add, categorically denied – that the will was read, and that the executor, Major G.K. Salmon, was granted police protection: whether from the crowds, or from possibly disappointed relatives, we are not informed. The provisions of the will, and the amount of money which it concerned, also vary much in the different accounts: £15,000, or otherwise £5,000, was 'left to the surviving sons and Norah' or 'divided among her children, Levi being left £100.' Three houses at Brighton, some jewellery, and ninety-seven five-pound notes, 'kept just handy by her' under the bed, were among the property. One paper states that £15,000 was left to an unnamed person. Another mentions 'considerable bequests to charity': yet another, that she died intestate. The Rector of Farnborough tells me that 'There has since been a dispute over the will,' and that 'there may be developments. The two cripple sons claim to have been defrauded'.

The Succession
There seem to be two elements more or less constant, of which the second is by far the most important: Money or property, possessed either by the individual or the family, generally comes into account. Urania Boswell was wealthy; and Morjiana Lee of Blackpool, who is apparently succeeding to Reni's high position as 'Queen of the Gypsies', has doubtless been successful financially. Selina Lee (wife of Job, Reni's brother), the new Queen of Kent, will presumably also be among the well-off class of Gypsies. But on the whole, family, and all it implies, has most to do with the succession. Not necessarily direct descent but the possession of blood in which flows the richest blend of the real old families, unmixed with gajo or mumper taint. If a good alliance can be added to this, so much the better. Let us test this in the three cases before us. Reni's father was Abraham Lee, 'the original Gypsy Lee' and her grandfather 'Fighting Zacki Lee'. If to this sufficiently illustrious descent we may add her

alliance with Levi Boswell, 'The Gypsy Chief', her social position is established. Morjiana Lee, the new Queen, is herself of Wood, Lee and Cooper stock, the daughter of Alice Wood and Henry Lee, with 'Blind Nelly' Wood and Peni Cooper for her grandmothers. An undoubted 'royal' lineage!

Predictions of the death of herself or her relations.
There is one other point concerning Reni which is not without interest. She bore the character of a prophetess with, apparently, more justification than the mere possession of lucrative dukkering powers. Especially she was able to foretell danger and death. The testimony to this really does seem too good to be lightly dismissed. Her prophecies relate to herself, her family, and a number of people, some of whom are well-known names. They may be classified as follows:-

On the Saturday before she died she said: 'On the third day from now I shall die and on that day it will rain.' Previously in 1924 she had said of herself: 'I shall die in nine years and it will be cold.' [She did – and it was.] Her brother Job added: 'On Friday she said that the storm-thrush would sing before her death. It sat in that tree there and sang on Saturday … when she died it left. I heard the death-bird crying in the night of Saturday. You might say it was an owl, but it is a different bird and you would never see it, no not if there were 20,000 of you, you wouldn't see that bird because it cannot be seen! It is the death-bird.'

Ten months ago she predicted that her son Levi would not live longer than February. He was buried on February 2nd at Bromley, Kent, his mother wishing that the two crippled sons Herbert and Kenza should ultimately occupy the spaces left in the family grave at Farnborough. The fulfilment of this prophecy is remarkable.

She has 'dated' her brother Job, who is to die in March 1936. Job says he is sure he will go then, for she was right also foretelling the deaths of his wife Selina's brother, and others whose departures she had foretold to the very day.

Predictions of events in the lives of the gaje
In 1897 she foretold that, 'Queen Victoria will see the leaves fall four times before she goes to her long rest'; that 'the King who comes after her will die long before my turn comes'; and that 'after that the world will change – not all at once, but we'll live to see strange things, you and I. Men will fly like birds, and swim under the water in boats shaped like fishes. They'll sit by their own firesides and listen to voices and music a thousand miles away, same as if it was in the room.'

At the previous Henley Regatta [1911] she warned Mr Vanderbilt most urgently not to sail in the maiden voyage of the 'Titanic', which was then being built. These seem to be the outstanding instances of a gift of foretelling the future believed in by herself and her relatives. Her reputation in this respect does really seem to be something more than that of a gosveri dukkerimangri which she has shared with many other Gypsy sybils; and while one's inherent scepticism makes one loath to give complete credence to the above assertions, an account of her funeral would be, perhaps incomplete without some mention of her claims.'

Sansparella Boswell (1865-1921)

Sansparella ('Sansby') Boswell was born in 1865. On 9 May 1898 Sansparella Boswell (33, spinster, 25 Bradley Street; father - Levi Boswell, hawker) married Nelson Lee (34, bachelor, labourer, 25 Bradley street) at St Luke's Church in the parish of Victoria Docks in the County of West Ham. Nelson signed the marriage certificate but Sansparella just made her mark. The witnesses were William Smith and Mary Buckley.

Sansparella had six children: Theodore Lee (born 20 November 1886), Nelson Lee (alias John Smith), Francis Lee ('Frank'), Ann Lee (born 1 April 1896, married Stanley Potter on 10 December 1923), Walter Lee (born 20 May 1897) and Louisa Lee (born 15 March 1898). Sansparella died in 1921, aged 56. We not know where she is buried.

On 7 August 1921, Louisa Lee (22, spinster, 10 Sabbuton Road, father - Nelson Lee, dock labourer) married Daniel Hunt (22, bachelor, hawker, 1 Rathbone Road, father - Charles Hunt, boiler maker) at St Luke's Church in the parish of Victoria Docks in the County of West Ham. They both signed the wedding certificate. The witnesses were Henry Gladding and Nancy Lee

Louisa had seven children: Daniel Hunt (married Mary), Gertie Hunt (married Kenny McLeod), Amy Hunt (married John Willing), Charlotte Hunt (married Elfie Ellis), Lylie Hunt (married Harry Bowers), Louisa Hunt and Charles Henry Hunt..

Charles Henry Hunt married Doreen Ivy Downs and they had two children: Kay Yvonne Hunt and Tony William Hunt. I met Kay Hunt (now Newman) and she gave me a lot of useful information about Urania Boswell, her great-great-grandmother.

Ada Boswell (1869-1939)

Ada Boswell was born in 1869. She married John 'Jack' Gumble (born 1858, dealer) and they had eight children: Levi (1887-1970), Randle (1893-1926), Kenzer (1895-1920), Lily (1906-1923), Bertie (1909), Jimmy, Rainie and Herbert (married Elvie, five children, lived in Plumstead).

John Gumble died on 25 May 1927, aged 69, at 35 Norton Road, Belvedere. He was buried at Plumstead Cemetery. Ada Boswell died on 10 December 1939, aged 69, at 138 New Road, Belvedere. She was also buried at Plumstead Cemetery.

Levi Gumble married Delilah Smith on 13 February 1915 and they had eleven children: Norah Rose (1912, married Joseph Buckley, eighteen children), Lilian (married Walter Eastwood, seven children), Rainie (1919, married Belcher Lee), Ada (1922, married Belcher Barnard, eleven children), Levi (1923, married Lucy Upton, seven children), Bertie (1925), Mary Ann Georgina (1926), James (1927-29), Lila (1930, married Edward Lee), Linda (1931, married Alan Dibsdull, three children) and Herbert (1932).

Ada Boswell and many members of her family lived on the Belvedere marshes, which had a large Gypsy settlement until it was washed away in the 1953 floods. Many Gypsies then settled in the nearby areas of Abbey Wood and Plumstead, which still have sizeable Gypsy populations today. For more information about the Belvedere Marsh Gypsy encampment see *Memories of the Marsh – a Traveler Life in Kent* by Betsy Stanley (Romany and Traveller Family History Society, 1998)

Percy Herbert Boswell (1872-1947)

Percy Herbert Boswell was born in 1872. There is a photograph of 'Albert son of Levi and Urania Boswell' taken by Fred Shaw at Locks Bottom, Orpington, Kent on 17 October 1912. The photograph shows 'Albert' sitting on a box in front of a camp fire in the Boswell yard at Tugmutton. A pail is suspended on a kettle crane and Albert is holding sticks to feed the fire. He is well wrapped up in a coat, scarf and hat. His weathered face is looking directly at the camera and his crutches are on the ground next to him. I am assuming that this is Percy Herbert Boswell who was crippled from birth; but it could equally be his brother, Kenzer James Boswell, who was also crippled from birth. Percy died on 23 March 1947 aged 75 at 7 Willow Walk, Farnborough. He was buried on 27 March 1947 at St Giles, Farnborough, in the same grave as his parents. The following inscription was added to the tombstone: 'Percy Herbert Boswell Son of above Died 23rd March 1947 Aged 75 years.'

Georgina Boswell (1877-?)

Georgina was born in 1877 at Kensal New Town, Middlesex. At the time of the 1891 Census she was a 14 year old domestic servant. Georgina later married a Mr Costin and she was present at her mother's death on 24 April 1933: 'The informant was Mary Ann Georgina Costin, daughter, 7 Willow Walk, Farnborough'. Georgina was also at the funeral of Urania Boswell on 11 May 1933. We do not know when Georgina died or where she is buried.

Kenzer Boswell (1877-1949)

Kenzer James Boswell was born in 1877. He was crippled from birth and an article about him appeared in *The Bromley Mercury* on 27 August 1926:

Farnborough Man as Donkey King – A Picturesque Figure

'Any day in midsummer there can be seen on Blackheath England's donkey king, Kenzer Boswell, a picturesque figure who for over 40 years has held the donkey stand opposite the main gates of Greenwich Park, and who has seen more young Englanders in the saddle than any man breathing.

Boswell is a true bred Romany, and proud of the facts that his mother (now an octogenarian) is the famous Gypsy Lee, and that when his father (Levi Boswell, the Gypsy chief) died two years ago he had a larger funeral than anybody can recollect, larger even than that of a king. He was eight years old when he started to help his father with the donkeys on Blackheath, for the family have had the stand for over 70 years. He is a bachelor and his home is at Willow Walk, Farnborough, where the Boswells live on a farm which they run, in a pretty thatched cottage of which Boswell speaks in terms of pride and affection. For 200 years his family has carried on the business of purveyors of fair tackle to country families in Kent in connection with their private sports gatherings, and he claims that they are known in almost every village.

The donkeys come over to Blackheath from Farnborough every morning and return at night. Things in this line, however, are nothing to enthuse about. Formerly he had nearly 60 donkeys, but nowadays they are expensive; before the war six animals could be bought for the price charged for one nowadays. Nor are the donkey seasons so good – there is no money about owing to the strike. Recollections of Blackheath mentioned by the subject of this notice cover the period when the Heath was under the care of the Metropolitan Board of Works, before the era of roundabouts and steam organs. In those days there were coconut shies, however, and the nuts were placed on tins, because the Board of Works would not allow a stake to be driven into the ground. Halcyon days, those, for the expert shots.

Fifty years ago there used to be horse and donkey riding, and other sports on the Heath on Sundays. Earlier the horse and donkey ride was from the Vanbrugh-park end to the main gates; then at Camomile Bottom; both are now done away with. Still, in these times Boswell's family own more donkeys than any other in the country, and he claims that he knows as much about those animals and about horses as any man in the kingdom.

Boswell explodes the Weller contention that nobody has ever seen a dead donkey. 'I've seen hundreds of them dead,' he remarked; 'at Grove Park I had 19 die in a day in a meadow into which they had been turned, and I have always believed they were poisoned.' The popular idea is that donkeys are hardy, need little care, and are content with short commons and a long stick. This belief is quite wrong. Boswell says that they are very delicate and require warmth and attention; they cannot stand the cold. He is his own vet and has never had outside advice for his animals in his life.'

Kenzer died on 22 April 1949 aged 72 at 7 Willow Walk. He was buried on 28 April 1949 at St Giles, Farnborough, in the same grave as his parents and his brother Percy. The following inscription was added to the tombstone: 'Also Kenzie Boswell, Who died April 22nd 1940 Aged 72 years.'

Norah Boswell (1879-1934)

Norah Boswell was born in 1879. She married Edwin Rose, and they had one child, Dorothea Rose (born 13 August 1897, baptized 12 September 1897 at Farnborough). Norah died on 16 March 1934 aged 55 at the Tugmutton encampment, Willow Walk, Farnborough. Her death was reported by *The Bromley Mercury*, on 16 March 1934:

Gypsy Queen's Favourite daughter – death at Farnborough

'Another of the famous Boswell Gypsy family will be buried at Farnborough today. She is Mrs Norah Rose, the youngest daughter of Mrs Urania Boswell, the late Gypsy Queen of Kent, whose favourite child she was. She died on Friday in the encampment at Tugmutton, Farnborough, where her mother died last May. It will be recalled that her youngest brother, Mr Levi Boswell died in Bromley only seven weeks ago. Mrs Rose had been in delicate health for some years and she appeared obviously ill at the funeral of her brother. When she took to her bed a fortnight before her death she sent for her only daughter, Mrs Walsh, who came over from Ireland and remained with her until the end. She was aged 55 and the wife of Mr Edwin Rose, of Lewisham. For many years she acted as housekeeper for her famous mother and until recently she also tended her two eldest brothers, Herbert and Kanza, who have been cripples since birth. She also leaves two sisters.

The funeral today will be as quiet as possible, the family having decided not to make such elaborate arrangements as were made for the funerals of the old queen and her son. Only two black horses, instead of the customary six, will draw the hearse. The cortege will leave the encampment at 2pm and the interment will be in Farnborough Churchyard at 2.30. It is hoped that Mr Eli West, the London City Commissioner to Gypsies, will conduct the service. Messrs W. Owen and Sons of Farnborough are the undertakers.' Norah was buried on 19 March 1934 at St Giles, Farnborough, in the same grave as her uncle Nathaniel. Her grave is on the other side of the path and hedge from that of her parents and brothers. It is said that she was buried 'the other side of the hedge' because she married a Gorjer (non Gypsy). Her funeral was reported by The *Bromley Mercury* on 23 March 1934:

Gypsy Queen's Favourite daughter – funeral at Farnborough

'Mrs Norah Rose, youngest daughter of Mrs. Urania Boswell, the late Gypsy Queen of Kent, whose death was recorded in last week's *Mercury*, was laid to rest in Farnborough churchyard on Friday, in the grave of her uncle Nathaniel Lee. Immediately opposite, on the other side of the path, is the grave of her father and mother. Comparatively little interest was taken in the funeral. No crowds lined the route of the procession as at the funeral of the old queen, although about fifty people gathered near the churchyard. Only a dozen or so saw the cortege leave the encampment at Tugmutton. The hearse was drawn by two black horses. Other members of the Lee and Boswell clans followed in two motor vans, while a number walked to the church. Altogether the mourners numbered about seventy. They included Mr. Edwin Rose, the dead woman's husband; Mr. and Mrs. Welch, son in law and only daughter; Messrs Herbert and Kenza Boswell, her crippled brothers; Mrs. Ada Gumbell, her sister; Mr. and Mrs. Job Lee, uncle and aunt; Mr. and Mrs. Leonard Lee; and Mr. and Mrs. Levi Dighton, cousins.

A service in the Parish Church was conducted by the Rector, the Rev. R.G. Griffith, and an address was given by Mr. Abraham West, the London City Missioner to Gypsies. 'It is not long since we laid to rest our queen mother and our brother Levi,' said Mr. West. 'Now we meet again to say farewell to our sister Norah. The early Christians had a beautiful way of parting with their loved ones. They never regarded death as something terrible, like a nightmare, but rather as a sleep, a bidding good night, assured that at the breaking of day they would rise to a blessed resurrection. Death, in my opinion, is sweet, in that it means the passing over from one life to another. We are laying Norah's tired body in the grave, but her soul goes marching on. It was often my privilege to sit and read and pray with Norah and never had I a more attentive listener.' Mr. West added that their warmest sympathy went out to those who would miss her very much. The interment was conducted by the Rector. Messrs Owen and Sons of Farnborough were the undertakers.

Dorothea (Dolly) Rose Boswell married Leo Welch, a coachman, of 25 Granville Road, Lewisham. They lived in Ireland. There is a photograph of 'Gypsy Lee's grand daughter Dolly Welch and husband Leo' taken at the seaside, and they have a boy child with them, possibly their son.

Levi Boswell (1882-1934)

Levi Boswell was born in 1882 and he later lived at 2 Walters Yard, Bromley High Street. On 15 April 1901 Levi Boswell (20, bachelor, horse dealer, 6 Moorlands Road, father – Levi Boswell, horse dealer) married Mozella Lee (20, spinster, 6 Moorlands Road, father – John Lee, horse dealer) at St Mary's, Plaistow. The witnesses were Seaman and Britannia Breeds. Levi had several children: Zacariah (born 1905, Marvels Lane, Bromley), Murzella (married Fred), Jack and Eileen (1919). Levi died on 29 January 1934, aged 52, at 25 Roslin Way, Burnt Ash Lane. His death was reported by the *Bromley Mercury* on 2 February 1934:

Gypsy Queen's son dies – Levi Boswell of Bromley

'Levi Boswell, youngest son of Mrs Urania Boswell, the late Gypsy Queen of Kent, died early on Monday at Roslin Way, Burnt Ash Lane, Bromley, aged 52, he had been ill a fortnight. He leaves a widow and four children. He was well known as a dealer and was a familiar figure in the Bromley district. Latterly he had occupied part of a house in Roslin Way, but on Monday his body was removed to a relative's house in Walter's Yard, High Street, Bromley, pending the funeral. It is understood that his children wished to have him buried in his parent's grave in Farnborough churchyard. This grave contains sufficient space for two more burials, but the old 'Queen' had it reserved for her two eldest sons, Herbert and Kenza, who lived at Farnborough. Herbert and Kenza have refused to allow their brother to be buried there, so the burial will be in Plaistow Cemetery, Bromley, today. The cortege will leave Walter's Yard at 2pm. It is anticipated that the funeral will be on a much less elaborate scale than that of the old 'Queen', who's burial last May was witnessed by hundreds of people from a wide area." Levi's death was also reported by the *Kentish Times* on 2 February 1934:

Death of Levi Boswell – Son of former Gypsy Queen

'Bromley will witness today an unusual spectacle – a Gypsy funeral – for Mr. Levi Boswell, youngest son of the late Mrs. Urania Boswell, former 'queen' of the Kent Gypsies, is to be buried with traditional pomp in Plaistow Cemetery this afternoon. There will be the usual six black, plumed horses to draw the hearse, and it is expected that many Gypsies will be present. It is hoped, too, that Mr. Abraham West, London City Missioner to the Gypsies, will assist the Rev. W. Gowans, Vicar of St Mary's, Plaistow, in conducting the funeral service.

Mr. Boswell, who had been living in Bromley for some years, and was a well known character in the neighborhood, died at 25 Roslin Way, Burnt Ash Lane, Bromley, on Monday, after a comparatively short illness. He had been suffering from bronchial pneumonia. He was 52 years of age, and the youngest son of the late king and queen of the Kent Gypsies. It will be recalled that the funeral of his mother in May last year at Farnborough churchyard attracted a huge crowd of sightseers to the village. He was conscious almost to the last, and gave directions for his funeral to members of his family who were with him. At his own request the body was removed to his old home, 2 Walters Yard, High Street, Bromley, where the coffin remained, surmounted by a burning candle until today. It was hoped that the funeral would take place at Farnborough in the same grave as the mother and father, but it was not found possible to overcome certain difficulties.

Mr. Levi Boswell formerly assisted his father in his business as a horse dealer, and since his death he has been in business for himself in the Bromley district. His favorite pastime was darts and he was a popular member of *The Duke's Head* darts team. The funeral procession will pause for a moment outside the public house on its way to the cemetery this afternoon. The service at the cemetery is expected to start at three o'clock. A touch of poignancy is added to the occasion by the fact that his family is making frantic efforts to trace his wife, Mrs. Mozella Boswell, and the youngest of his four children, Eileen Boswell, aged 15, who disappeared some four years ago and had not seen him since. It is hoped that they may be found in time for them to be present at the funeral. Arrangements for the funeral have been entrusted to Messrs Francis Chappell and Sons, of High Street, Bromley.'

Levi was buried on 2 February 1934 at Plaistow Cemetery, Bromley, Kent. His funeral was reported by *The Bromley Mercury* on 9 February 1934:

Gypsy Queen's son buried – Impressive Spectacle at Bromley – favourite pony follows hearse

'With time honoured Gypsy ceremonial, Levi Boswell, youngest son of Mrs Urania Boswell of Farnborough, the late Gypsy Queen of Kent, was buried in Plaistow Cemetery, Bromley, on Friday. Levi, as recorded in last week's *Mercury* died the previous Monday at 25 Roslin Way, Burnt Ash Lane, Bromley, after suffering for about a fortnight with bronchial pneumonia. Aged 52, he had lived in the Bromley district for many years and was widely known as a dealer. Before he died he made a request that his body should be removed to his old home at 2 Walter's Yard, High Street, Bromley. This was done and, in accordance with Gypsy custom, members of the family took it in turn to keep an unceasing watch over the open coffin which was surmounted by a burning candle.

The unusual spectacle of a Gypsy funeral attracted many hundreds of people, and additional police were on duty to control the crowds. Walters Yard was so packed with people it was only with difficulty that the hearse, drawn by the customary six black horses, could approach the house, and in order that the hearse could be turned it was necessary to unhitch the two leaders. Each horse was covered with purple trappings, and riding on the outside leader was a man wearing a jockey costume of purple velvet. The hearse, surmounted by black plumes, was almost covered with a mass of wreaths. One, placed in a prominent position at the back, was in the shape of a large horseshoe, containing a representation of a horse's head and a silver riding whip. The inscription, in silver letters read: 'From Murzella and Fred' – his daughter and son in law.

'Nigger', Levi's black favourite pony, followed his master to the grave. He was led immediately behind the hearse by a cousin of Levi's, Leonard Lee, son of Job Lee, the only brother of the late queen. Near relatives, including Levi's two eldest brothers, Herbert and Kenza, who have both been cripples from birth, came next in two coaches, each drawn by a pair of black horses, and about a hundred members of the Boswell and Lee clans followed on foot. Efforts have been made without result to trace Levi's wife, and the youngest of his four children, a girl, who went away about four years ago and had not been seen by him since.

Traffic was held up as the procession moved down the High Street, through lines of people standing on the pavements four and more deep. A brief halt was made in the Market Square as the cortege came abreast of the *Duke's Head* public house. It was here that Levi indulged in his favourite pastime of dart playing, and his fellow members of the team stood outside at the salute. Further crowds of people were gathered all along the route, through West Street, College Road and Burnt Ash Lane.

Members of the family were, with one or two exceptions, the only people admitted to the cemetery chapel, and they filled the little building. A simple service, comprising Scriptural readings and prayers, was conducted by Mr Abraham West, London City Missioner to the Gypsies, who gave a touching address.

'We have met once again under a cloud,' he said. 'It is not long since we met in Farnborough to say farewell to our dear old mother, Urania Boswell, and now, within a few months, we have met to say farewell to her boy, Levi. Very few of us expected to meet again so soon in such circumstances. We were looking, rather, another way. It seems so strange that the younger should be taken before the elder, but we just have to bow to the will of God and the laws of nature. Here we pay humble tribute to one who has been called to his rest. And our sympathies go out to those who were nearest and dearest to him.' The hymn, 'Abide With Me', was sung at the graveside, the committal being conducted by Mr West. Messrs Francis Chappell and Sons carried out the funeral arrangements.' Levi's funeral was also reported by the *Kentish Times* on 9 February 1934:

Funeral of Levi Boswell – crowds watch Gypsy ceremony

'Crowds numbering several hundreds witnessed an unusual spectacle in Bromley on Friday afternoon, when the funeral took place of Mr Levi Boswell, youngest son of the late Mrs Urania Boswell, former 'queen' of the Kent Gypsies. The death of Mr Boswell at the age of 52 years was reported last week.

The funeral cortege started from Walters Yard, Bromley, and large numbers of sight seers gathered there in the afternoon to watch the procession leave. The large hearse, topped with nodding black plumes, was drawn by six coal black horses, each draped with a purple pall and an outrider dressed in a velvet suit and jockey cap rode at the front. The coffin was heaped high with masses of wreaths and flowers, notable among them being a huge wreath in the shape of a horseshoe with a whip and horse's head from his daughter and her husband. Behind the hearse followed his own pony, Nigger, led by Mr Leonard Lee, a cousin of Mr Boswell. Behind this again came two coaches, each drawn by a pair of black horses, draped in purple, and these were followed by a large number of Gypsy relatives on foot.

Outside in the High Street, large crowds had assembled, and all along the route to Plaistow Cemetery, where the internment took place, the roads were lined with people, eager to see so unusual a procession. The sombre cavalcade, headed by police officers who controlled the traffic, made its way out of Walters Yard, into the High Street and paused for a moment outside the *Dukes Head* public house in the Market Square, where a number of Mr Boswell's old friends stood at attention, hat in hand, to pay their last tribute. Thence the procession continued down West Street and College Road to the cemetery in Burnt Ash Lane. Here it was met by Mr Abraham West, London City Missioner to the Gypsies, who performed the last rites.

The tiny cemetery chapel was thronged by Mr Boswell's Gypsy kindred, while outside further crowds of spectators had gathered round the graveside. Mr West, who perhaps knows the Gypsy people more intimately than any man alive, recalled in his address that it was not long since they had last met in Farnborough churchyard to say farewell to their mother, Urania Boswell. Now, within a few months they were met again to say farewell to her boy Levi. Very few of them expected they would meet again so soon in such circumstances. Nothing could rob them of the affection of their warm Gypsy blood, and they had all gathered there to sympathise with those who were mourning a loved one.

Among the family mourners were Mr Z. Boswell (son), Mrs Maud Boswell (daughter in law), Mr Jack Boswell (son), Mr and Mrs F. Caple (son in law and daughter), Mr and Mrs P. Friend (brother in law and sister in law), Mr and Mrs Leonard Friend (brother in law and sister in law) and Mr Jimmy Friend (brother in law). Others who were at the service included his two crippled brothers, Herbert and Kanza, his sister Norah and Mr Job Lee (uncle).

Among those who sent wreaths and other floral tributes were Mr and Mrs Z Boswell, Mr Jack Boswell, Mr and Mrs Ellis, Mr and Mrs F. Caple, Mr Bob Raby, Mr Sid Grey, Mr Fred Thompson, 'A few friends', G and J Causten, Members of *Dukes Head* dart club, Mr Turner and family, 'Neighbours of Walters Yard', Mrs Breeds and family, Mr and Mrs Friend, Mr and Mrs Luke, Mr and Mrs Underwood and Mrs Buckland, Mr Jimmy Poulton and family, Bob Davis and Bob Tilly, Rose and George Wells, Mastrel Products and Co., Mr and Mrs Cooper, Mr and Mrs Botton, Herbert, Ada, Kenza and Norah Boswell, Albert and Prescilla Botton, Mr W.R. Jewell, Mrs Ranson and Dot, Mr J. Lowne, Mr J. Goodman, 'Anonymous', Mr Toby Brittain, Mr Walter Smith, 'E.B.T.', Mr Bert Harries, Mr W.A. Jowers, 'A.F.A.', Mr L. Summers, Mr W. Cotman, Arthur, "A Friend', Mrs R. Chatfield, Mr F. Vallence, Mr J. Lewis, 'G.A.G.', 'Rags', and Mr J. Summers. The arrangements for the funeral were entrusted to Messrs Francis Chappell and Sons, High Street, Bromley.'

Zacariah Boswell lived in Sidcup and died on 20 January 1977, aged 72. He was buried at Bromley Hill cemetery, next to his mother.

9. Fellow Travellers

- James Dighton (1800-73)
- Daniel Coates (1810-70)
- Edmund Arnold (1851-?)
- John Brazil (1819-?)
- George Eastwood (1819-?)
- James Pettigrove (1829-1907)
- George Reynolds

This chapter looks at some other Gypsy families who were associated with the Patemans, Farnborough and Tugmutton Common, through marriage, as friends and neighbours, and as fellow travellers on the roads of Kent. I am particularly indebted to Bob Collins who supplied me with much of the information for this chapter.

James Dighton

James Dighton (1800-73) = Eliza Lee (1800-50)
- James Dighton (1819-1906)
- Justinia Dighton (1824)
- John Dighton (1830)
- Saunders Dighton (1831)
- Isabella Dighton (1834)
- William Dighton (1837)
- Matilda Dighton (1839)
- Laurence Dighton (1842)
- Henry Dighton (1846-73)
- Andrew Dighton (1848)

Justinia Dighton married Sakey Boswell and they had four children: Jack, Levi, Kate and Mary. Levi Boswell married Urania Lee and they lived at Tugmutton for many years next door to James and Jane Pateman (see The Boswells).

James Dighton junior (1819-1906) married Duanna Lee (1812-97) and they had ten children: Nathan (1845), Solomon (1846), Eliza (1848), Elijah (1849), Oliver (1851), Deliah (1855), Noah (1858), Phoebe (1859), Walter (1861) and Priscilla (1866). James Dighton also had two children with Duanna Lee's sister, Elizabeth: Andrick (1856) and William (1862).

On 22 August 1881 Phoebe Diton (22, spinster, Croydon, father – James Diton, hawker) married Walter Pateman (22, bachelor, hawker, Croydon, father – Robert Pateman, hawker) at Croydon parish church. The witnesses were Andrew Diton and Ebenezer Whittaker.

Solomon Dighton (1846-1903) married Patience Smith (1848-1932) and they had ten children: Celia, Delia, Mary, Lavinia, Jenter, Dorwainer, Florence, Albert (1877), Jack (1880-1918) and Henry (1884-1949).

In 1881 there were four Diton families living in caravans on Mitcham Common: James Diton (61, Mitcham, general dealer), his wife Misel (Elizabeth, 61, Hereford, Hawker) and their children William (19) and Andrick; Solomon Diton (37, Plumstead, skewer maker), his wife Patience (33, Suffolk, skewer maker) and their children Celia (5), Deliah (10), Albert (4) and Lavinia (2); Noah Diton (30, Plumstead, peg maker) his wife Lydia (24, Ipswich) and their children James (5) and Walter (1); Nathan Diton (44, Farningham, hawker) his wife Urane (35, Watford, hawker) and their children Noah (17), Agne (8), Massey (5) and Alice (2); and Duanna Diton (67, Hereford, hawker) and her children Noah (23), Deliah (26), Phoebe (22), Walter (20) and Priscilla (15).

Also living on Mitcham Common in 1881 were: Robert Pateman (60, Hoo, skewer maker) and his sons Walter (21) and Robert (13). Walter Pateman married Phoebe Dighton later that year; Charles Lee (21, Rochester, skewer maker) and his wife Louisa (20). Louisa was Walter Pateman's younger sister.

Albert Dighton (1877-1931) married Alice Huggett (1884-1951) and they had thirteen children: Florence (1899), Alice (1902), Genty (1904), Harriet (1906), Patience (1910), Nellie (1912), Henry (1915), Jack (1917), Lily (1919), Samuel (1921), Walter (1924), Phyllis (1925), Agnes (1927).

Henry Dighton (1915-66) married Oliver Hodder (1917) and they had five children: David (1936), Valerie (1938), Barry (1948), Trevor (1949) and Alan (1953). Barry Dighton kindly supplied me with all the information in this section. Barry has conducted extensive research into his Gypsy family history and has found many references to his Dighton ancestors in the *Journal of The Gypsy Lore Society* and the works of George Borrow. Barry writes:

'My Gypsy connections seem to have been severed when my grandfather Albert Dighton married my *gorgio* grandmother (who was 15 and pregnant at the time!) in 1899. Thereafter we were housebound. My great grandfather Solomon Dighton was married to Patience (Mary) who was one of Rev Hall's chief informants. She in turn was the daughter of Samuel Roberts' (and George Borrow's) Clara Heron, wife of Cornelius Smith, and sister to the infamous Riley Bosvil.'

Liney Ditton

On 28 October 1912 Liney Ditton (29, spinster, 208 Chatham Hill, father – John Ditton, deceased, licenced hawker) married Major Coates (27, bachelor, licenced hawker, 208 Chatham Hill, father – William Coates, licenced hawker) at Christ Church, Luton, Kent. The witnesses were Noah Ditton and Macy French. Major Coates was born on 9 March 1885 in a tent on the Common at Mitcham. His mother was Fanny Coates, a licensed hawker. The name of his father was not given. Major was baptised on 3 May 1885 at Mitcham. His parents were William and Fanny, and his father was a hawker. Major and Liney had two children. Nathan Coates was born on 9 November 1913 at 183 Beacon Road, Chatham. His father was a licensed hawker. William Coates was born on 7 June 1916 at 183 Beacon Road, Chatham. His father was a general labourer.

Fanny Dighton

On 25 August 1934 Fanny Dighton (24, spinster, Chelsfield, father – Walter Dighton, farm labourer) married Mark Coates (25, bachelor, farm labourer, Chelsfield, father – Mark Coates, farm labourer) at Chelsfield, Kent. The witnesses were Sarah Ann Dighton and H. Ayres. Mark was born in 1909, the son of Mark Coates and Rebecca Lee. Fanny and Mark had four children. Mark Coates was born on 14 October 1937 in a Caravan at Millers Farm, Chelsfield. His father was a general labourer. Mark died on 4 May 1941, aged three, in the isolation hospital at Bromley. The cause of death was diphtheria and his father was a general labourer at Corks Meadows, St Pauls Cray. James Coates was born on 24 November 1939 at Corke's Meadow, St Pauls Cray. His father was a hawker.

Walter Coates was born on 6 June 1942 in a Caravan at Millers Farm, Chelsfield. His father was a timber loader. William Coates was born on 2 March 1946 at Corke's Meadow, St Pauls Cray. His father was a street hawker.

Daniel Coates

Daniel Coates (1810-70) = Phoebe Reynolds (1817-90)
- Daniel Coates (1844-?)
- Sarah Coates (1847-?)
- William Coates (1848-1929)
- John Coates (1859-1946)

Daniel Coates was born in 1810 and married Phoebe Reynolds. Phoebe was the daughter of William and Elizabeth Reynolds. Phoebe was baptised on 9 November 1817 at Mayfield, Sussex. Daniel Coates died on 2 June 1870 at Epsom Common. He was a 60 year old marine store dealer. The cause of death was 'laceration of the scalp and other injury to the head by falling off a cart when under the influence of liquor accidentally and in five minutes.' An inquest was held on 4 June 1870. On 3 April 1881 Phoebe Coates and her children John and Sarah were living in tents on Mitcham Common. Mary and Brigilda Coates were living in a neighbouring tent. Phoebe Coates died on 4 December 1890, aged 78, at the Workhouse Infirmary, Croydon. The cause of death was chronic bronchitis. The informant was N.W. Wilson, Superintendent Workhouse Infirmary.

Daniel Coates was born in 1844. In 1881, Daniel Coates (37, Ilford, General Dealer) was living with his son James (8, Mitcham) on Mitcham Common. James Coates had a daughter, Begonia, who died on 28 February 1895, aged 2 months, in a van, at Whitehorse Lane, South Norwood. Her father was a hawker.

William Coates

William Coates was born in 1848. On 14 November 1870 William Coates (of full age, bachelor, hawker, father – Daniel Coates, deceased, hawker) married Jane Eastwood (of full age, spinster, father – Benjamin Eastwood, hawker) at St James Church, Bermondsey. The witnesses were two members of the Groombridge family. Jane Eastwood was born in 1849. Her father was Benjamin Eastwood. William and Jane had eleven children: William (1871), Martha (1872), Walter (1874), Caroline (1876),

Augusta (1879), Daniel (1881), Mark (1882), Benjamin (1885), Jane (1888), Elizabeth (1891) and John.

William Coates was born on 17 October 1871 at The Downs, Epsom. His father was a hawker. He was baptised on 12 November 1871 at St Martin's, Epsom. Martha Coates was born on 11 December 1872 at Dunton Green, Otford, Kent. Her father was a general hawker. Martha died on 3 February 1873, aged seven weeks, at 20 Albion Cottages, Tonbridge Wells, Kent. The cause of death was 'atrophy from birth' and the informant was William Coates, licenced hawker.

Walter Coates was born on 2 April 1874 at Common Side, Mitcham, Surrey. His father was a licenced hawker. Walter died on 8 September 1876 aged 2 years at Pullens Farm, Horsmonden, Kent. The cause of death was 'diarrhoea 10 days, exhaustion' and the informant was William Coates, hawker.

Caroline Coates was born on 25 October 1876 at Riverhead, Sevenoaks, Kent. Her father was a hawker. On 30 May 1916, Caroline Coates (43, spinster, 44 De Burgh Road Wimbledon, father – William Coates, hawker) married Stephen Collins (44, bachelor, hawker, 44 De Burgh Road, father – William Collins, deceased, hawker) at All Saints Church, Wimbledon, Surrey. The witnesses were Ianthe Coates and A.G. Balliston.

Augusta Coates was born on 20 April 1879 at The Downs, Epsom. Her father was a hawker. In the 1901 census Augusta (22) was living with Albert Collins (20) in a caravan at Prince's Road, Mitcham. Living in a neighbouring caravan were Albert's father, William Collins (60) and his wife Betsy (60). On 17 July 1916 Augusta Collins (38, spinster, 40 De Burgh Road, father – William Coates, hawker) married Albert Collins (39, bachelor, hawker, De Burgh Road, father – William Collins, deceased, hawker) at All Saints Church, Wimbledon, Surrey. The witnesses were A. Lee and A.G. Balliston.

On 3 April 1881 William and James Coates were living in a tent on Mitcham Common with their children William, Caroline and Augusta. Daniel Coates was born on 20 May 1881 in a tent on the Common at Mitcham, Surrey. His father was a hawker of brooms and mats. On 24 July 1881 Daniel was baptised at Christ Church, Epsom.

On 6 May 1916 Daniel married Betsy Arnold and they had six children. Mark Coates was born in 1882. Benjamin Coates was born on 11 December 1885 in a house cart at Locks Bottom, Farnborough, Kent. His father was a pedlar.

Jane Coates was born on 11 May 1888 in a caravan on the Common, Mitcham, Surrey. Her father was a licensed hawker. Jane was baptised on 22 July at All Saints, Orpington, and her father was a hawker. Jane died on 23 February 1890 in a van at Purley Way, Croydon, aged 21 months. The cause of death was broncho pneumonia and the informant was William Coates, licenced hawker.

Elizabeth Coates was born on 5 April 1891 at Epsom. On 31 March 1901 William and Jane Coates were living in a house cart at Orpington with their children Daniel, Mark, Benjamin, Elizabeth and John. William Coates died on 20 January 1929, aged 81, and was buried at All Saints, Orpington. Jane Coates died on 14 June 1919, aged 80, and was also buried at All Saints.

John Coates

John Coates was born on 11 May 1859 in a cart in the Abridge Road, Lambourne, Essex. His father was a licensed hawker. John married Eliza Cooper, who was born in 1863 in Shirley, Surrey, the daughter of Uriah and Margaret Cooper. In 1881 Uriah Cooper (70) was living with his wife Margaret (40) and their children Eliza (18), Cinderella (16), Henry (12), John (6), Constantina (4) and Levindia (11 weeks) in a tent at the High Road, Chipstead, Surrey. John and Eliza Coates had eleven children: Margaret (1882), Walter (1883), Cinamenta (1885), Beecham (1886), John (1888), Harry (1889), Phoebe (1890), William (1892), Sarah (1893), Nellie (1896) and Patience (1899).

Margaret Coates was born on 2 November 1882 at Banstead, Surrey. On 3 April 1904 Margaret Coates married Harry Collins (born 25 November 1883) At All Saints, Eyke, Suffolk. Margaret died on 15 March 1949 at Eyke, Suffolk and was buried at All Saints. Harry Collins died on 25 January 1966 at Primrose Farm, Biggin Hill, and was buried at Biggin Hill cemetery.

Walter Coates was born in 1883 at Mitcham, Surrey. On 29 September 1907 Walter Coates (23, bachelor, labourer, Orpington, father – John Coates, labourer) married Emma Amelia Rogers (20, spinster, Orpington, father – James Rogers, labourer) at All Saints, Orpington. The witnesses were Edward and Lenda Ashdown. Walter and Emma had one child: John Coates was born on 21 August 1908 at Cray Valley Cottage Hospital, St Pauls Cray. His father was a farm labourer of Tubbendens Farm, Orpington. Walter Coates died on 22 February 1964 and was buried at St Giles, Farnborough, Kent. Emma died on 10 April 1981 and was buried at St Giles.

Cinamenta Coates was born on 24 October 1885 at 7 Queens Road, Mitcham, Surrey. Her father was a bricklayer's labourer. Cinamenta died on 2 November 1885 at 7 Queens Road, Mitcham, age 9 days. The cause of death was premature birth (7 months) and the informant was John Coates, bricklayer's labourer. Robert Beecham Coates was born on16 September 1886 at Farnborough, Kent. He was baptised on 10 October 1886 at St Giles, Farnborough, as Beauchamp, son of Jack and Eliza Cooper. His father was a labourer at Farnborough. John Coates was born on 4 April 1888 at 22 Sibthorp Road, Mitcham, Surrey. His father was a hawker of flowers. John Coates died on 6 April 1888 at 22 Sibthorp Road, aged 2 days. The cause of death was premature birth, 6 months, and the informant was John Coates, a bricklayer's labourer. Henry Coates was born on 13 January 1889 in a shed at Farnborough, Kent. His father was a pedlar. John was baptised on 10 February 1889 at St Giles, Farnborough. His father was a labourer at Farnborough.

Phoebe Coates was born on 1 July 1890 in a tent at Farnborough. Her father was a farm labourer. Phoebe was baptised on 13 July 1890 at St Giles. Her father was a labourer at Farnborough. Phoebe died on 17 December 1909 at 6 Cobden Road, Farnborough, aged 19 years. The cause of death was chronic valvular disease of the heart and dropsy 2 months. Her father was a farm labourer. On 5 April 1891 John and Eliza were living in a tent at Mitcham with their children Margaret, Walter, Beecham,

Harry, Phoebe and Lucy (sister). William Coates was born on 11 February 1892 in a house cart at Farnborough. His father was a general labourer. John was baptised on 10 April 1892 at St Giles. His father was a labourer at Farnborough. William died on 16 April 1900, aged 8, at Grain on the Hoo Peninsula in Kent. The cause of death was chronic heart disease and broncho pneumonia. His father was a farm labourer at Grain.

Sarah Coates was born on 10 November 1893 at Darrick Common, Orpington. Her father was a farm labourer. Sarah was baptised on 14 January 1894 at St Giles. Her father was a labourer at Darrick Common. Sarah died on 16 August 1911, aged 18, at 6 Cobden Road, Farnborough. The cause of death was enteritis 17 days and toxaemia meningitis. She was a spinster and a farm labourer. Norah Ellen Coates was born on 21 August 1896 at Farnborough. Norah was baptised o 11 October 1896 at St Giles. Her father was a labourer at Farnborough. On 25 December 1914 Norah Ellen Coates (18, spinster, 6 Cobden Road, Farnborough, father – John Coates, farm labourer) married William Rogers (24, bachelor, farm labourer, 10 Cobden Road, father – James Rogers, farm labourer) at St Giles. The witnesses were Walter Coates and Emma Amelia Coates. Norah Ellen Rogers died on 15 November 1977 at Maidstone, Kent, aged 81. She was buried at St Giles in the same grave as William James Rogers and Emma Rogers (died 8 March 1927, aged 22 months).

Patience Coates was born on 24 October 1899 in a house cart at Chelsfield, Kent. Her father was a licensed hawker. Patience died on 8 December 1904, aged 5, in a house cart at Tiles Farm, Orpington. The cause of death was whooping cough 10 days and broncho pneumonia. Her father was a field labourer. John Coates died on 29 April 1946 at 6 Cobden Road, Farnborough, aged 86. He was a farm labourer and the cause of death was senile myocarditis. The informant was Jane Wilkinson, grand daughter. John was buried at St Giles, Farnborough. Eliza Coates died on 13 September 1951 at 6 Cobden Road, Farnborough, aged 89. She was the widow of John Coates, agricultural worker (retired). The cause of death was coronary occlusion. The informant was E.A.Coates, daughter in law, 8 Park Parade, Crofton Road, Farnborough. Eliza was buried at St Giles, Farnborough, in the same grave as her son Henry (died 1926) and John Coates.

Robert Beecham Coates

On 26 July 1913 Robert Coates (25, bachelor, farm labourer, 6 Cobden Road, Farnborough, father – John Coates, farm labourer) married Rose Lee (21, spinster, 6 Cobden Road, father – James Lee, farm labourer) at St Giles, Farnborough. The witnesses were John Matthews and Nellie Coates. Robert and Rose had four children. Robert Coates junior was born on 15 April 1914 at Willow Walk, Farnborough. His father was a farm labourer. Robert Coates junior died on 16 November 1957, aged 43, at Farnborough Hospital. The cause of death was congestive cardiac failure. He was a builder's labourer of 6 Cobden Road, Farnborough. The informant was T. Coates, brother, of 5 White Lion Cottages, Locks Bottom. Nora Coates was born on 21 January 1917 at Wimbledon. Jane Coates was born on 16 October 1919 at 40 De Burgh Road, Wimbledon. Her father was a general labourer. Thomas Coates was born on 24 April 1923 at Locks Bottom House, Farnborough. His father was a farm labourer of Tiles Farm, Orpington. His mother was Rose Coates, formerly Backey. We are not sure if this was Rose Lee by another name or a different woman altogether. The informant was E.H. Croucher, occupier, Locks Bottom House. Rose probably died some time between 1923 and 1938.

On 26 February 1938 Robert Coates (40, widower, market gardener's salesman, 6 Cobden Road, Farnborough, father – John Coates, general labourer) married Sarah Ellen Ribbens (25, spinster, 16 Epsom's Cottages, Fordcroft, St Mary Cray, father – Charles Ribbens, general labourer) at Bromley Register Office. The witnesses were G. Dutton and C. Ribbens. Robert gave his age as 40 but he was 52. Sarah was living at 16 Epsom's Cottages. Robert and Sarah had two children. Patricia Coates was born on 2 July 1935 at Farnborough Hospital. Her mother was a field worker of 16 Epsom Cottages, St Mary Cray, Orpington. The name of her father is not given. Patricia died on 2 June 1948, aged 12 years, at Farnborough Hospital. The cause of death was pericarditis and rheumatic fever. The informant was S.E.Coates, mother, of 9 Cobden Road, Farnborough, 'now the wife of Robert Coates, a hawker.'

John Henry Coates was born on 15 March 1938 at Farnborough Hospital. His father was a hawker of 16 Cobden Road, Farnborough. John Henry died on 17 September 1939, aged 17 months, at Farnborough Hospital. The cause of death was shock from scalds (16 hours), misadventure, no post mortem. An inquest was held on 19 September 1939. His father was a flower hawker of 9 Cobden Road, Farnborough. Robert Coates senior died on 13 November 1956, aged 71, at 9 Cobden Road, Farnborough. He was a night watchman, County Council, retired. The cause of death was cardiac failure and the informant was S.E. Coates, widow of the deceased.

Benjamin Coates

On 28 June 1916 Benjamin Coates (32, bachelor, general dealer, 40 De Burgh Road, father – William Coates, hawker) married Annie Collerson (29, spinster, 40 De Burgh Road) at All Saints Church, Wimbledon, Surrey. The witnesses were Alice Steward and A.G. Balliston. Benjamin may have got married in June 1916 because conscription was introduced in May 1916 and he was eligible to be called up.

Benjamin Coates appears to have had a number of wives or partners. One of them could have been Ianthe Coates who died on 12 October 1954, aged 67, at 75 Harrow Manorway, Belvedere. The cause of death was acute pulmonary oedema, cardiac failure and hypertension. Ianthe was the wife of Benjamin Coates, general dealer. The informant was M. Anderson, daughter, 78 Albert Road, Belvedere. Some of the families who had to leave the Belvedere Marsh Gyspy encampment after the floods of 1953 were accommodated at Crabtree Manorway, Belvedere.

Sarah Coates was born in 1910. Sarah died on 7 July 1911, aged 9 months, in a caravan at Fairfield, Orpington. The cause of death was pneumonia and diarrhoea. Sarah was the daughter of Benjamin Coates, hawker and farm labourer of 6A Seaton Road, Mitcham. We do not know who the mother was. It could have been Annie Lee (alias Collerson?) who was the mother of Benjamin's next child. Ben Coates junior was born on 18 December 1912 at Higgs Farm, Orpington. His father was a hawker. Jim Coates was born on 19 August 1921 at 4 St Andrews Cottages, Orpington. His father was a general dealer and his mother was Priscilla Carpenter, late Pateman, formerly Arnold, a general dealer. Priscilla was the widow of Walter Pateman. Walter was killed in 1917 and Priscilla married John Carpenter in 1919. Benjamin Coates lived with Priscilla at 117 Lower Road, Orpington from 1927-1931 when they moved to 82 Wellington Road, where they both lived until their deaths.

Louisa Coates was born on 18 March 1930 at 1 New Road, Belvedere, Erith. Her mother was a flower seller but her father's name was not given. Joseph Coates was born on 6 December 1931 in a caravan at 1 East Road, Belvedere, Erith. Her mother was a licensed hawker but her father's name was not given. East Road formed part of the Belvedere Marsh Gypsy Encampment which was swept away by the great flood of 1953. Benjamin Coates senior died on 8 April 1970, aged 84, and was buried at All Saints, Orpington, in the same grave as his parents. Priscilla Coates died on 21 February 1971 at Orpington hospital. She was buried on 2 March 1971 at All Saints, Orpington. Her grave, which also contained three of her children by Walter Pateman, was next to the grave of Benjamin Coates and his children. Priscilla and Benjamin had known each other since at least 1901 when Priscilla Arnold and her family were living in a house cart at Orpington and Benjamin Coates was living with his family in a neighbouring house cart.

Mark Coates

On 24 July 1916 Mark Coates (34, bachelor, hawker, 40 De Burgh Road, father – William Coates, hawker) married Rebecca Lee (28, spinster, 40 De Burgh Road, father – John Lee, hawker) at All Saints Church, Wimbledon, Surrey, The witnesses were Sarah Jelley and A.G. Balliston. Mark and Rebecca had ten children: Elizabeth (1906), Betsy (born 7 October 1907, Mitcham), Mark (1909), Thomas (born 21 March 1912, Romford), Rose (1919), William (born 4 October 1919, Slade Green), Edward (born 4 December 1921, Orpington), Caroline (born 6 December 1923, Belvedere), Daniel (1926) and Steve (born 24 August 1928, Farningham).

Elizabeth Coates was born in 1906. On 3 August 1925 she married Daniel Arnold at Orpington. Mark Coates was born in 1909. On 25 August 1934 he married Fanny Dighton and they had four children. Thomas Coates was born on 21 March 1912 at 21 Hart Street, Barking Town, Essex. His father was a hawker. Elizabeth, Mark junior and Thomas were born before their parents got married in 1916. Maybe they got married in July 1916 because conscription was introduced in May 1916 and Mark was eligible to be called up. This might explain why their next child, Rose Coates, was not born until 1919. William Coates was born on 4 October 1919 (he could have been a twin of Rose?) in a caravan at Francis farm, Slade Green, Dartford. His father was a hawker and ex private in the 1st Surrey Regiment which suggests that our theory about the 1916 marriage and gap between the birth of children is correct. Edward Coates was born on 4 December 1921 at Crofton Farm, Orpington. His father was a farm labourer.

Caroline Coates was born on 6 December 1923 at 121 Occupation Road, Belvedere, Erith. Her father was a licensed hawker. Occupation Road formed part of the Belvedere Marsh Gypsy encampment. Situated immediately north of the railway line, west of Belvedere Station, this flat, low lying area of the Erith Marshes was firmly established as a Traveller encampment in about 1902, although oral testimony suggests that, long before it was parcelled off into plots, it was already in regular use as a stopping place. On 1 February 1953 the River Thames burst through the bank in eleven places and the Belvedere Marsh Encampment was swept away for good. It was remembered by Betsy Stanley in *Memories of the Marsh: a Traveller life in Kent*. Betsy lived at 37 Occupation Road. Daniel Coates was born in 1926. Steve Coates was born on 24 August 1928 in a caravan at Coldharbour Farm, Buton Street, Farningham, Kent. His father was a licensed hawker.

Henry Coates

On 1 September 1917 Henry Coates (28, bachelor, soldier, 6 Cobden Road, Farnborough, father – John Coates, farm labourer) married Rose Smith (20, spinster, 12 Cobden Road, father – Eli Smith, farm labourer) at St Giles, Farnborough. The witnesses were James and Sinnie Smith. They probably got married in September 1917 because Henry was a soldier, and this might explain why their first child was not born until 1919. Mary Elizabeth Coates was born on 23 November 1919 at 6 Cobden Road, Farnborough. Her father was a farm labourer. Mary died on 9 August 1921, aged twenty months, at 12 Cobden Road. The cause of death was broncho pneumonia. Her father was a farm labourer. Joseph Allen Coates was born on 3 September 1922 at 12 Cobden Road, Farnborough. His father was a farm labourer. Henry Coates died on 13 January 1926 at 46 Ouseley Road, Balham, aged 37 years. He was a farm labourer of 1 Kings Mews, Vant Road, Tooting. The cause of death was pulmonary tuberculosis and the informant was N. Rogers, sister, of 6 Cobden Road, Farnborough, Kent. This was Norah Ellen Coates, who married William Rogers in 1914. Henry was buried at St Giles, Farnborough.

Edmund Arnold

Edmund Arnold (1851-?) = Selina Brazil (1858-?)
- Edmund Arnold (1876-?)
- Selina Arnold (1879-?)
- Emma Arnold (1882-?)
- Betsy Arnold (1885-?)
- Priscilla Arnold (1887-1971)
- Sarah Arnold (1891-?)
- Albert Arnold (1893-1902)
- William Arnold (1900-?)
- Daniel Arnold (1904-?)
- Rose Arnold (1907-1916)

Edmund Arnold was born in 1851 at Cudham, Kent the son of Joab and Emma Arnold. In 1851 John Arnold (56, master basket maker, Cudham) was living with his wife Ann (50, Halsted) and daughter Eliza (20, Sundridge) at The Hill, Sundridge, Kent. Also living at The Hill were James Arnold (30, master basket maker, Shoreham), his wife Harriet (28, Woolwich) and their children, Stephen (6, Woolwich), Alice (4, Milton) and Lillace (11 months, Dartford). In 1861 Joab Arnold (37, agricultural labourer, Eynsford) was living with his wife, Emma (40, Bexleyheath), and their children Edmund (14, agricultural labourer, Sundridge), Selia (13, Sundridge), Thomas (7, scholar, Sundridge) and Caleb (4, scholar, Sundridge) at The Hill, Sundridge.

In 1881 Alfred Arnold (43, hawker, Canterbury) was living with his wife Frances (45, Hadlow), and their children Benjamin (12, Maidstone), Sylvia (10, Chatham) and

Mercy (3, Boxley) at Pevenden Heath, Boxley. They were described as 'Gypsies, caravan 2' – there were 3 other caravans containing the Penfold, French and Walker families. It is interesting to note that Alfred Arnold and his family were captured twice on the 1881 census – at Boxley, Hollingbourne and at King Street, Maidstone. At Maidstone they were described as traveling hawkers and their place of birth was Brenchley. Benjamin's age was given as 10 and Silvia's was 8. Mercy was given the middle name Everton.

Edmund Arnold was born on 24 February 1876 at Godstone, Surrey. His mother was Selina Arnold (Hawker) but the name of the father (Edmund Arnold) was not given. Edmund junior was baptized on 5 March 1876 at Crowhurst, Surrey.

In 1881 Edmund Arnold (33, labourer, Cudham) was living in a house cart with his wife Selina (21, born at sea) and their children Edmund (5, Sevenoaks) and Selina (2, Edenbridge) at Ide Hill, Sundridge. Joseph Ince and his wife Selina were living in the neighbouring house cart.

In 1891 Edmund Arnold (46, general labourer, Woolwich) was living with his wife Selina (30, East Grinstead) and their children, Edmund (15, general labourer, Edenbridge), Selina (14, Caterham), Emma (8, scholar, Edenbridge), Betsy (6, scholar, Tunbridge Wells), Priscilla (4, scholar, Tunbridge Wells) and Sarah Ann (2 months, Southborough) at Kings Cottage, London Road, Southborough. Also living with them was Priscilla Brazil (84, boarder, widow, Hastings). This could have been Selina's mother.

In 1901 Edmund Arnold (50, agricultural labourer, Hyde Hill) was living with his wife Lena (45, Lingfield) and their children, Emma (19, Hyde Hill), Betsy (16, Tunbridge Wells), Pryss (13, Tunbridge Wells), Sarah Ann (10, Tunbridge Wells), Albert (8, Peckham) and William (1, Orpington) in a house cart at Orpington. William and Jane Coates and their children, including Daniel (20), Benjamin (15) and Elizabeth (10), were living in a neighbouring house cart. It is possible that Priscilla met Walter Pateman at this time, or later when they were both working as farm labourers.

Betsy Arnold

Betsy Arnold was born in 1886. On 6 May 1916 Betsy Arnold (30, spinster, hawker, Crofton Old Farm, Orpington, father – Edmund Arnold, farm labourer) married Daniel Coates (35, bachelor, farm labourer, Crofton Old Farm, Orpington, father – William Coates, hawker) at Bromley Register Office. The witnesses were Priscilla Pateman and Emma Dabner. Daniel was born in 1881, the son of William and Jane Coates. Daniel and Betsy had seven children. Daniel Coates junior was born in 1902. Daniel died on 31 December 1915 at Crofton Old Farm, Orpington, aged 13 years. The cause of death was pleurisy and pneumonia. The informant was Daniel Coates, farm labourer. Daniel Coates junior was born in 1902, fourteen years before Daniel senior and Betsy Arnold got married. In 1902 Daniel senior was 21 and Betsy was 16 and so it was technically possible. Also, Daniel senior was at Crofton Old Farm in 1914 and 1918 for the birth of two of his children, so it is reasonable to suppose that he was also there in 1915 for the death of Daniel junior.

We do not know why there was such a big gap between the birth of Daniel junior in 1902 and that of Daniel senior's next child in 1910. Albert Coates was born on 30 July 1910 in a caravan at Crofton Heath, Orpington. His father was a hawker. Lena (otherwise Selina) Coates was born in 1913. Lena died on 23 February 1932, aged 19, in a caravan at Corke's Meadow, St Paul's Cray. The cause of death was acute gastro enteritis (influenza), haemorrhage and exhaustion. Lena was a spinster field worker and daughter of Daniel Coates, general labourer. Benjamin Coates was born on 9 December 1914 at Crofton Hall Farm, Orpington. His father was a farm labourer.

Maybe Daniel and Betsy got married in May 1916 because conscription was introduced and Daniel was eligible to be called up. This would explain the gap between the birth of Benjamin in 1914 and Rose May in 1918. Rose May Coates was born on 20 May 1918 at Crofton Old Farm, Orpington. Her father was a farm labourer. Priscilla Coates was born on 3 February 1920 at 4 St Andrews Cottages, Orpington. Her father was a general dealer. Priscilla Coates died on 10 April 1936, aged 16, in a caravan at Corke's Meadow, St Pauls Cray. The cause of death was acute oedema of the lungs and chronic nephritis. Priscilla had no occupation and was the spinster daughter of Daniel Coates, a street hawker. Cecilia Coates was born on 14 June 1923 at 5 Fulcher's Buildings, St Mary Cray. Her father was a general labourer.

Priscilla Arnold

Priscilla Arnold was born on 25 February 1887 at Ford Farm, Penshurst, Kent. Her father was a general labourer. On 24 February 1909 she married Walter Pateman at Bromley Registry Office and they had five children: Walter (1909), Albert (1910), Lena (1912), William (1913) and Edmund (1915). Walter Pateman was killed in action in February 1917. On 17 March 1919 Priscilla Pateman (30, widower, Lower Road, Orpington, father – Edmund Arnold, farm labourer) married John Carpenter (40, widower, labourer, Lower Road, father – Thomas Carpenter, printer, deceased) at All Saints, Orpington. The witnesses were Peter and Sarah Brant.

We do not know what happened to John Carpenter but from 1921 Priscilla was living with Benjamin Coates and they had a son. Jim Coates was born on 19 August 1921 at 4 St Andrews Cottages, Orpington. His father was a general dealer and his mother was Priscilla Carpenter, late Pateman, formerly Arnold, a general dealer. On 3 June 1944 James Coates (22, bachelor, contractor, 82 Wellington Road, father – Benjamin Coates, contractor) married Dorothy Gwendoline Duffin (21, spinster, engineer, 76 Avalon Road, father – Thomas Duffin, labourer) at All Saints, Orpington. The witnesses were Thomas Duffin and B. Coates. James and Dorothy had one child: Priscilla Coates was born on 5 December 1944 at 82 Wellington Road. Her father was a cartage contractor.

Priscilla Carpenter died on 21 February 1971, aged 84, at Orpington Hospital. The cause of death was fulminating bronchopneumonia. She was the widow of Carpenter, occupation unknown, 82 Wellington Road, St Mary Cray. The informant was James Coates, son.

Priscilla Coates was buried on 2 March 1971 at All Saints, Orpington. It is interesting to note that on her death certificate her name was given as Carpenter and on her burial record it was given as Coates. She was buried in the same grave as her children

Albert, Edmund and William. Her grave is close to that of Benjamin Coates and his parents. A gravestone was erected in 2007 (presumably by her son James Coates, or by her grandson James Pateman) with a line drawing of a horse and trap and the epitaph: 'Here lies Priscilla Coates and her three sons Billy, Edmund and Albert. Gone but not forgotten.'

Albert Arnold was born in 1893 at Peckham. Albert died on 18 February 1902 in a house cart, Crofton, Orpington, aged 8 years. He was the son of Edmund Arnold, a farm labourer. He died of pneumonia and the informant was Selina Arnold, mother, present at the death. Albert was buried on 22 February 1902 at All Saints, Orpington. He was buried in the same grave as Walter Pateman (the son of Walter and Priscilla Pateman).

Daniel Arnold was born in 1904. On 3 August 1925 Daniel Arnold (21, bachelor, labourer, 113 Lower Road, Orpington, father – Edmund Arnold) married Elizabeth Coates (19, spinster, Crofton Old Farm, father – Mark Coates, farm labourer) at All Saints, Orpington. The witnesses were John Smith and Betsy Coates.

Rose May Arnold was born in 1907. Rose May died on 10 February 1916 and was buried at All Saints, Orpington. She was buried in the same grave as Lena Pateman (the daughter of Walter and Priscilla Pateman).

John Brazil

John Brazil (1819-?) = Priscilla? (1821-?)
- Elizabeth Brazil (1840-?)
- Mathew Brazil (1845-?)
- Sarah Brazil (1847-?)
- Mary Brazil (1850-?)
- William Brazil (1853-?)
- James Brazil (1856-?)
- Ann Selina Brazil (1858-?)

John Brazil was born in 1819 and he married Priscilla (born 1821).

In 1851 John Brazil (32, traveler, not known) was living with his wife Priscilla (30, not known) and their children Elizabeth (11, Dean Hill, Sussex), Matthew (6, not known) and Sarah (4, Crowborough, Sussex) on the south side of the High Road at Peasmarsh in Essex. Also traveling with them was Sarah Brazil (17, sister, unmarried, not known).

In 1861 John Brazil (47, Tinman, Wadhurst) was living in a caravan with his wife Priscilla (43, Brighton) and their children, Matthew (13, Hever), Mary Ann (11, Rotherfield), William (8, Rotherfield), James (5, ?) and Anne (3, Lindfield) at Leigh. Anne's full name was Ann Selina, and this was Priscilla's mother. George Eastwood (42, mat maker, Burwash) was living in a neighbouring caravan with his wife, ten children, grand daughter and niece. William Brazil (70, mat maker) was living in another nearby caravan with his wife Jane (70), their sons James (33) and Matthew (27) and their grand daughter Sarah (12).

In 1871 John Brazil (54, hawker, Wadhurst) was living with his wife, Priscilla (44, Hastings) and their children James (15, ?) and Ann Selina (12, Lindfield) at Fletching, Sussex. William Brazil (20, ?) was living in tents and carts with his wife and two children at Buggers Bush, Boxted, Surrey. Benjamin Brazil (41, hawker, Leigh) was living in the same encampment with his wife and five children.

In 1881 John Brazil (69, traveling hawker) was living with his wife Prescilla (53), children Matthew (34), Selina (32) and William (24) in a travelling van at Hartfield. Also travelling with them were Matthews' children Cordelia (13) and James (11). They were travelling with the Newman family: Charles (45), Henry (15), Priscilla (13), Caleb (9) and John (5). Ann Brazil (60, hawker) was living with her niece at Heathfield. William Brazil (30, hawker, Heathfield) was living with his wife and four children at Hastings.

In 1891 Priscilla Brazil (27, general hawker, Croydon) was living with her three children at Brighton. William Brazil (36, hawker, Heathfield) was living with his wife and ten children at Battle, East Sussex. Ellen Brazil (58, flower hawker) was living with her three children at Ore, Sussex. James Brazil (36, hawker, Crawley) was living with his wife, ten children and mother at Worthing.

In 1901 William Brazil (steam round a bout proprietor) was living with his wife and seven children in a traveling caravan at Hastings. This formed part of a large encampment which also included William Brazil (21, general hawker, Hastings), his wife and son. Matthew Brazil (44, general dealer, Whitstable) and his wife Phoebe (40, manageress of lodging house, Whitstable) were living at Lewes. Walter Brazil (24, licenced hawker, Tunbridge Wells) was living with his wife at Alkham.

Mathew Brazil was born in 1845 and married Lena Collins and they had three children. Cordelia Brazil was born on 27 October 1868 at Bexhill. Her father was a hawker. James Brazil was born on 11 June 1870 at Hatch Lane, Tenterden. His father was a hawker. Henry Brazil was born on 1 January 1878 in a caravan on the Common at Mitcham. His father was a hawker of pegs.

James Brazil

James Brazil was born in 1856 and married Rebecca Mears. They had twelve children: James and Mary (1873), Jane (1875), Priscilla (1877), Phyliss (1880), Sarah (1882), Emily (1884), Matthew and Mary (born 18 April 1886, Brighton), Job and Patience (born 21 April 1890, Egham) and Maria (born 28 January 1897, Farnham).

In 1901 James Brazil (36, hawker, Crawley) was living with Rebecca (38, Mersham, Kent) and their ten children in a caravan and tent in a field at Broadwater, Worthing, Sussex.

Ann Selina Brazil married Edmund Arnold. Phoebe Brazil married William Eastwood and their daughter, Emma Eastwood, was born on 9 October 1860 at Old Place Farm, Sandhurst. Her father was a general labourer.

William Brazil married Caroline Eastwood and they had two children: Fanny Brazil (born 26 March 1879, Leaves Green); and Thomas (born 1 August 1884, West Firle).

Tom Brazil married Naomi Eastwood and their daughter, Grace Brazil, was born on 22 April 1913 at North Bensted. Her father was a hawker of baskets and wares.

James Brazil married Priscilla Coates and their daughter, Margaret Brazil, was born on 24 May 1913 in a caravan at 50 De Burgh Road, Wimbledon. Her father was a licensed hawker.

Jane Brazil married Benjamin Eastwood and they had seven children: Jane (born 1 January 1850 at Hever, Kent; labourer); Mary and Martha (born 30 April 1852 at High Halstow, Hoo, Kent; agricultural labourer); Emma (born 14 July 1857 at East Grinstead; pedlar); Fanny (born 11 October 1860 at Old Place farm, Sandhurst, Kent; general labourer); Tom (born 15 September 1867 at Badsell Tudely, Kent; licensed hawker); Benjamin (born 4 October 1874 at Hawkhurst, Kent; hawker).

George Eastwood

George Eastwood (1819-?) = Phoebe Brazil (1821-?)
- Francis Eastwood (1840-?)
- William Eastwood (1841-?)
- Benjamin Eastwood (1843-?)
- Jane Eastwood (1848-?)
- Mary Eastwood (1850-?)
- Phoebe Eastwood (1851-?)
- Richard Eastwood (1853-?)
- Caroline Eastwood (1857-?)
- Phillis Eastwood (1857-?)
- Emma Eastwood (1860-?)
- A… Eastwood (1863-?)
- John Eastwood (1865-?)

George Eastwood married Phoebe Brazil. They had 12 children: Francis (1840); William (born 1 April 1841, Hadlow; hawker); Benjamin (born 29 July 1843, in a van situate in Scrubbs Lane, Maidstone; hawker); Jane (1848); Mary (1850); Phoebe (1851); Richard (born 13 May 1853, Boxley); Caroline and Phillis (born 14 December 1857, Barnes Common; mat maker); Emma (born 9 October 1860, Cranbrook); A… (1863); and John (born 5 July 1865, Claygate).

In 1861 George Eastwood (42, mat maker, Burwash) and his family were living in caravans at Leigh, Kent: wife Phoebe (40); children Frances (21), William (20), Benjamin (17), Jane (13), Mary (11), Phoebe (10), Richard (7), Philly (3), Emma (6 months); grandchildren Elizabeth (3), Mercy (6 months); and niece Elizabeth (21). They were travelling with two Brazil families: John and Priscilla; and William and Jane.

In 1871 George Eastwood (53, pedlar, Burwash) and his family were living in caravans on Barming Heath at East Barming, Kent: Phoebe (52), Jane (22), Richard (17), Phillis (14), Emma (10), A… (8) and John (4). They were travelling with: William Eastwood (30, pedlar, Tonbridge) and his wife Esther (34); Benjamin Eastwood (27, pedlar, Maidstone) and his wife Priscilla (32).

In 1891 there were three Eastwood families living in caravans at Perry Street, Northfleet, Kent: Flora (52, Hawker, Raleigh); Mark (26, general dealer, East Tel…), Emma (25), John (5) and Mark (7 months); John (26, hawker, Raleigh), Ada (23), John (5), Benjamin (3) and Walter (8 months).

In 1891 there were also two Eastwood families living in house carts and caravans at Lowfield Street, Dartford, Kent: James (36, hawker, Maidstone), Mary (35), James (15), Eelia (13), John (11), Alice (4) and Harriet (4 months); William (30, Dartford), Elizabeth (30), William (11), James (8), Britania (6), Mary Ann (4) and Elvenia (1).

They were travelling with two other families: William Wingrove (34, labourer, Dartford), Phoebe (30), William (10), Mark (8), Thomas (6), Phoebe (4), George (2) and Annie (2 months); William Johnson (28, horse slaughterer, Dartford), Harriet (28), Annie (7), Harriet (5), Phoebe (3) and Caroline (2).

In 1891 another Eastwood family was living in a caravan at Newhithe Lane, East Malling: William (52, licensed hawker, Bexleyheath), Esther (54), Charlotte (13), and William (16). They were travelling with Joseph Cooper (39, licensed hawker, Chalk, Gravesend), James (16), Alfred (12), Eliza (7), Job (4), George (1) and Elizabeth Hope (lodger, 38).

There are connections between the Coates and Eastwood families. Jane Eastwood (1849-1929) married William Coates (1848-1929). Mark Eastwood married Mary Ann Coates and they had a son, Thomas Eastwood (born 16 August 1864 at Stoke, Hoo, Kent; his father was a licensed hawker). Thomas Eastwood married Mary Ann Coates and they had a daughter, Brigolia Eastwood (born 13 June 1896 at Farnborough, Kent; her father was a general labourer).

Naomi Eastwood

On 23 October 1933 Naomi Eastwood (20, spinster, Stokes Yard, father – Benjamin Eastwood, general dealer) married Benjamin Coates (21, bachelor, hawker, Stokes Yard, East Ham, father – Benjamin Coates, general dealer) at St Bartholemew's, East Ham. The witnesses were Herbert Tumble and Britannia Eastwood. Benjamin was born in 1912, the son of Benjamin Coates and Annie Lee. Naomi and Benjamin had five children.

Brittania Coates was born on 26 April 1934 in a caravan at 82 New Road, Belvedere, Erith. Her father was a licensed hawker. This formed part of the Belvedere Gypsy Encampment which was swept away by the floods of 1953.
Benjamin Coates junior was born on 23 April 1938 in a caravan at 10 East Road, Belvedere, Erith. His father was a licensed hawker.

Violet Coates was born on 28 September 1943 at Paris Farm, East Malling. The family might have been down in Kent for the hopping. Her father was a farm labourer.

Daniel Coates was born on 9 April 1949 at Farnborough Hospital. His father was a general dealer of Chalk Pit, Ruxley, Sidcup. James Pateman was born at Chalk Pit, Ruxley, in 1942 and his father, Albert Pateman, was living there in a vardo in 1947.

John Coates was born on 7 May 1951 at 20 Masons Hill, Bromley. His father was a general dealer of Chalk Pit, Ruxley, Sidcup.

James Pettigrove

James Pettigrove (1829-1907) = Isabella (1833-1929)
- Alfred Pettigrove (1862-?)
- Henry Pettigrove (1865-1915)
- Francis Pettigrove (1871-1919)
- Elizabeth Pettigrove (1879-?)

Galer: 'But with the name of Pettigrove my romance deepened. I was in the circus ring with its horses and sawdust, I was on the flying boats and the galloping horses. There is hardly a village in Kent that does not know of Pettigrove's galloping horses. Garden fetes, flower shows, rejoicings – could there have been a great day unless Pettigrove's swing boats or steam roundabouts were there? One thinks of those old days when, as children, we waited for the arrival of that wonderful and magic procession that came into the village on the night before the great day. What wonderful galloping horses, what a splendid array of brass all polished up – ready for tomorrow.'

From Galer's description it seems that Pettigrove's Fairground was a regular visitor to St Mary Cray and other local villages. On 31 March 1901 Pettigrove's roundabouts were recorded in the Census at Lower Road, Orpington:

Caravan No.1: Henry Pettigrove (29, travelling showman, London, Walworth), his wife Polly (28, Buckinghamshire, Slough) and their children, Jessie (13, Middlesex, Hounslow) and James (11, Kent, Maidstone).

Caravan No. 2: Alfred Pettigrove (39, showman, Hertfordshire, St Albans), his wife Fanny (36, Kent, Tunbridge Wells), and their children Isabella (14, St Mary Cray), Sarah (6, Kent, Westerham), Matilda (4, Kent, Gravesend), Frank (2, Kent, St Mary Cray) and Fanny (1, London, Westminster) plus Ernest Borrett (servant, 26, Kent, Riverhead).

Caravan No.3: James Pettigrove (74, showman, London, Walworth), his wife Isabella (68, London, Walworth), and their children Francis Pettigrove (28, Berkshire, Abingdon) and Elizabeth (22, London, Hammersmith) plus William Point (servant, 52, London, Battersea) and Joe Mills (servant, 48, Kent Malling).

Caravan No.4: James Sanders (36, showman, London, Stepney), his wife Mary (32, Middlesex, Ham Green) and their children Mary Ann (8, Kent, Sidcup), James (6, Middlesex, Hounslow) and Isabella (2, Kent, Gravesend).

Living nearby were 24 persons 'found in huts and tents at Lone Barn, East Hall'.

It is interesting to note that Alfred Pettigrove had a servant and James Pettigrove had two servants. In a history of Keston village there are two photographs of Pettigrove's Fairground with the caption: 'One of the more popular attractions to young and old on a visit to the village was Granny Pettigrove's colourful fairground with its swings and steam driven roundabouts. It occupied the site of Mrs Swatton's and Daisy Eaglestone's tea rooms after their demolition. The site was subsequently a caravan park and now Windmill Close'. Keston village was very close to Farnborough and Locks Bottom. Isabella was presumably Granny Pettigrove. There is a photograph of Isabella Pettigrove (taken in 1927) who arrived in Orpington from Hatton Garden with her husband William.

Several members of the Pettigrove family are buried in All Saints churchyard, Orpington: Henry Pettigrove (born 17 November 1865; died 23 December 1915); Polly Pettigrove (died 2 February 1952 aged 85 years); Francis Pettigrove (died 25 June 1919 aged 48 years); James Brittendene Pettigrove of Westerham (died 23 August 1907, aged 78 years). A news item in the Orpington Journal in 1929 reported that 'Mrs Isabella Pettigrove 'the oldest show woman in the world' dies at the age of 100 and is buried in the elaborate family vault at Orpington.'

Pat Loveridge has written a useful *Calendar of Fairs and Markets held in the nineteenth century* (2003) which gives you a good idea of how many fairs and markets were held across the country. These provided many opportunities for families such as Pettigrove's Fairground to travel around and make a living. Ray Galer refers to the Statutory Fairs of St Mary Cray. Edward I granted a Statutory Fair to be held at St Mary Cray on the Festival of the Feast of the Blessed Virgin Mary, which fell on 15 August. As the Market House on Market Meadows was blown down in a great storm on 26 November 1703, and never rebuilt, it seems that this Statutory Fair fell into disuse. But the Michaelmas Statutory fair continued and was probably visited by Pettigrove's Fairground:

'Now my friend, Michaelmas day was a great day in the countryside, a real holiday. Many a Statutory Fair was held on this day in many a town and country village. A Statutory Fair is different from an ordinary fair, for it was granted by the King to the town or village through the power of the local monastery or local church, and they brought in much money. They had legal right – their own law court, called the Court of Pie Powder, with its own particular laws, which were duly carried out. A Statutory Fair was generally granted on the day upon which the Festival of the saint was kept – by which the church is named – and, of course, as there were many churches dedicated to St Michael and All Angels, naturally Michaelmas Day was a great day in many a town and village.'

George Reynolds

George Reynolds = Charlotte Busby

- John Reynolds (1835-?)
- Phoebe Reynolds (1840-?)
- Alice Reynolds (1843-?)
- Louisa Reynolds (1846-?)
- Elvy Reynolds (1847-?)
- George Reynolds (1853-1937)
- Mercy Reynolds (1855-1940)
- Jane Reynolds (1861-1939)

William and Elizabeth Reynolds had several children: John (1800), Lydia (1810), Phoebe (1817); Daniel, Able and George.

John Reynolds (1800) married ? and they had three children: Charles (1832), Mary (1836) and John (1850). In 1861 John Reynolds (61, licensed hawker) was living with his children Charles (29, Rye), Mary (25, Rye) and John (11, Kent) in a caravan at Plumstead Road. Thomas Wheeler (35, licensed hawker, Kent) was living with his wife Hester (33, Crawley) and their five children in a neighbouring caravan.

Lydia Reynolds (1810) married a traveller names James Matthews from Ditchling in Sussex. They had a daughter, Phoebe, baptised on 3 July 1836 at Cocking, Sussex. Phoebe Reynolds (1817-90) married Daniel Coates (1810-70) and hey had four children: Daniel (1844), Sarah (1847), William (1848) and John (1859).

Daniel Reynolds married Jane ? and they had a daughter, Phoebe Elizabeth, baptised on 11 August 1847 at Saint Giles, Reading, Berkshire.

Able Reynolds married Sarah Jackson and they had a son, Cain, born on 8 March 1838 at Battle, Sussex.

George Reynolds married Charlotte Busby on 16 May 1837 at Ridgmont, Bedford, England. They had eight children: John (1835), Phoebe (1840), Alice (1843), Louisa (1846), Elvy (1847), George (1853), Mercy (1855) and Jane (1861).

Phoebe Reynolds was born on 24 December 1840 in the parish of Brasted, Sevenoaks. Her father was George Reynolds, tin man, and her mother was Charlotte Reynolds, formerly Jones. Phoebe was baptised on 3 January 1841 at Brasted, Kent.

Alice Reynolds was born on 30 July 1843 at Chelsfield. She married Elias Hedges and their first child was born in 1865 and registered at Dartford, Kent. Alice died in 1923 and was buried at Hoddesdon, Herts.

Louisa Reynolds was baptised on 1 February 1846 at Stanstead.

Elvy Reynolds was baptised on 18 July 1847 at St Mary Cray.

George Reynolds

George Reynolds was born on 4 May 1853 at the Common, Ightham, Kent. His father was a hawker and his mother's name was given as 'Charlotte Reynolds formerly Jones'. George was baptised on 24 July 1853 at All Saints Church, Orpington. His father was a labourer. George married Mary Ann Pateman (1851) and they had five children: John (28 February 1875), George (1877), James (1879), Thomas (1880) and Elvy (1888).

In 1881 George was living with his family in a van at Piggenden's lane, Farnborough, Kent. In 1891 and 1901 George was living at Tugmutton, Farnborough. In 1901 his son, Thomas Reynolds, was working as a bricklayer's labourer in Portsmouth with Henry and Noah Pateman (Mary Ann's nephews). In 1902 George lived at 3 Tugmutton. In 1910-14 he lived at 3 Willow Walk. In 1910-11 his son, James Reynolds, lived at 4 Willow Walk. In 1911 his son, George Reynolds junior, lived at 8 Willow Walk. In 1914 his son, Thomas Reynolds, lived at 4 Willow Walk.

George Reynolds died on 28 October 1937 aged 84. Mary Ann Reynolds died on 15 May 1929 aged 79. Thomas Reynolds died on 18 June 1964 aged 83. They were all buried in the same grave at St Giles, Farnborough.

Mercy Reynolds

Mercy Reynolds was born at Crockenhill, Kent and baptised on 26 August 1855 at All Saints, Orpington. Her father was a labourer. Mercy Reynolds married William Pateman (1857-1921) and they had eight children: Mary (1876), Henry (1880), Noah (1883), Walter (1886), Alice (1889), Phoebe (1892), William (1894) and Amy (1896).

In 1881 Mercy was living in a van on the side of the road at Orpington Lane, Farnborough, with William, Mary and Henry. Noah, Walter and Alice were born in a house cart on Farnborough Common. In 1890 Mercy moved to Stows Cottages, Church Road, Farnborough, and this is where Phoebe, William and Amy were born. In 1901 Mercy moved to 4 Cobden Road, Farnborough. From 1924-28 Mercy lived at Chislehurst Road, Orpington. Mercy lived at 61 Chislehurst Road from 1929-39.

Mercy Pateman died on 3 January 1940 at the County Hospital, Farnborough, aged 84 years. Her address was 61 Chislehurst Road, Orpington, and she was the widow of William Pateman, farm labourer. The cause of death was 'broncho pneumonia following fractured ribs due to a fall in the street (9 days). No P.M. Misadventure.' Mercy was buried on 9 January 1940 at All Saints, Orpington. She was buried in the same grave as her husband, William Pateman, who died in 1921.

Jane Reynolds

Jane Reynolds was born: in St Mary Cray, Kent in 1861 (1881 Census); in Sittingbourne, Kent in 1856 (1891 Census); in 'Lidden' (Lyde?), Kent in 1859 (1901 Census). Her death certificate says she was 78 when she died in 1939, which would make her birth year 1861. So we can assume she was born in Kent some time between 1856 and 1861.

Jane Reynolds married James Pateman (1846-1926) and they had eighteen children: Betsy (1880), Emmie (1882), Phyllis (1883), Hannah (1884), Robert (1885), Mary Ann (1886), Charlotte (1887), Phoebe (1889), Jane (1890), Celia (1892), John (1893), Polly (1894), Betsy (1896), Elvy (1897), George (1899), Daisy (1901), Rose (1903) and William (1904).

In 1881 Jane was living at Bastard Green, Farnborough, with James and Betsy. From 1882-85 she lived at Tugmutton, Farnborough. Mary Ann was born at Stone's Cottages, Farnborough, in 1886. Jane lived at Tugmutton from 1887-1900. This address changed to 5 Tugmutton from 1901-1908; Willow Walk from 1909-14; and 5 Willow Walk from 1915-39.

Jane Pateman died on 25 March 1939 at 5 Willow Walk, Farnborough. She was the 78 year old widow of James Pateman a 'greengrocer master'. She died of myocardial degeneration and chronic bronchitis (she smoked a clay pipe for much of her life). The informant was 'R.Pateman, son, 1 Colegate Cottages, Farnborough.' This was Robert Pateman (1885-1960). Jane was buried on 1 April 1939 at St Giles, Farnborough, in the same grave as her daughter, Phyllis, who died in 1902.

I have four photographs of Jane Pateman. One is taken in a photographer's studio. Jane is middle aged, sitting in a chair with her arm on a table. Her hair is parted in the middle which makes her look quite severe. She is wearing a white blouse and a long black skirt. This skirt had a large pocket where Jane kept her Foxes mints.

The other three photographs were taken when she was much older. She is going on a charabanc outing and she is wearing a hat, white blouse and full length black skirt and coat. In one photograph she is sitting with her grandson William David (1930) on her lap, surrounded by a large group of people, including her son William (1904) and wife Doris, her daughter Daisy (1901) and husband Jack Baker, and her daughter Rose (1902) and husband Boysie Rye.

John Reynolds

John Reynolds (1835) married Mary Ann Breeds (1841) and they had several children: Charlotte (1866), William (1 July 1866), Anny (1871), Macey (10 December 1871, married Taylor), George (1874), John / Jack (1878), Elvy (8 June 1880), Seaman (1881) and Thomas (1890).

In 1881, 1891 and 1901 John Reynolds was living with his family at Tugmutton, Farnborough. In 1902 he lived at 6 Tugmutton. In 1910-14 he lived at 6 Willow Walk.

William Reynolds was born in 1866. *Kentish Times* 17 April 1914: 'Keep Smiling. William Reynolds, Tugmutton, Farnborough, was charged with being drunk on licensed premises at the New Inn, Farnborough, on the 11th inst. Acting sergeant 206P stated that at 10.30 on Friday evening he saw the prisoner staggering about High Street, Farnborough. He walked towards the New Inn and entered. Witness followed him in and brought him out. He had not been served. Prisoner, smiling broadly: I am very sorry to say he is telling a story. The Chairman: Have you anything to say to the Court? Prisoner: Nothing at all, sir. He was fined 10s and 2s 6d costs.'

George Reynolds was born on 3 April 1874. He married Mary Ann ? (1874, Somerset) and they had three children: George junior (1893), John (1898) and William (1900). In 1901 George was living with his family at Worley's Hole, Farnborough. In 1913-14 he was living at 8 Cobden Road, Farnborough. George senior died on 29 August 1928 aged 55. Mary Ann died on 10 May 1952 aged 80 years. They are both buried at St Giles, Farnborough.

John / Jack Reynolds was born on 1 February 1878. He married Annie Irish and in 1902 he was living at 2 Worley's Cottages, Farnborough.

Seaman Reynolds was born on 20 August 1881. He married Eliza Loft (1887), the sister of William Loft (1890) who married Mary Ann Pateman (1886). Seaman and Eliza had seven children: Britania (1908, married Peter Loveridge), William (1910, married Margaret House, six children), Seaman (1912, married Ruth? three children), John (1915, married Dorothy ?, one child), Thomas (1918, married Mary Stewart, two children), Rose (1921-2000, married Laurence Abbott, three children), and Amelie (1925, married Joe Francis, three children). In 1913-14 Seaman was living at 4 Tea Tree Cottages, Farnborough. Seaman died on 14 May 1941 aged 59. Eliza died on 25 December 1966 aged 79. They were both buried at St Giles, Farnborough.

Thomas Reynolds (1890) married ? and they had four children: Elvie (married Leonard Stillman, two children), Louise (married Fred Saunders, two children), Frances (married Seaman Reynolds, one child) and Nellie (married Fred Woodgate).

Cherie Batty gave me some photographs of the Reynolds family: a studio photograph of Elvie Reynolds as a young woman; Seaman and Francis Reynolds (nee Pateman) with son David; Bill Reynolds, in military uniform; William Pateman, Laurence Abbott, Jack Reynolds, Jimmy Reynolds, Seaman Reynolds and Charlie Percival in a pub.

There is also a group photograph of: brothers Jack Reynolds, Thomas Reynolds and Seaman Reynolds (senior) with his wife Eliza Alice Loft; siblings Seaman Reynolds (junior), Amelia Reynolds (aka Milly), William John Reynolds, Rose Alice Reynolds and husband Laurence Abbott, and Britania Reynolds and husband Pete Loveridge; William Pateman and his wife Doris Abbott.

There is a photograph of Bill Reynolds, Elsie Beaney, Caroline Smith, Minnie Jones, Harry Beaney and Pickles Beaney.

There is a long association between Farnborough and the Reynolds family. In 1881 John Reynolds was living at Tugmutton Common and George Reynolds was living at Piggenden's Lane. In 1891 George and John Reynolds were living at Tugmutton. In 1901 George Reynolds was living at Worley's Hole. In 1902 John Reynolds was living at Worley Cottages. In 1910 George, James and John Reynolds were living at Willow Walk. In 1911 J. Reynolds was living at 1 Nile Cottages, Farnborough and another J. Reynolds was living at 5 Nile Cottages. In 1913 S. Reynolds was living at Tea Tree Cottages and G. Reynolds was living at Cobden Road. In 1914 J. Reynolds was living at 3 Poplar Cottages, Sevenoaks Road.

10. Chronology

1846 – 17 July: James Pateman born in a tent on Cooling Common, Cliffe, Kent
1846 – 26 July: James Pateman baptised at St Helen's, Cliffe
1857 – William Pateman born at Rochester, Kent
1871 – 2 April: James and William Pateman at Beckenham on Census Day
1876 – Mary Pateman born at Crockenhill, Kent
1880 – Henry Pateman born at Crockenhill
1880 – 22 November: Betsy Pateman born at Star Lane, St Mary Cray
1881 – 3 April: James Pateman at Bastard Green, Farnborough on Census Day
1881 – 3 April: John Pateman lodging at Orpington Lane on Census Day
1881 – 3 April: William Pateman in van on side of Orpington Lane on Census Day
1881 – 13 November: Betsy Pateman died at Tugmutton aged 12 months
1881 – 19 November: Betsy Pateman buried at St Giles, Farnborough
1882 – 20 March: Emmie Pateman born at Tugmutton, Farnborough
1883 – 21 April: Phillis Pateman born at Tugmutton
1883 – 13 May: Noah Pateman born at Locks Bottom
1883 – 26 June: John Pateman died at Broad Street Green, aged 38
1883 – 28 June: John Pateman buried at St Giles
1884 – 28 April: Hannah Pateman born at Tugmutton
1884 - 7 September 1884: Hannah Pateman died at East Peckham, aged 4 months
1885 – 30 May: Robert Pateman born at Tugmutton
1886 – 9 May: Walter Pateman born at Farnborough
1886 – 17 July: Mary Ann Pateman born at Stones Cottages, Farnborough
1887 – 17 June: Farnborough Commons Protection Committee formed
1887 – 19 September: Charlotte Pateman born at Tugmutton
1889 – 16 April: Phoebe Pateman born at Tugmutton
1889 – 6 July: Alice Pateman born at Farnborough
1889 – 13 July: Alice Pateman baptised at St Giles
1890 – 4 August: Jane Pateman born at Tugmutton
1891 – 5 April: James Pateman at Tugmutton on Census Day
1891 – 5 April: William Pateman at Church Road, Farnborough on Census Day
1892 – 1 January: Phoebe Pateman born at Stow Cottages, Farnborough
1892 – 22 January: Alice Pateman died at Fulcher's Square, St Mary Cray, aged 50
1892 – 14 February: Phoebe Pateman baptised at St Giles
1892 – 30 May: Celia Pateman born at Tugmutton
1893 – 5 September: John Pateman born at Locks Bottom
1893 – 8 October: John Pateman baptised at St Giles
1894 – 1 November: William Pateman born at Farnborough
1894 – 23 December: Polly Pateman born at Locks Bottom
1894 – 24 December: Celia Pateman died at Starts Hill, aged 2
1895 – 8 January: Celia Pateman buried at St Giles
1895 – 13 January: William Pateman baptised at St Giles
1895 – 7 September: Mary Pateman married Elias Lewis at St Giles
1896 – 17 February: Amy Pateman born at Farnborough
1896 – 10 May: Amy Pateman baptised at St Giles
1896 – 26 September: Betsy Pateman born at Locks Bottom
1897 – 13 August: Betsy Pateman died at Hockenden, St Mary Cray, aged 10 months
1897 – 17 August: Betsy Pateman buried at Star Lane Cemetery, St Mary Cray
1897 – 26 December: Elvy Pateman born at Farnborough

1898 – 1 February: Charles Lewis born at Farnborough
1898 – 13 February: Elvy Pateman baptised at St Giles
1899 – 1 April: George Pateman born at Tugmutton
1900 – 7 January: Boysey Rye born at Cudham
1900 – 21 June: Polly Pateman died at Willow Walk age 6
1900 - 26 June: Polly Pateman buried at St Giles
1900 – 22 November: William Pateman died at Swanley age 7
1900 – 4 December: John Pateman died at Tugmutton aged 7
1900 – 8 December: John Pateman buried at St Giles
1901 – 31 March: James Pateman at Tugmutton on Census Day
1901 – 31 March: Phillis Pateman at 2 Wellclose Villas on Census Day
1901 – 31 March: William Pateman at Cobden Road on Census Day
1901 – 31 March: Noah and Henry Pateman at Portsmouth on Census Day
1901 – 25 May: Daisy Pateman born at Wellbrook Road
1901 - 28 September - Mary Pateman died at Cobden Road, Farnborough, aged 23.
1902 – 22 April: Phillis Pateman died at Willow Lane age 20
1902 – 28 April: Phillis Pateman buried at St Giles
1902 – 1 June: Noah Pateman married Annie Honeysett at St Pauls Cray
1902 – 9 November: Henry Pateman married Lottie Tilley at All Saints, Orpington
1903 – 3 January: Rose Pateman born at Wellbrook Road
1904 – August: William Pateman born at Tugmutton
1904 – 27 August: Emmie Pateman married William Fenton at St Giles
1904 – 20 November: William Pateman baptised at All Saints, Orpington
1909 – 24 February: Walter Pateman married Priscilla Arnold at Bromley
1910 – 29 January: Charlotte Pateman married James Bassett at St Giles
1910 – 27 August: Robert Pateman married Phyllis Rose Lockyer at St Giles
1911 – 27 January: Robert Henry Pateman born at 9 Willow Walk
1911 – 7 August: Alice Pateman married Jesse Lee at Bromley
1911 – 20 December: Robert Henry Pateman baptised at St Giles
1911 – 25 December: Phoebe Pateman married Charles Smith at All Saints
1912 – 28 December: Jane Pateman married James New at St Giles
1914 – 11 October: Phyllis Daisy Pateman born at 1 Colegate Cottages
1914 – 28 November: Phyllis Daisy Pateman baptised at St Giles
1914 – 26 December: Phoebe Pateman married Frederick Pankhurst at All Saints
1915 – 30 October: Mary Ann Pateman married William Loft at St Giles
1917 – 27 February: Walter Pateman killed in action at Bouchavesnes, France
1918 – 17 November: Phyllis Daisy Pateman died at 1 Colegate Cottages, aged 4
1918 – 23 November: Phyllis Daisy Pateman buried at St Giles
1921 – 23 April: George Pateman died at Orpington, aged 22
1921 – 28 April: George Pateman buried at St Giles
1921 – 24 October: William Pateman died at Chislehurst Road, Orpington, aged 65
1921 – 29 October: William Pateman buried at All Saints, Orpington
1922 – 23 December: Elvy Pateman married Edward Whiffen at Bromley
1924 – 14 October: William George Pateman born at 1 Colegate Cottages
1924 – 30 November: William George Pateman baptised at St Giles
1926 – 29 May: James Pateman died at 5 Willow Walk, aged 79.
1926 – 5 June: James Pateman buried at St Giles, Farnborough
1928 – 31 March: Daisy Pateman married Jack Baker at Bromley
1928 – 25 December: Rose Pateman married Boysey Rye at St Giles
1929 – 16 November: William Pateman married Doris Abbott at Bromley

1930 – 20 May: William David Lawrence Pateman born at 5 Willow Walk
1930 – 6 July: William David Lawrence Pateman baptized at St Giles
1936 – 26 December: Amy Pateman married Charles Chown at All Saints
1938 - 30 July: Robert Henry Pateman married Doris Rushbrook at Bromley
1939 – 25 March: Jane Pateman died at Willow Walk aged 78
1939 – 1 April: Jane Pateman buried at St Giles
1940 – 3 January: Mercy Pateman died at Orpington aged 84
1940 – 9 January: Mercy Pateman buried at All Saints, Orpington
1948 – 22 September: Boysey Geoffrey Rye died at Bromley, aged 48
1949 – 24 November: Noah Pateman died at Orpington age 66
1949 – 28 November: Noah Pateman buried at All Saints, Orpington
1950 – 16 April: Elvy Pateman died at Fordcombe, Kent, aged 52
1953 – 6 June: Elias Lewis died at Bromley
1956 – 18 February: Emmie Pateman died aged 74, buried at St Giles
1960 – 9 April: Robert Pateman died at 320 Crofton Road, aged 74
1961 – 5 February: Henry Pateman died at Cray Valley Hospital, aged 81.
1961 – 10 February: Henry Pateman buried at All Saints
1961 – 11 June: Lottie Pateman died at 3 Felstead Road, age 77
1961 – 16 June: Lottie Pateman buried at All Saints
1961 – 10 October: Annie Pateman died at Orpington aged 81
1961 – 14 October: Annie Pateman buried at All Saints, Orpington
1966 – 9 August: William Pateman died at Farnborough Hospital aged 61
1967 – 29 September: Phyllis Rose Pateman died at Maidstone aged 80
1976 – 27 October: Daisy Baker died at Bromley aged 75
1982 – 20 December: Doris May Pateman cremated at Beckenham
1990 – 22 February: Robert Henry Pateman died at Bromley, aged 79
1990 – 2 March: Robert Henry Pateman cremated at Beckenham
1990 – 29 March: Rose Pateman died at Herne Bay, aged 90

11. Family Trees

James Pateman (1846-1926) = Jane Reynolds (1861-1939)
- Betsy Pateman (1880-1881)
- Emmie Pateman (1882-1956)
- Phillis Pateman (1883-1902)
- Hannah Pateman (1884)
- Robert Pateman (1885-1960)
- Mary Ann Pateman (1886-?)
- Charlotte Pateman (1887-?)
- Phoebe Pateman (1889-?)
- Jane Pateman (1890-?)
- Celia Pateman (1892-1894)
- John Pateman (1893-1900)
- Polly Pateman (1894-1900)
- Betsy Pateman (1896-1897)
- Elvy Pateman (1897-1950)
- George Pateman (1899-1921)
- Daisy Pateman (1901-1976)
- Rose Pateman (1903-1993)
- William Pateman (1904-1966)

William Pateman (1857-1921) = Mercy Reynolds (1855-1940)
- Mary Pateman (1876-1901)
- Henry Pateman (1880-1961)
- Noah Pateman (1883-1949)
- Walter Pateman (1886-1917)
- Alice Pateman (1889-?)
- Phoebe Pateman (1892-?)
- William Pateman (1894-1900)
- Amy Pateman (1896-?)

12. Sources

Dorothy Anderson (1993) *Farnborough History*

J.H.B. Blandford (1913) *Farnborough and its Surroundings*

Silvester Boswell (1973) *The Book of Boswell:* autobiography *of a Gypsy*

British Pathe News, Http://www.britishpathe.com/

Bromleage (April 1976) *The Recording of the Tombstones in Farnborough Churchyard*

Raymond Buckland (1998) *Gypsy Witchcraft and Magic* (1998)

Simon Evans (2004) *Stopping Places*

Ray Galer: *Fantasies of St Mary Cray* (1946); *Romances of St Mary Cray* (1947); *Historical Sketches of St Mary Cray* (1948); *Traveler's Joy in St Mary Cray* (1950)

James Greenwood (1881) Lo*w Life Deeps*

John Guy (Byegone Kent, Vol. 23, No.10) *The Forgotten Landscape of the Hoo Peninsula*

Edward Hasted (1797) *History of Kent*

Barbara Hodson (1999) *Farnborough old village: a brief history*

Roger Huntley (1978) *Farnborough: village among ferns upon the hill*

Gwen Jones and John Bell (1992) *Oasthouses in Sussex and Kent: their history and development*

Gillian Kemp (1997) *The Romany Good Spell Book*

Pat Loveridge (2003) *A Calendar of Fairs and Markets held in the nineteenth century*

Philip Macdougall (1989) *The Book of Medway - The story of Rochester, Chatham and Strood*

Alan Major (1999) *Goldings, Napoleons and Romneys*

Alan Major (1994) *Hidden Kent*

Trevor May (1998) *The Victorian Domestic Servant*

Monica North (2002) *Dickens Country*

Passing Through, www.passing-through.co.uk

Robinson (1973) *Farnborough Board Schools 1873-1973: a short history*

Muriel Searle (1990) *Farnborough and Downe in old picture postcards*

Muriel Searle (1994) *Orpington in old picture postcards*

Margaret Smith (2001) *Cooling – a Dickens of a Village*

Betsy Stanley (1998) *Memories of the Marsh – a Traveler Life in Kent*

E.B.Trigg (1975) *Gypsy Demons and Divinities: the magic and religion of the Gypsies*

Brian Vesey-Fitzgerald (1973) *The Gypsies of Britain*

Sadie Ward (1991) *The Countryside Remembered*

Fred Whyler (1985) *Farnborough, Green Street Green and Locks Bottom*

Fred Whyler and Alan Robinson (2000) *Farnborough - Continuity and Change*

Other publications by the same author

Canadian Corner – a brief history (2000)

Orpington and the Great War (2001)

Seven Steps to Glory: Private Pateman Goes to War (2002)

Charles Dickens and Travellers (2003)

What Dark History is This? William Pateman and the Gordon Riots (2004)

Hoo, Hops and Hods: the life and times of Robert Pateman (2007)

Corkes Meadow: the life and times of Noah Pateman (2007)